THE DATE OF THE EXODUS

IN THE LIGHT OF EXTERNAL EVIDENCE

THE DATE OF THE EXODUS

IN THE LIGHT OF EXTERNAL EVIDENCE

BY

J. W. JACK, M.A.

WIPF & STOCK · Eugene, Oregon

Wipf and Stock Publishers
199 W 8th Ave, Suite 3
Eugene, OR 97401

The Date of Exodus
In the Light of External Evidence
By Jack, J.W.
ISBN 13: 978-1-5326-4165-7
Publication date 10/5/2017
Previously published by Edinburgh, T. & T. Clark, 1925

PREFACE

IN this book the author has endeavoured to reach historical results through external evidence, particularly of an archæological nature, combined with a critical view of the Old Testament records. It is well known that archæology and Old Testament history cannot be separated without injury to the latter. This is specially true where the latter concerns such a subject as the Exodus and its various historical problems. Only by the application of trustworthy external evidence can these be properly understood and interpreted. It is the author's conviction that the more such evidence is available, the greater will be the gain to Biblical history and to the cause of true religion. He has therefore endeavoured in this volume to advance along archæological lines, using the results of the most recent discoveries in Egypt, Palestine, Asia Minor, and the East. At the same time he has kept in touch with genuine Biblical criticism, which after all is not the invention of modern scholars, but the legitimate interpretation of the Biblical records by them. Nothing but harm can be done to religion by unreal conceptions of the Old Testament. Not only does the revelation of God in Old Testament times suffer, but Christianity does so along with it, for the latter cannot rightly be separated from the former. Proper Biblical criticism, assisted by archæological results, makes the story of Israel the most vivid and real of all ancient histories.

Others have already written largely on the date of the Exodus, and the author has necessarily had to traverse a good deal of ground familiar to readers. Some people may be inclined to think that nothing new can be said on the subject. But Biblical science and archæology do not stand still, and this progress—marvellous within recent years—must be the author's justification for the appearance of this new work. We are able now to look at the Exodus in a light totally different from that of forty years ago. The new knowledge of the ancient history and languages of the Middle East, which has crowded on us thick and fast within the last few years, and the documentary discoveries at Tell el-Amarna, Boghaz Keui, and elsewhere, which have given us historical revelations of the most trustworthy kind, have enabled us to interpret the Exodus aright and place it in its proper historical setting as part of a larger Semitic movement. The author has sought to put the reader, as far as practicable, in possession of the latest facts on the subject. Some writers try to vindicate the Old Testament narrative by making statements on Egyptian history and archæology which prove on examination to be incorrect or unjustifiable. Those who do this only discredit the Old Testament. He has tried to avoid this by stating his facts with all possible care and resting his arguments at every point on valid historical evidence. The numerous Boghaz Keui documents which have not yet been translated or published will no doubt reveal many surprises, even in regard to the Hebrew race and the Israelite nation. The author, however, feels sure that any further information will only confirm the conclusions advanced in these pages. He is not without hope that the book may lead some, who may have given too easy an assent to other views, to come nearer at least to the position he advocates. He does not wish to be ultra-dogmatic, and some scholars may differ from him on certain questions, for there are still many unsettled problems and wide divergences of opinion, but he feels convinced that there are strong arguments in favour of the view he puts forward. In spite of all uncertainties, there is an impressive accumulation of facts which cannot be ignored.

The period dealt with in the volume is the most interesting and most highly illuminated in all ancient history. We see the Hittites, Amorites, Babylonians, Egyptians, and Israelites all coming into contact. The land of Canaan, as the bridge between Egypt and the various nations of Asia, becomes specially important. The Israelites appear on the scene for the first time in history, and in their entry into Canaan we see their relation to and co-operation with other Semitic races. The whole period, covering the Exodus and the Conquest, deals with events of the greatest interest and importance to the Biblical student. As this is an age when large numbers of people are interested in historical research, the author hopes that on this account alone the book may prove acceptable to many people.

He has endeavoured to make it as little technical as possible, so that it may be useful to the larger class of average readers as well as to Biblical scholars. Owing to the nature of the subject, it has not been possible to avoid certain philological and historical discussions, and the use of Hebrew and other forms of Semitic language, but these have been kept within strictest limits. Hebrew, Greek, and foreign quotations have been put as far as possible into the footnotes. In this way he has tried to steer a middle course between a work which only experts could understand, and one too 'popular' to be of much use to those really interested in the subject. As a rule, customary and recognized spellings of ancient names have been retained, but where usage varies, the more correct forms have been adopted. In Babylonian, Egyptian, and other languages, *sh* has been used generally instead of *š*, except in the transliteration of texts. The ordinary *h* has been kept for the guttural *ḥ* (Hebrew ח, Arabic ح) as well as for the hard breathing, while the symbol ḫ has been adopted instead of *kh* for the harder guttural, except in Egyptian names and a few others where the latter has become more familiar. The Semitic and Egyptian ע (*ʿain*) is marked by ʿ in cases where custom has not dispensed with it.

A large number of authorities on the subject, including British, German, French, and American, have been consulted in the preparation of the volume. The reports and transactions of the learned Associations, and especially those of the Egypt Exploration Society, have afforded valuable information. The author is glad to express his indebtedness to all these, and also to such reliable Egyptologists as Sir E. A. Wallis Budge, Sir W. M. Flinders Petrie, Professor T. Eric Peet, Dr. H. R. Hall, Dr. A. H. Gardiner, Mr. Sidney Smith, and others for information contained in their works or articles, as well as to Böhl, Dhorme, Thureau-Dangin, Weidner, and many other foreign scholars. With some of these authorities, both British and foreign, he has had much correspondence on points of importance, particularly on the Ḫabiru-SA-GAZ question. He feels particularly indebted to the younger generation of Egyptologists, who have begun their researches at the point reached by their predecessors many years ago, and through the richness of modern discovery have reached results somewhat different and in many cases more correct. In matters of Biblical criticism, the author feels under much obligation to such eminent Biblical scholars as Professor C. F. Burney, Dr. S. A. Cook, Professor S. R. Driver, Professor Adam C. Welch, and others. By the last-named he has also been helped personally with literature and in other ways. He has mentioned in the footnotes some of the principal authorities whose works he has consulted. If he has been unable to make due acknowledgment to all such, it is because of the multiplicity of the sources, and the inadvisability of burdening the book with excessive references and thus confusing the reader. As far as possible, he has worked out historical facts and theories to his own conclusions. At the same time the references will be found sufficiently numerous to allow a reader who may not have access to one source to be able to consult another.

The author has only to add that this volume is the result of conscientious research, and of an earnest desire to arrive at the truth. It is many years since he began to study the question discussed in these pages, and during this long time he has been enabled to consult most of the important works dealing with it. He ventures to hope that his labour will not have been entirely in vain. He feels it unnecessary to offer any apology for this somewhat personal statement; for when a writer on such a debatable subject asks the attention of Biblical and Egyptological students, he is required to show that by industry and research he has entitled himself to a hearing. He feels at the same time that he has no further claim than this, and he therefore most diffidently asks for his work the indulgence of his readers.

J. W. J.

August 1925.

CONTENTS

LIST OF EGYPTIAN KINGS

DYNASTIES XVIII. AND XIX.: *c.* 1580–1210 B.C.

IN the first column the usual names of the kings are given. In the second will be found the Greek transliterations from Manetho's lists. The dates in the third column are those of Dr. H. R. Hall, whose scheme of dating follows the higher Sothic limit, while those in the fourth column are Professor Breasted's, who adopts the lower Sothic limit. The two columns of dates, it will be noticed, differ only slightly for these two Dynasties. It is in the later dates assigned to the XIth and XIIth Dynasties, and consequently to all that precede these, that the difference is more apparent. According to Dr. Hall, the commencement of the XIIth Dynasty, for instance, must be placed about 2212 B.C., while Professor Breasted assigns it to about 2000 B.C.

In this volume we have adopted Dr. Hall's scheme of dates up to the reign of Amenhotep III. From this time onward to the reign of Ramesses II. we have used the revised dates of this particular period furnished by Professor Langdon and Dr. Alan H. Gardiner (*Journal of Egyptian Archæology*, 1920, p. 204), who base their view on the details in the Treaty between Hattushilish III. and Ramesses II., and on additional Egyptian material from a collation by Sethe. These dates, it is found, agree better with the recent discoveries in Hittite and Babylonian history.

EIGHTEENTH DYNASTY

		Hall.	Breasted.
Ahmose I.	Amosis	1580–1558	1580–1557
Amenhotep I.	Amenophis	1558–1545	1557–1501
Thutmose I.	Tethmosis	1545–1514	
Thutmose II.	Khebron	1514–1501	
Queen Hatshepsut	Amensis	1501–1479	1501–1447
Thutmose III.	Mephres Misaphris Misphragmouthosis	1479 (1501) –1447	
Amenhotep II.	Amenophis	1447–1420	1447–1420
Thutmose IV.	Touthmosis	1420–1412	1420–1411
Amenhotep III.	Horos	1412–1376	1411–1375
Amenhotep IV. (Akhenaten)		1380–1362	
S'akere (Smenkhkere)	Akenkheres	1362–1360	1375–1350
Tutankhamūn	Khebres	1360–1350	
Ai II.	Akherre	1350–1346	
Harmhab	Harmais	1346–1322	1350–1315

NINETEENTH DYNASTY

Ramesses I.	Menophres	1321	1315–1314
Seti I.	Sethōs	1321–1300	1314–1292
Ramesses II.	Ramesses	1300–1233	1292–1225
Merenptah	Amenophath	1233–1223	1225–1215
Amenmose	..	1223–1220	1215
Ramesses Siptah Queen Tausret	Thouōris	1220–1214	1215–1209
Seti II	Sethōs	1214–1210	1209–1205

LANGDON-GARDINER DATES

Amenhotep III.	1419–1383	..	..
Akhenaten	1383–1366	..	..
Three short reigns	1366–1358	..	..
Harmhab	1358–1324	..	..
Ramesses I.	1324–1322	..	..
Seti I.	1322–1301	..	..
Ramesses II.	1301–1234	..	..

Map I

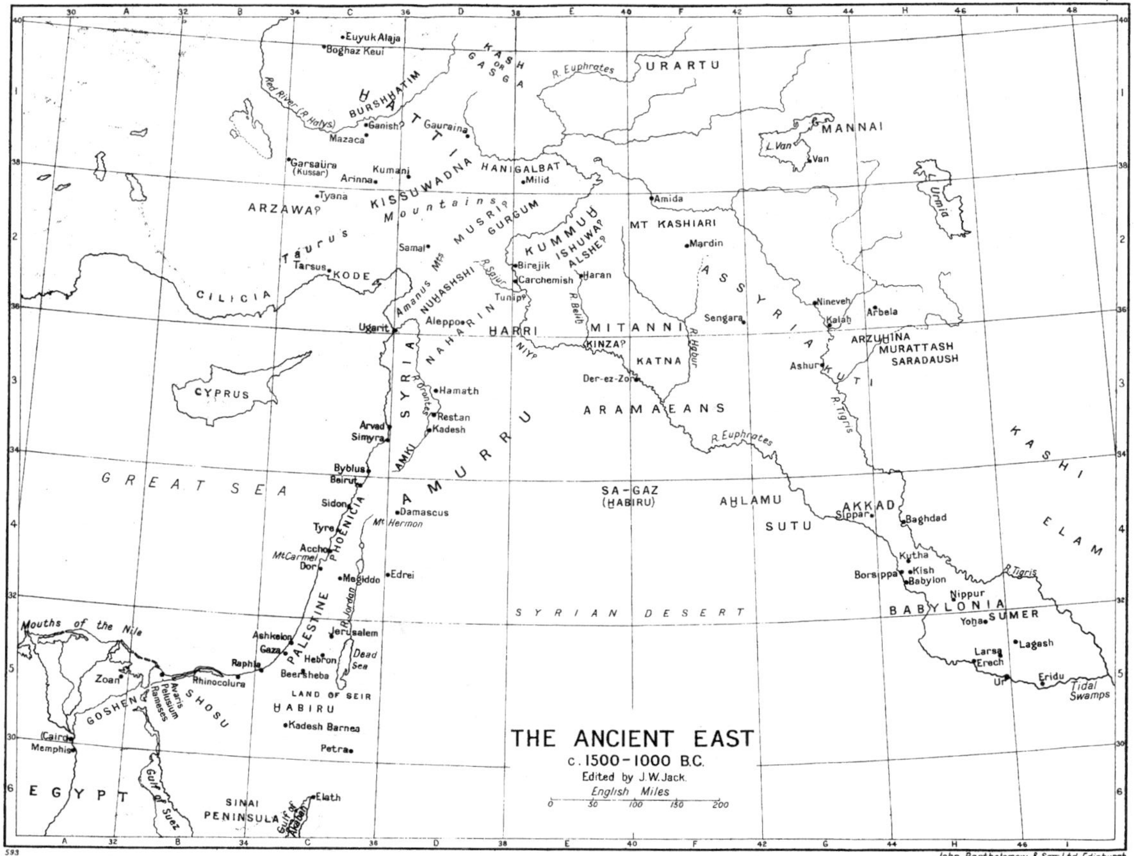

John Bartholomew & Son, Ltd. Edinburgh.

THE DATE OF THE EXODUS
IN THE LIGHT OF EXTERNAL EVIDENCE

CHAPTER I

THE DATA

THE period of Egyptian history at which the Exodus of the Israelites took place can only be determined inferentially. This is due mainly to our lack of knowledge on important aspects of the case and to the consequent difficulties involved. For one thing, the Book of Exodus does not mention the name of any of the Pharaohs at the time, the first Pharaoh named in the Bible being " Shishak, king of Egypt " (1 Kings xi. 40, xiv. 25), who reigned several hundred years later ; [1] and owing to the general fixity of Egyptian institutions no distinctive evidence as to the age in which these Pharaohs lived can be gathered from the manners and customs mentioned in the book.

It is well known, too, among scholars that we do not possess a contemporary account of the Exodus and the subsequent events ; for, if these had been still fresh in the minds of the Israelites or their immediate descendants when the book was written, we

[1] Known as Sheshonk I., the first king of the XXIInd or Libyan Dynasty, who ascended the throne *c.* 945 B.C. The Pharaoh Merenptah (*c.* 1230 B.C.) may be referred to in Josh. xv. 9, xviii. 15, where the " well of the waters of Nephtoah " may be an incorrect reading for " the well of Merenptah," as Sayce has pointed out (*Expository Times*, xxix. p. 73). The error is due to a mistake in the Hebrew pointing, מֵי נֶפְתּוֹחַ having been put for מינפתוח (Menephtah or Merenptah). The arrival of " the captains of the archers of the well of Merenptah which is in the highlands " is announced in a letter to the Egyptian government from one of its officials on the Canaanite frontier in Merenptah's third year. (Cf. *Select Papyri of the British Museum*, plates v. and vi.)

should have had more particulars in the narrative—not only the personal names of the Pharaohs, but the place where they held their court, the names of some of the officers and task-masters, and other definite and specific items of information. Contemporary writers of history are generally more exact and detailed. The narrative of the Exodus contains material written down several centuries later, presumably in the schools of the prophets, and thus represents an age already distant. It was probably compiled in its present connected form only about the fifth century B.C., nearly nine hundred years after the Israelites are supposed to have sojourned in Egypt. If we had to deal with an historical record such as that contained in the Book of Kings or the Books of Samuel, where we have documents contemporary, or nearly so, with the events narrated, and consequently sound historical data (generally speaking) together with Assyrian annals to enable us to reach satisfactory conclusions, we should find ourselves standing on firmer ground. But it is quite different with the records which deal with the period immediately preceding the monarchy and which are concerned with the sojourn of the Israelites in Goshen, their conquest of Canaan, and their gradual settlement in the land.

The narrative of Exodus, moreover, is part of a great composite work, the Hexateuch, which contains in one complex whole all that had been preserved of Old Testament writings regarding the early history of the Israelites. In such a narrative we come into contact with documents which have been repeatedly copied, interpolated with new matter, and expanded with traditions. It is generally possible to distribute the material among four different schools of writing, the Yahwistic, Elohistic, Deuteronomic, and Priestly (known respectively to Biblical scholars as J, E, D, P). These documents differ from each other in the use of the Divine names, in their style and vocabulary, in their theological attitude, and in the accounts they give of the same events. The relative age of them is shown by the order just given, the periods of the first two overlapping; and each of them has its own individual standpoint, as each of the Synoptic Gospels has its own picture of the life of Christ. None of the documents appears in its original form as a connected whole. They have all been annotated and condensed by later editors, and fused by them into a general narrative; and this editorial work has been a repeated process by successive scribes, belonging to different periods in Israel's history and even to 'different schools of thought,' if one might so express it. All this editing and re-editing was necessary, that the religious lessons taught by the history might appeal to the people of respective generations. Just as all history, such as that of the Reformation in our own land, has to be occasionally rewritten in the course of the ages, owing to new aspects which have developed through the lapse of time, so the religious teachers of Israel, who were the chief conservators of its historical traditions, took the surviving documents, wove them into connected form, and applied them to the religious and political condition of their own day. Hence we have a substratum of ancient narratives, presenting more or less variant traditions, and generally annotated and connected together, sometimes wrongly, certain critics believe, by later editors. All this makes it difficult to arrive at the detailed facts required for the fixing of a date for the Exodus, and helps to account for the various and divergent views put forward by scholars.[1]

[1] An explanation of the various documents may be helpful to non-Biblical students, as some knowledge of the matter is necessary for a proper understanding of questions connected with our subject. J is so termed as exhibiting a preference for the Divine name Jehovah (or Yahweh, as it should properly be), and appears to have been produced by the prophetic school of Judah, *c.* 850–750 B.C. E, on the other hand, generally uses the Divine title *Elohim*, 'God,' and has emanated from the northern kingdom of Israel, *c.* 800–750 B.C. D represents the work of the Deuteronomic redactors or revisers, who are believed to have been connected with the southern kingdom of Judah and to have done their work not long after the promulgation of the Law (*i.e.* the nucleus of Deuteronomy) in the eighteenth year of Josiah (621 B.C.), though Professor Welch holds that the Deuteronomic code emanated from the northern kingdom of Israel over a century earlier, about the time of Amos and Hosea (Welch, *The Code of Deuteronomy*, 1924). The revisions are the product of a reforming prophetical atmosphere, in which history was looked at from a moral and spiritual aspect. They bear traces of the same thoughts and language as we find in the Book of Deuteronomy. P is the work of the priestly or legalistic school, who transformed the people from the monarchical system to an ecclesiastical one under high priests. Their writings date from the latter

For another thing, neither the papyri already discovered nor the monuments and tombs of Egypt give us the slightest record of the Exodus, or even of the Oppression, which must have extended over a considerable period. There is one mention of Israel ('*Ysir'al* people') on a monument erected by Merenptah, king of Egypt, about 1230 B.C., in which it is stated that "Israel is desolated, her seed is not." The reference is a genuine one, admitted by practically all Egyptologists, but it does not shed much light on the Exodus, and indeed has only created further difficulties in some minds. Some Biblical scholars see a mention of Moses in the somewhat obscure inscriptions left in the Sinai mines by a polytheistic overseer, who is believed by them to have lived in the time of Queen Hatshepsut (*c.* 1514–1479 B.C.). The inscriptions in question were discovered by Flinders Petrie in 1905. Attempts at decipherment have been made by Alan Gardiner,[1] Cowley,[2] Sethe, and others, and fairly extensive monographs have been written on the subject by Grimme and Völter. But the identification of the various letters is not certain, though most writers seem agreed. The supposed name 'Moses' is more probably MNSH. This latter spelling, however, is recognized as a possible alternative form of his name (cf. Judg. xviii. 30, where this form may occur). Nevertheless, it might represent one of a hundred different individuals, and doubtless has no connection whatever with the leader of the Israelites.

part of the Exile or later (*c.* 500–300 B.C.), though based on older material. They consist largely of artificial chronology, of genealogies and statistics, of religious formulas, and of an insistence on the *minutiæ* of worship and ceremonies.

This theory, however, of the component parts of the Old Testament must not be regarded as rigid and unbending, for the religion of Israel did not advance in separate clear-cut stages, or by elaborate reconstructions. The Old Testament in its present form is the result of a very complicated process. Still, in its broad general aspect and guiding principles, the theory referred to is recognized by Biblical scholars as correct. Cf. Welch, "The Present Position of Old Testament Criticism," in *Expositor*, xxv. (1923), pp. 344 ff.

For the more recent developments on the composition of the Hexateuch, cf. R. Smend, *Die Erzählung d. Hexateuch*, 1912; Eichrodt, *Die Quellen d. Genesis von neuem untersucht*, 1916; Eissfeldt, *Hexateuch-Synopse*, 1923.

[1] *Journal of Egyptian Archæology*, 1916, pp. 12 ff.

[2] *Ibid.*, pp. 17 ff.

Names of places called 'Jacob-el' and 'Joseph-el' occur in the list of conquests made by Thutmose III. in Palestine (*c.* 1479 B.C.); but apart from this and from the mention of 'Israel,' we may regard it as certain that there is no Egyptian reference anywhere to any of the persons or events connected with Israel's early history. Abraham, Jacob, Joseph, and Moses are all clearly connected with Egypt in the Biblical narrative, but with the exceptions mentioned no Egyptian records make reference to any of these persons. No inscriptions or documents of any kind have yet been discovered which place the Exodus within the contents of Egyptian history by bearing witness to its occurrence.

Indirectly, however, on *a priori* grounds, we are in a much better position now for dealing with the matter than we could have been a few years ago. The increase of knowledge on ancient Egyptian history has been very considerable. One has only to compare the older editions of works on Egypt with the modern ones to observe the enormous advance made. The successive landmarks in the advance are quite apparent, beginning with Brugsch's *Egypt under the Pharaohs* (German edition, 1877), and ending with the latest editions of Breasted, Petrie, and others. No portion of this history has been more fully examined and explored within the last few years than that into which the Oppression and the Exodus must have fallen. Sarcophagus, stele, papyrus, and tablets have now spoken with much clearer accent, and their writings and inscriptions have yielded up much authentic history regarding the dwellers by the Nile. Among available Egyptian documents are the lists of kings which have been found inscribed in the temples at Karnak, Abydos, and Sakkarah, and which date from the XVIIIth and XIXth Dynasties. They contain the names of 61, 76, and 47 kings respectively. The two latter lists compiled in the reigns of Seti I. and Ramesses II. are remarkably accurate, based evidently on a careful study of the ancient official archives. Tombs and papyri of the same period have preserved shorter lists and give us valuable contemporary chronologies. The sequence of names in these is not always correct, and only a selection from the full series is given as a rule, but the lists are invaluable for historical guidance. In addition, there are lists in a dilapidated papyrus of the Ramesside period, now preserved at Turin, which no doubt enumerated when complete all the kings up to the Hyksos Dynasty. Every year excavations are being made and tombs are being discovered containing inscriptions. As a rule, the inscriptions, especially the public ones, are rather one-sided, consisting largely of a glorification of the reigning Pharaoh, his deeds of valour, and the cities and districts he managed to subjugate in Asia and other regions.[1] Most trustworthy information has been furnished, in particular by the discovery of the Tell el-Amarna Letters in 1887, followed about twenty years later by the discovery of the rich store of Hittite archives at Boghaz Keui in Asia Minor. These historical tablets have disclosed a multitude of new facts of the greatest interest and importance. The Hebrews and other ancient people now come before us with a fulness which Biblical experts a generation ago would hardly have believed. We can now read the historical facts of the Mosaic age, the inner life and conditions, the high politics, the religious beliefs, the international intercourse, the psychology and philosophy, and the ebb and flow of life and thought. We have a new background for our Palestinian history, and are able to reconsider the course of Israel in the light of the wider historical drama. Our views of ancient history have had to be considerably modified, while special illumination has been cast on that portion of history which concerns the Oppression and Exodus of the Israelites.

An immense mass of Egyptian and Greek tradition gathers round Moses or the Israelites in Egypt. Many of the stories have been collected in the works of Josephus, Philo, Eusebius, Hecatæus of Abdera, and other historians, in the Targums and Rabbinical commentaries, and in the pseudepigraphical

[1] Cf. Valdemar Schmidt, *Recueil Champollion*, 1922, p. 161, "On ne rencontre jamais, à aucune époque de l'histoire d'Égypte, sur aucun monument, la moindre mention d'un événement malheureux, d'une défaite, d'une perte d'aucune sorte."

writings ascribed to Moses.[1] Traditions are also found in the Koran and other Arabian works.[2] Many of these traditions, by adding to the miraculous in the life of Moses, endeavour to increase his unique spiritual position. Josephus, for instance, describes the childhood and youth of Moses. Pharaoh's daughter's name was Thermutis; the child was of Divine form (μορφῇ θεῖον), and refused to be suckled by Egyptian nurses; the princess persuaded the Pharaoh to put his crown on the infant's head, but the latter threw it down and trod on it. When grown up, Moses is stated to have led a successful campaign against the Ethiopians, and to have ultimately married Tharbis, the daughter of the Ethiopian monarch. This last statement is no doubt a legend connected with his Cushite wife (Num. xii. 1). Philo refers to Moses in the same strain, and gives details of his education in the learning of Egypt, Greece, Assyria, and Chaldæa. Both in Josephus and Philo there are many tedious expansions of the Bible story, with long speeches put into the mouths of Moses and others, after the manner of Tacitus, Thucydides, and similar historians.

In a fragment from the historical works of Hecatæus, as preserved in Diodorus,[3] we have some legendary accounts of the Sojourn and Exodus. Hecatæus was a Greek historian and philosopher who lived for some time at the court of Ptolemy I. (323–283 B.C.), and who accompanied this monarch in his expedition to Syria. He records that the Jews had formerly dwelt in Egypt, but had been forced by the Egyptians to quit the country on account of a plague that was thought to be due

[1] See Josephus, *Ant.* ii.–iv., ix., x., and *Contra Apion.*, i. 14, 26 f.; Philo, *Vita Moysis*; Eusebius, *Præp. Evangelica*, x. 13; Hecatæus, in Diod. Sic. xl. 3; Lysimachus of Alexandria, in Josephus, *Contra Apion.*, i. 34; Chœremon of Naukratis, in Josephus, *Contra Apion.*, i. 32; Diodorus Siculus, xxxiv. 1; Tacitus, *History*, v. 3–5. For a list of the pseudepigraphical books of Moses, see Charles, *Assumption of Moses*, pp. xiv–xvii.

[2] For the Jewish and Mohammedan legends, see Stanley, *Jewish Church*, i. pp. 86 ff.; the Koran, *Suras* ii., vii., x., etc.; Gustav Weill, *The Bible, the Koran, and the Talmud*; Hershon, *Genesis, with a Talmudic Commentary* (under 'Moses,' in Index iii.); D'Herbelot, *Bibliothèque Orientale, Moussa ben-Amram.*

[3] Diodorus, xl. 3 (*Exc. Photii*, pp. 542 ff., French edition).

to their presence. The Jews, it is stated, offered sacrifices to their own gods, and despised the Egyptian ones, with the result that the latter inflicted the plague on the land as a chastisement. The Jews were expelled and the plague ceased. A number of the expelled people, especially the more renowned of them, led by Kadmos and Danaos, fled to Greece, where they settled permanently; the remainder, who formed the large majority, marched to Palestine under the leadership of Moses, where they made Jerusalem their capital and founded a large temple. No date or epoch is given for the Sojourn or Expulsion. It is evident that this story of Hecatæus could not have come from Jewish sources, but must have been a legendary one furnished by the Egyptians themselves.

We have also important historical events recorded by Manetho, an Egyptian priest and writer who was a native of Sebennytus, in the Delta, and who lived during the reign of Ptolemy II. (Philadelphus), 285–246 B.C. He was commissioned by the king to collect all that was known of Egyptian annals and translate them into Greek. He must have been conversant with the literature of ancient Egypt, and he had access to monuments which in those days must have been in a state of perfect preservation. His original writings, under the name of *Aigyptiaca* (*Αἰγυπτιακά*), perished unfortunately at a very early period, and are only known to us through the garbled versions of other ancient writers. Until the remarkable discoveries of Champollion, his work was our sole authority on ancient Egyptian history, with the exception of sketches given by Herodotus and Diodorus. The mistakes of his copyists have caused considerable divergence in his records, but in general his work has proved of much use to later historians. His statement of Dynasties and kings, in three books, extending from Menes, the first king, to the conquest of the eastern world by Alexander, agrees fairly well with modern discoveries, though it is undoubtedly erroneous and fabulous in some respects.[1]

[1] For further information, see C. Müller, *Fragmenta Historicorum Græcorum*, ii. 511–616; A. Weidemann, *Ägyptische Geschichte* (Gotha, 1884), pp. 121 ff.; J. Krall, *Festgaben für Büdinger* (Innsbruck, 1898).

Josephus quotes from him,[1] although it is doubtful whether he ever saw Manetho's works himself.[2] The statement quoted is to the effect that a priest of Heliopolis, named Osarsiph, who afterwards became Moses, raised a revolt of persons afflicted with leprosy and other diseases, who had been settled on the borders of Egypt to deliver the land from their presence. They were defeated and driven out of Egypt by 'Amenophis,' the king. In another chapter (32), Josephus quotes a similar story from Chœremon, an Alexandrian scribe living shortly before the Christian era, the leaders of the Jews being Moüses Tisithen and Joseph Peteseph. In a later chapter (34), a third version of the story is quoted from Lysimachus, who is otherwise unknown, but is certainly still later than Chœremon. There are some Biblical scholars and Egyptologists who regard this story of the expulsion of the lepers from Egypt as a correct version of the Exodus and abide by Manetho's statement of names and places, but it is safer to regard many of its details as mere legendary lore.

No doubt there are in all this mass of ancient tradition some important facts, not otherwise known, which may explain obscurities in the Biblical record and fill up gaps in the story. It is at least singular that the three ancient documents which relate the Exodus, *viz.*, those of the Bible, Hecatæus, and Manetho, make mention of a plague or plagues as furnishing a reason to the Egyptian government for the expulsion of the Israelites, although all the documents differ as to details. According to the first two sources, it was the Egyptians who were affected; according to Manetho, it was the Israelites. So far, however, as the solving of the date of the Exodus is concerned, all the legends gathering round Moses or the Exodus, with the single exception of Manetho's statements (to which we shall afterwards return), may be ignored.

The fact that the Book of Exodus is by no means a contemporary narrative and that there is no mention of the Israelites on Egyptian monuments (except in the one case

[1] *Contra Apion.*, i. 26.

[2] Cf. Ed. Meyer, *Ägyptische Chronologie*, p. 72.

referred to), does not, however, discredit the story of Israel's sojourn and servitude in Goshen, or their Exodus from it. It makes the problem, no doubt, more difficult of solution, but it does not indicate, as some critics would have us believe, that the story is false, and indeed does not affect the problem in that way at all. It must be remembered that greater historical events have happened in the land of the Pharaohs and left absolutely no trace in our imperfect Egyptian records. The Israelites were not the only people who sojourned for a long time in Egypt, or who were enslaved to work on Pharaoh's buildings, for there are many pictures on the monuments of people who formed part of a *corvée* and were certainly not Jews. We see them making bricks under the superintendence of a taskmaster and performing other servile work; and the story of Israel might well be lost to the Egyptians amid a dozen similar memories. Besides, fresh light may appear any day in the discovery of further inscriptions or papyri. Important antiquities are being unearthed by numerous individuals and societies. In spite of all the Egyptian articles in the museums of London, Turin, Berlin, Cairo, and elsewhere, Egypt is only half excavated. Probably more inscriptions still exist under the ground than above it. This is particularly true of the Delta, which was the main scene of the events of the Exodus. This tract of the country is as yet almost an unknown book to us, so far as those early days are concerned, for nearly all our discoveries have come from Middle and Lower Egypt.

Further, it is far from likely that any nation would have placed in the forefront of its records an experience of hardship and slavery in a foreign country, unless this had been a real and vital part of its national life. No nation, certainly, would ever invent the report that it had been in servile bondage to another. The whole story is bound up so closely with the revelation of Yahweh and the religion of Israel that it is hardly likely to be a pure invention. The Jewish records show that it imprinted itself deeply in the memory of later generations. Everything else stands in the background compared with the Egyptian bondage and the deliverance thence. In song, psalm, and prophecy, it echoed down the history of Israel till its close, and could no more be forgotten than the British nation can forget the Great War or the American nation its struggle for Independence. According to critics the narrative of the Exodus has been enriched by the editors with many strange details, and has acquired a miraculous element during the centuries that intervened between the events and the age of the writers. Codes of laws also, which are really of late origin, have been thrown back to the earlier period, in order to give them the stamp of authority. The story has been made the foundation for the institutions of subsequent ages, and been adapted from time to time to later ideals. But after separating what the critics believe to be the later accretions from the earliest records and removing all elaborations due to the development of religious and social institutions, we still have sufficient acceptable traditions left to uphold the Exodus. The majority of Egyptologists and Biblical critics recognize it as an historical event. "That there is a kernel of history in the traditions of Israel's stay in Egypt is not to be doubted." [1] "That Israel was in Egypt under one form or another no historian could possibly doubt; a legend of such tenacity, representing the early fortunes of a people under so unfavourable an aspect could not have arisen save as a reflexion, however much distorted, of real occurrences." [2] "With regard to the main fact that at some time or other certain of the people who subsequently came to be known as the Hebrews dwelt in Egypt for a period, and afterwards entered or re-entered Canaan, there is hardly a dissentient voice." [3]

[1] Professor D. D. Luckenbill, *American Journal of Theology*, xxii. (1918), p. 40.

[2] Gardiner, "The Geography of the Exodus," in *Recueil Champollion* (1922), p. 204. At the same time Gardiner believes that "the Hyksos invasion and the subsequent expulsion of the Hyksos afford quite sufficient basis for the origination of the legend."

[3] Professor T. Eric Peet, *Egypt and the Old Testament*, p. 21. Cf. also Stade, *Geschichte des Volkes Israel*, p. 130; *Die Entstehung des Volkes Israel*, Giessen, 1899; Renan, *Histoire du peuple d'Israel*, i. p. 161; Ewald, *History of Israel*, English translation, ii. pp. 15–228; Wellhausen, *History of Israel*, pp. 429–438; Kittel, *History of the Hebrews*, English translation, pp. 227 ff.; Cornill, *History of the People of Israel*, pp. 41–43.

The admitted facts, after the removal of all supposed post-exilic elaborations, are simple and reliable. Briefly put, they amount to this—that the Israelites were a Semitic people, some or all of whom sought admission into Egypt[1] under pressure of famine. They were placed in the land of 'Goshen,' but after a period of serfdom they finally escaped from it or were driven out of it under the leadership of Moses; and after some years of migration, they gained possession of Palestine, where they established themselves as a religious and political nation. We have, however, no undisputed Egyptian authority for the name 'Goshen,' which seems to rest entirely on Scriptural evidence, but it is admitted by critics that it lay in the eastern Delta region and included the present Wady Tumîlât valley. Heinrich Brugsch, the celebrated hieroglyphic scholar, identified it incorrectly with an ancient Egyptian town Pi-Sopd or Pi-Sapdu ("the house of the god Sopd," now the village *Saft el-Henneh*), the capital of the XXth nome of the Delta.[2] Gardiner pointed out, however, that GSMT (the vowels being uncertain), which Brugsch applied as a name to the town, should probably be SHSMT (Shesmet), and apparently had no connection with the district of Goshen.[3] There was a Goshen in South Palestine

[1] The idea of Winckler (*Altorientalische Forschungen*, 1893, pp. 24 ff.), that the land in which the Israelites sojourned was not Egypt (Hebrew Mizraim, cuneiform *Musr*, *Misr*, or *Misri*), but a supposed North Arabian district called Musr or Musri, has now been discredited by scholars. Reminiscences of wanderings in the Arabian tract, he held, had become confused with the name of Egypt. For a statement of the theory, see Cheyne, *Encyclopedia Biblica*, 1433 f.; and for a refutation of it, see Budge, *Hist. Eg.* vi., Preface, with Ed. Meyer and B. Luther, *Die Israeliten u. ihre Nachbarstämme*, and Bissing, *Recueil de Travaux*, 1912. It is impossible to believe that the whole Egyptian part of the Book of Exodus (found independently in the early statements of both J and E), with its frequent mention of the Pharaoh and its explicit references to Raamses, Succoth, and other places, has been 'faked up' by some redactor.

[2] *Dictionnaire Géographique*, p. 427. Cf. also pp. 876, 1348; *Zeitschrift für ägyptische Sprache*, xix. (1881), pp. 15–18.

[3] Gardiner, *Journal of Egyptian Archæology*, v. (1918), p. 218 ff. Naville takes a different view, *op. cit.*, x. (1924), p. 32; but until further evidence is forthcoming, Gardiner's conclusion seems preferable.

(Josh. x. 41, xi. 16), believed by most scholars to have been in the vicinity of the 'River of Egypt' (*Wady el-ʿArîsh*), about 50 miles south-west of Gaza, and a few scholars incline to the view that some movement of the Israelites from this eastern extension of Egypt is at the basis of the Biblical story of an Exodus. But this theory seems to have little to support it. Some close connection between the Israelites and Egypt proper stands out clearly in the traditions. The theory fails to account for the nature and fundamental data of the Exodus, and is opposed to statements which have every appearance of fact. Goshen must therefore have been somewhere in the eastern Delta. It could not have been a large tract of country. It must have been bounded on the north and south by deserts, and probably covered only about 100 square miles at the most. Within this enclosed tract, somewhat triangular, the great majority of the Israelites must have dwelt, with their flocks and herds, much the same as the bedouins of the present day. They would have their sheiks and tribal leaders, councils of elders, rudimentary worship, and other organization. To the Egyptians they would, no doubt, be of little importance, being insignificant in number, of poor social and political standing, and simply one of the many bedouin tribes who had settled in the pasture lands of the eastern Delta. They were shepherds, and every shepherd was "an abomination unto the Egyptians." This is probably the reason why they are never mentioned in Egyptian history; for even Moses, from the Egyptian point of view, was no more than a leader of alien nomads. As they might, however, form a pact with the enemies of Egypt in the case of invasion (Ex. i. 10) from the east, and thus expose the land to another Asiatic conquest, they were transformed into public serfs and made slaves of the state.

We are not concerned here with the route taken at the Exodus. Whether it was direct to Kadesh-Barnea (*ʿAin Kudeis*), about 50 miles south of Beersheba, or the traditional route by the Gulf of Suez, or the extreme northern route along the shore between the Mediterranean Sea and Lake Serbonis (as Professor Peet, Dr. Hall, and others hold)[1] does not affect the question as to the date. Some reference, however, must be made to the numbers involved, as these, apart from questions of credibility, have an indirect bearing on some theories of the date. The number of men is stated to have been 600,000, besides children and a mixed multitude (Ex. xii. 37 (J); Num. xi. 21 (J)); or, according to the first census of the twelve tribes taken in the desert (Num. i. 46, ii. 32), 603,550 males above twenty years old, besides 22,000 Levites above one month old, or 8580 between thirty and fifty years old (Num. iii. 39, iv. 48). It is incredible that this vast number of people, amounting in reality to about 2,000,000, could have made the march to Kadesh under the circumstances depicted. As Doughty observes, the convoy would be about 200 leagues long. Nor could they have maintained themselves for a generation in the desert between Goshen and Canaan. That there is very serious difficulty in the numbers is evident from a closer examination of them. According to Num. iii. 43, there were only 22,273 first-born boys, or 44,546 families allowing for first-born girls. This would mean that only one man in thirteen had a family. In other words, there were twelve unmarried men to every family. Some critics have escaped the difficulty by regarding the numbers as wholly fictitious, or making some purely arbitrary reduction. No doubt events which have been handed down through many centuries in the form of traditions told

[1] Peet, *Egypt and the Old Testament*, pp. 134 ff.; Hall, *Palestine Exploration Fund Quarterly*, 1923, p. 126; Sir William Willcocks, *From the Garden of Eden to the Crossing of Jordan*, p. 62; Schleiden, *Die Landenge von Suês*, 1858; Brugsch, *L'Éxode et les Monuments Égyptiens*, Leipzig, 1875.

This theory of the route has difficulties. The translation 'Reedy Sea' for 'Red Sea' (*Yam Sūph*), adopted by these scholars, though undoubtedly correct, would apply as much to Lake Timsâh as Lake Serbonis (cf. Driver, *Exodus*, p. 111). The theory of Gardiner (*Recueil Champollion*, 1922, p. 210), that the author of the Exodus narrative, whose geography was not perfect, mistakenly identified 'Raamses' with Tanis, and that he assumed the Exodus to have started from the latter place, would explain many difficulties. The 'Reedy Sea' would correspond with the south-eastern portion of Lake Manzala. Both Peet's and Gardiner's theories on the matter are at least worth considering, though they appear open to many difficulties.

and retold round the camp-fire and beside the well, are bound to undergo some amount of modification, embellishment, or corruption in the process. Other scholars, again, greatly reduce the numbers by translating the Hebrew word *elef* (אֶלֶף) by 'families,' instead of by 'thousands' as generally rendered. Thus, instead of 74,600 of the tribe of Judah, we would have seventy-four families, amounting to 600 people. In this acceptation the 'thousands' forming the numbers of the various tribes of Israel at the time of the Exodus and again at the second census taken later in the wanderings (Num. xxvi.) would simply be the number of tents in a tribe, and the 'hundreds' would be the number of the people. The first census would thus work out at 598 tents, with 5550 people, showing an average tent-group of about nine persons. Instead of the vast multitude, which has always been a difficulty, we need not suppose on this theory that more than 6000 people were involved. This number is certainly more in accord with the size of Goshen, and would not likely affect Egypt to any great extent one way or another.[1] It also agrees better with some of the Biblical traditions. According to J (*e.g.* Ex. i. 10) the Hebrews constituted a comparatively small community, and according to E (Ex. i. 15) they were so few that two midwives were sufficient for them. At the same time, not all Hebrew scholars are prepared to admit that in passages of this nature the word *elef* should bear the meaning of 'families' or 'tents.' When the word is used otherwise than as a numeral, it seems to denote a larger unit than a family or household, and represents a whole clan, or several branches of kinsmen within a clan (cf. Judg. vi. 15; 1 Sam. x. 19 ff.; Mic. v. 2). Even in this sense it is very rare, and is not found in statistical lists.[2]

There is another view of the matter that is taken. It is significant that all the passages ordering and describing the

[1] For an elaboration of this theory, accepted by Flinders Petrie and some other scholars, cf. Petrie, *Expositor*, 1905; *Researches in Sinai* (1906), pp. 207 ff.; *Egypt and Israel*, pp. 40 ff.

[2] Cf. Driver, *Exodus*, p. 101 n.; MacNeile, *The Book of Exodus*, p. 75.

numbering of the people according to their various tribes (Num. i., xxvi.) are part of the Priestly Document (P), dating as late as the latter part of the Exile. The whole style of this document, which is almost exclusively concerned with the externals of religion—priesthood, sacrifices, feasts, numbers, and legislative enactments—shows by its stiffness, artificiality, and conciseness of treatment that it is dealing with a past long dead, and not with the perpetuation in written form of a still living tradition. It is thought, therefore, by some that the priestly redactors, in treating of the census at the time of the Exodus, are reading back into ancient history both the numbers and organic unity of the twelve tribes as realized in later times. This reading back of subsequent facts into early history is believed to be a common practice with the priestly redactors. In the JE documents, for instance, the spies confine their investigations to the Negeb and the hill country immediately to the north of it; but according to P they explore the whole land "from the wilderness of Zin unto Rehob, to the entering in of Hamath" (Num. xiii. 21), *i.e.* the whole of the territory that belonged to Israel centuries afterwards when the monarchy was at the zenith of its splendour. So, in the case before us, the complete tribal system, some think, did not probably exist before the Conquest of Canaan. The likelihood is that originally there were only Leah and Rachel tribes, and that at some time just before or after the Conquest these tribes broke up into organic divisions which eventually went to the formation of the twelve tribes (Leah = Reuben, Simeon, Levi, Judah, Isaachar, Zebulun; Rachel = Joseph, Benjamin). As the sons of concubines, the Zilpah tribes (Gad and Asher) and the Bilhah tribes (Dan and Naphtali) were not looked upon as real parts of Israel at the time of the Exodus, but were regarded as additions afterwards.[1] The perfect organic unity of the tribes, depicted in Num. i. and Num. xxvi., with the numbers of each tribe on leaving Goshen, must therefore, some believe, be assigned to a much later date.

[1] Cf. Professor W. H. Bennett, in *Hastings' Dictionary*, iv. pp. 810 f. (article "Tribes").

It is evident we can never know the true relation of the tribes of the Exodus to the twelve tribes afterwards known as Israel, so long as we have no contemporary documents, but there is a general consensus of opinion among Biblical scholars and Egyptologists that the Exodus from Egypt did not include the whole of the tribes. Jacob, for instance, bought ground at Shechem; indeed, he conquered the town and held pasturing grounds in the district (Gen. xxxiii. 19, xxxvii. 12, xlviii. 22). The story, too, of Jacob's daughter, Dinah, the tribal fortunes of Reuben, Judah's marriage with the Canaanite, and other traditions of the patriarchs and their deeds, seem to imply a permanent settlement in Canaan. Perhaps there has been a considerable body of tradition of this nature which has disappeared in favour of the sojourn in Egypt, as we have it. Whether or not, facts prove that some of the Israelites remained behind when the rest went down to the land of the Pharaohs. Burney holds that only the Rachel or Joseph tribes sojourned in Egypt, while Simeon, Levi, and some elements of Judah were in the desert region near Kadesh-Barnea, and Asher, Zebulun, Issachar, Reuben, Gad, Dan, and Naphtali were in Canaan all along, the first three being located in the far north, between Phœnicia and the Sea of Chinnereth (Gennesaret).[1] The Joseph tribes alone under the leadership of Joshua attacked Canaan from the east, along the line marked out by Jericho, Ai, Gibeon, Beth-horon, and the vale of Aijalon; while Simeon, Levi, and Judah, augmented by the Kenites, Calibbites, and other elements, made an independent thrust from the south, conquered the territory of Arad and settled down in it, afterwards advancing their conquests farther north into the hill country. Thus, according to this view, Joshua was not the leader across Jordan of a united Israel, composed of the twelve tribes, but only of a certain section (the Joseph tribes), and the remaining tribes entered Canaan by other means and at other periods.[2] Whether these views be correct or not,

[1] *Israel's Settlement in Canaan* (Schweich Lectures, 1917), pp. 36, 84, etc.
[2] *Op. cit.*, p. 31.

2

there is good evidence for believing that the tribes which formed the Exodus did not include the whole of Israel,[1] and consequently the numbers given by P, if not explained on the basis of 'families,' must be assigned, some critics think, to a much later date.

Before proceeding further, it is necessary that the writer should state his view as to the date of the Exodus, and give the lines on which he hopes to proceed in the following pages. Nowadays there are at least three main schools of thought on the matter: (1) The one which dates the Exodus during the XVIIIth Dynasty, about 1445 B.C., just after the long reign of Thutmose III. and during that of his son, Amenhotep II. If we allow for the 'wilderness wanderings,' the entry into Canaan would correspond with the attacks of the Ḫabiru mentioned in the Tell el-Amarna Tablets (*c.* 1400–1366 B.C.). There is not much difference between this view and the one advocated by Dr. H. R. Hall and a few other scholars,[2] except that they believe the Israelites to have left Egypt with the Hyksos (*c.* 1580 B.C.) or shortly afterwards, and to have lived a nomadic life of about 200 years in the desert previous to entering Canaan as the Ḫabiru. (2) The school which connects the Exodus with the religious revolution attempted throughout Egypt by Amenhotep IV., otherwise known as Akhenaten (*c.* 1383–1366 B.C.). According to this view, which is strongly advocated by Mr. Arthur Weigall, the Israelites were driven out at the close of the revolution, or at the commencement of the restoration under Harmhab (*c.* 1358–1324 B.C.). This would place the Exodus about 1350 or 1345 B.C., being about a century later than the date suggested by the first school. (3) The traditional school, which dates it more than a century later still, during the XIXth Dynasty, by regarding Ramesses II. (*c.* 1301–1234 B.C.) as the great Oppressor of the Israelites, and the Exodus as having taken place during the reign of his son, Merenptah (*c.* 1233–1223 B.C.), or even later still, during

[1] For a fuller discussion of this matter, see Paton, *Biblical World* (American), xlvi. pp. 82–88.

[2] *The Ancient History of the Near East*, 5th ed., 1920, pp. 403 ff.

the reign of one of his immediate successors.[1] In support of this view, it is held that the name of the store city 'Raamses,' built by the Israelites (Ex. i. 11), shows that the Exodus must have happened after Ramesses II. came to the throne. As the Egyptian armies, too, were constantly raiding Canaan down to the time at least of Ramesses III., who ascended the throne as late as 1204 B.C., and yet there is absolutely no mention of such attacks in the Biblical records, it is held that the entry of the Israelites into the land must have been after this date.[2]

The writer belongs to the first of these schools. While not laying weight on Biblical chronology, which is recognized as artificial and of uncertain value, especially for pre-monarchic times, he finds that the earliest date (*c.* 1445 B.C.) satisfies best all the conditions involved, and that the difficulties in the way of it, emphasized so much by some critics, are non-existent, or at all events easily explainable. The difficulties to be considered by all three schools are at least five in number: (1) The chronological, which must be so treated as not to do violence to admitted data; (2) the fact of the Ḫabiru invasion of Palestine, which must be satisfactorily solved without resort to fanciful explanations; (3) the question as to Pithom and Raamses having been built by the Israelites during their sojourn in Egypt; (4) the fact that Egyptian armies frequently raided parts of Palestine

[1] Some scholars would place it later than the traditional school. Kittel, Maspéro, Wiedemann, and others would date it during the period of weakness and general anarchy at the close of the XIXth Dynasty. MacCurdy (*Hist. Proph. and Mon.*, i. p. 204), Eerdmans (*Vorgeschichte*, pp. 74 f.), and others would even put it in the XXth Dynasty. Eerdmans places it as late as 1130 B.C. But these scholars entangle themselves in serious chronological difficulties. Eerdmans, indeed, makes his theory impossible, as he finds it necessary to allow only about eighty years for the whole period from the Conquest to the accession of David in 1009 B.C. These extra late dates are considered in Chapter XI., on Chronology.

[2] One or two scholars, such as Professor Tofteen (*The Historic Exodus*, 1909, Chicago), combine the first theory with this one, thus making two Exoduses, the first at the end of the reign of Thutmose III. and the second after Ramesses III. But there is no ground for such a view, which appears forced and contradictory to genuine tradition.

down to the early years of Ramesses III. (*c.* 1204–1172 B.C.); (5) the fact that Merenptah's stele (*c.* 1228 B.C.) refers to 'Israel' as a people already settled in Palestine. Taking all these difficulties into consideration, it seems to the writer that the third school of thought, while claiming support from (3) and (4), *viz.* the building of Pithom and Raamses and the later raids into Palestine, does so without sufficient justification, and at the same time offers no reasonable solution to the remaining three difficulties. The views of this school were of much value so long as there was no authentic information to the contrary from Egyptian or other contemporary sources. It was natural to regard Ramesses II., who built so much in the Wady Tumîlât, as the Pharaoh of the Oppression, and his weak successor, Merenptah, who precedes a period of Egyptian decline, as the Pharaoh of the Exodus. But since the discovery of the Tell el-Amarna Letters referring to Canaan being invaded by Ḫabiru, and of Merenptah's stele mentioning the Israelites, such views have lost much of their weight, even among the most conservative scholars. The second school is no better. It has no ground for the view that the Exodus resulted from Akhenaten's religious revolution. There is, in fact, no connection between the Atenism of that king and the religion of Israel, as we hope to show later; and this second theory does not offer a much better explanation of the difficulties than the third one. The theory of the first school, on the other hand, satisfies excellently all the conditions. It is certainly in agreement with the Biblical chronology, it accounts easily for the Ḫabiru invasion, it is in accord with the statement on Merenptah's stele, and it is not at all inconsistent, as we hope to show, with the building of Pithom and Raamses, nor with the Egyptian raiding of Palestine. It affords remarkable harmonies of date and circumstances, without any kind of makeshift. It is noteworthy, too, that Manetho and almost all ancient historians and chronologers, who would, no doubt, derive their information from Egyptian sources, whether legendary or otherwise, place the Exodus under the XVIIIth Dynasty, not the XIXth. It seems unlikely that Manetho, especially, would make a mistake as to the particular Dynasty under which the Exodus occurred.

In the following chapters the writer, before treating of the first-named theory, will deal successively with the arguments advanced for the third and second.

CHAPTER II

PITHOM AND RAAMSES

ONE of the arguments on which great stress is laid in support of the traditional or late-date theory is the fact mentioned in Scripture (Ex. i. 11 (J)) that the Israelites during their sojourn in Egypt built the 'treasure or store' cities Pithom and Raamses (or Rameses),[1] and as these are supposed to have been connected with Ramesses II. (*c.* 1301–1234 B.C.), it is assumed that the Exodus cannot have taken place till after his reign. For this reason, among others, the Exodus has been assigned by many experts to the reign of Merenptah, the immediate successor of Ramesses II. or even later. Brugsch, Ebers, Rawlinson, Driver, Sayce, Petrie, Burney, and many others take up this position. "Unless we deny the historical accuracy of Ex. i. 11," says Professor Sayce, "the date of the Exodus is definitely fixed."[2]

In 1923 the members of the University Museum of Philadelphia, under Dr. Fisher, discovered a stele of Ramesses II. at Beisân (the ancient site of Beth-shean, near the Sea of Galilee) containing a reference to the building of the town of Rameses in the Delta, in which some 'Semites' are stated to have taken part.[3] The daily newspapers and even some

[1] They are termed עָרֵי מִסְכְּנוֹת in the Hebrew, usually rendered 'treasure (A.V.) *or* store (R.V.) cities'; but scholars are not agreed as to the exact meaning of the expression. The Septuagint makes them πόλεις ὀχυραί, 'strong *or* fortified cities,' and further adds, "and On, which is Heliopolis" (τήν τε Πειθὼ καὶ Ῥαμεσσὴ καὶ Ὦν, ἥ ἐστιν Ἡλίου πόλις). The expression עָרֵי מִסְכְּנוֹת occurs in 1 Kings ix. 19, where the only Septuagint version (A) which has this section puts πόλεις τῶν σκηνωμάτων, 'cities of abode.'

[2] *Hastings' Dictionary*, iii. p. 887*a*.

[3] *The Museum Journal*, Philadelphia, xiv. (1923), No. 4, p. 234.

authoritative Journals distorted this detail into the information that the stele narrates the building of the store city of Rameses by the *Israelites*, and thus the discovery of the stele was regarded as another corroboration of the late-date theory! Considering the great importance of the city of Rameses, to which additions were made continually during this king's reign, we should expect that a large number of captives would be employed in the works. Quite naturally many of these, probably the large majority of them, would be of Semitic race; and, as any one can see, this is really all that the inscription implies.[1]

A closer examination of the whole argument for these two cities being built by the Israelites during their sojourn in Egypt shows that the proof is not so convincing as it might appear. Lagarde, Hommel, and others hold, on what seem to be good grounds, that there stood originally in the text "Pithom of (the province of) Raamses" (*viz.* in distinction from other places called Pithom). Lagarde has made a careful critical comparison of this verse in the ancient copies, including the Syrian. His arguments are too technical to refer to here, but he concludes that "Pithom of Raamses" is the correct reading (וְאֶת פִּתֹם רַעַמְסֵס).[2] If this be so, 'Raamses' cannot be taken here as the name of a town: it is an explanatory addition only, reminding us of its use in Gen. xlvii. 11 ("in the land of Rameses"),[3] and the writer must be using the name proleptically, as the author of the verse in Genesis was doing (for it is admitted the name did not exist in the time of Joseph or the Hyksos).

[1] The stele, which has been described as "a masterpiece of poetic literature" (*The Journal, loc. cit.*), consists of twenty-four lines wholly devoted to a panegyric of the king, who was like "a lion among the goats," "an eagle among birds," his enemies "flying like feathers before the wind." The brief line stating that Ramesses used Semites in the building of his name-city is tucked away in the midst of all this flowery language.

[2] P. de Lagarde, *Mitt.*, iv. pp. 149 ff.; cf. also Hommel, *Expository Times*, x. p. 212.

[3] Similarly, the Greek version of Gen. xlvi. 28 ff. also mentions Rameses as the land into which Judah was sent to meet Joseph at the city of Heroonpolis (τὸν δὲ Ἰούδαν ἀπέστειλεν ἔμπροσθεν αὐτοῦ πρὸς Ἰωσὴφ συναντῆσαι αὐτῷ καθ' Ἡρώων πόλιν εἰς γῆν Ῥαμεσσῆ).

But even apart from this construction of the text, the argument is weak. The city of Rameses of course existed, for we have indubitable Egyptian evidence of it, and the Israelites are said to have started from it when they left Egypt (Ex. xii. 37; Num. xxxiii. 3). No doubt it took its name from one of the Ramesside Pharaohs, and as Rameses I. was merely an ephemeral king, it probably took its name from Ramesses II. But to assume on this account that it was founded and built as late as the reign of this Pharaoh is unwarranted. Geographical names occurring in a narrative written many centuries after certain events took place are often much later than those events. Modern historians trained in scientific methods of accuracy do not make such mistakes. They never attribute to past ages the names, social conditions, and phases of thought which are current at the time of their writing—not even when their object is to inculcate the lessons of past ages to their contemporaries. But Jewish historians, not accustomed to such accuracy, were prone to do this, both in their civil and religious writings.[1] The union of the twelve tribes, the single sanctuary, the laws regulating sacrifices and the priesthood, and numerous other usages were all read into bygone history as if they had actually existed in those early ages. The word 'Pharaoh' (Egyptian *Per-ʿo*), for instance, literally meaning 'The Great House,' is applied in the story of Joseph to the reigning monarch; but it is known not to have been adopted as the king's official designation until about the XVIIIth Dynasty, several centuries later than Joseph. Similarly, the title Zaphnath-paaneakh, given to Joseph by Pharaoh, as well as the names Potiphar and Asenath, are later still than the XVIIIth Dynasty. In Gen. xiv. 14 we read that Abram pursued the captives of his brother as far as Dan; but we know that the name of the city at the time was Laish (or Leshem), and the name Dan was only given to it later, at the time of the Danite migration northward (Josh. xix. 47; Judg. xviii. 29). In 1 Chron. xxix. 7 (R.V.) we read of a reckoning in Darics (אֲדַרְכּוֹנִים),

[1] Cf. Professor MacFadyen on "Telescoped History," ***Expository Times***, xxxvi. (1924), pp. 103 ff.

which was a Persian coin not introduced until the fifth satrapy,[1] but it is here represented as a current coin in the time of David, many centuries earlier. In all such cases the writers, who lived and wrote after the changes referred to had taken place, used the newer names or designations as being better known to their contemporaries, just as we find it often said that "the Romans built York," whereas we know that the name under which they built it was Eboracum (the Latinized form of the early British name Evrawc), the name York being a much later appellation.

In the same way, the name Rameses, applied to the city by the narrator of the Exodus, may not have been adopted till long after the city was built, and indeed till long after the Israelites had left Egypt. Dr. Hall is undoubtedly correct when he says, "The name Rameses, as that of a store-city, may have been conferred by a scribe writing long after the Mosaic period." [2] Because the city was called 'Rameses' when the earliest Jewish records were written (*c.* 850 B.C.), it does not at all follow that it was so called when the Israelites built it. There is absolutely no proof that this was its original name, and therefore we cannot argue that its foundation was laid as late as Ramesses II., or even his immediate predecessors. We have evidence that this Pharaoh strengthened and greatly improved various Delta towns. He added enormously, for instance, to Zoan or Tanis, so much so that Naville calls him its "second founder." Possibly the same was the case with the city of Rameses, which may have been already ancient before he ascended the throne. It was his habit to give his name to the work and monuments of his predecessors, for there is abundant evidence that he habitually erased their names, including the name of his father, and substituted his own. What more likely, in view of all these considerations, than that 'Raamses' was simply an older city which this great and ambitious monarch rebuilt and strengthened, and to which he transferred his own name? At all events, there seems little ground for using the building

[1] Babelon, *Les Origines de la Monnaie*, xx f.
[2] *Ancient History*, p. 403, n. 3.

of the city as an argument in favour of a late date for the Exodus.

Professor Luckenbill, while he admits that the Israelites must have entered Canaan during the Amarna period, yet in order to account for the building of these two cities by them, holds that one or more of the southern tribes (Levi or others) must have sojourned in Egypt in the day of Ramesses II.[1] There is surely no ground for such an artificial hypothesis. Though the southern tribes were probably independent to a large extent of the northern tribes (the Joseph ones) in their general movements and developments, Pithom and Rameses could hardly have been built by one or two tribes two centuries after the rest of Israel had taken possession of Canaan.

The excavations which have been made with a view to finding the city of Rameses do not give us much light. It is known to have existed somewhere in the Delta. Flinders Petrie believes that he has located it at the modern village of Tell er-Retâbeh (or Tell Rotâb), in the Wady Tumîlât, where he found scenes on the temple wall descriptive of Ramesses II. slaughtering prisoners before the god Tũm, lord of Theku, a granite stele of the same king recording victories in the south over the eastern bedouins, a double statue in red granite of Ramesses II. and the god Tũm, some foundation works of Ramesses III., and some scarabs and minor objects going back to about the IXth Dynasty (about 2500 B.C.).[2] According to Petrie, an official here was over the foreigners of Theku (Thuku), which he identifies with Succoth (or ' booths ') ; and this official, he thinks, was probably the superintendent of the Israelites.[3] " All these discoveries," he says, " exactly accord with the requirements of

[1] *American Journal of Theology*, xxii. (1918), p. 41.

[2] Petrie, *Hyksos and Israelite Cities*, plates xxviii.–xxxvi., with pp. 28–34.

[3] *Egypt and Israel*, pp. 33 f. If Succoth (סֻכּוֹת) be a Semitic word, it might become ' Theku ' (Tkw) in Egyptian, for the Hebrew consonants *s* and *c* correspond perfectly with the Egyptian *t* and *k*, and the Egyptians frequently dropped the final *t*; but the identification is not accepted by all Egyptologists, and may be regarded as doubtful (cf. Gardiner, *Journal of Egyptian Archæology*), v. (1918), p. 266 n. ; Peet, *Egypt and the Old Testament*, p. 88).

the city of Raamses, where both the second and third kings of that name are stated to have worked. . . . The absence of any other Egyptian site suitable to these conditions, which are fulfilled here, makes it practically certain that this was the city of Raamses named in the Exodus." [1] But there seems to be little evidence, as Professor Peet says,[2] in these discoveries for regarding the site as that of the city of Rameses, for there is nothing in them to prove the name of it; and even though it be Rameses, as Petrie believes, there is nothing to prove that it was founded by Ramesses II. "The claim," says Gardiner, "is uncorroborated by any inscriptional testimony whatsoever." [3]

Peet, Gardiner, Hall, and others incline to the view that the city of Rameses is identical with Pi-Ramesse ('House of Ramesses'), the Delta capital of the XIXth Dynasty, which they conjecture occupied the site of the Avaris of the Hyksos and was at or near the later Pelusium, on the easternmost branch of the Nile.[4] The city is known to have been a favourite resort of the kings, especially of Ramesses II., who no doubt used it for training his soldiers and inspiring terror in his Asiatic enemies. It was the centre of the revenue administration. Here were the great public offices and hither the taxes were brought. It possessed temples of Amūn, Re, Ptah, Sutekh, and other deities.[5] It was the city to which the messengers of the Hittite king, Hattushilish III., brought (about 1280 B.C.) the silver tablet containing the peace treaty. The papyri give lyrical descriptions of the country around it: [6] "It is a fair spot, there is not the like of it. . . . The residence is agreeable to live in, its fields are full of all good things; it is furnished with abundant

[1] *Hyksos and Israelite Cities*, p. 28.

[2] *Egypt and the Old Testament*, p. 83.

[3] "The Delta Residence of the Ramessides," in *Journ. of Egypt. Arch.*, v. (1918), pp. 127 ff., 179 ff., 242 ff.

[4] Pelusium was built in the time of Psammetichus I. (c. 651–610 B.C.), when this king assigned it to his Ionian and Carian mercenaries (Herodotus, ii. 154). A brief history of the city and its neighbourhood is given by Dr. W. F. Hume, *Cairo Scientific Journal*, ix. p. 54.

[5] Clédat, *Notes sur l'Isthme de Suez*, pp. 162 ff.

[6] *Pap. Anastasi III.*, 11; cf. Gardiner, *Journ. of Egypt. Arch.*, v. p. 185.

provisions every day . . . its meads are verdant with herbage . . . the fruit is like the taste of honey in the cultivated fields; its granaries are full of wheat and spelt; they draw near to the sky, onions and leeks in the . . . clusters of flowers in the grove, pomegranates, apples, and olives, figs from the orchard." Such was the residence city of the Ramesside kings, and Gardiner inclines to believe that either the 'Raamses' of the Bible is to be identified with this city, "or else it is a town unknown to the Egyptian monuments, the existence of which is merely postulated."[1] Though Gardiner admits that "more satisfactory testimony is required on almost every point,"[2] there may be truth in what he says. It seems to be corroborated by Manetho, the Egyptian historian, whose account of the Exodus, though untrustworthy in many particulars, states that after the Israelites had been working in the quarries for a long time in a miserable state, the king set apart the city of Avaris for their use, and that it was from there that they were ultimately driven out and pursued.[3] It is also noteworthy that in the official Targums of Palestine and of Jerusalem, which are regarded as excellent Aramaic translations of the Hebrew, the name Raamses or Rameses in the various passages where it occurs is replaced by the name Pelusium ('Pelusin'). Instead, for instance, of "The children of Israel journeyed from Rameses to Succoth" (Ex. xii. 37), we read, "The sons of Israel moved forth from Pelusin towards Succoth." But whatever view we take of the site of the city, the main point in our argument is that there is no proof of the city dating only from the reign of Ramesses II. In calling it by this name, the writer or compiler of the Biblical narrative naturally made use of the current appellation of his own day. The standpoint is that of the *writer* of the narrative, not that of the *event* recorded.

[1] "The Delta Residence of the Ramessides," *op. cit.*, p. 261; cf. also iii. pp. 99 ff., x. pp. 87 ff.; *Bibliothèque de l'école des Hautes Études*, No. 234; Hall, *Ancient History*, p. 405; Peet, *Egypt and the Old Testament*, p. 85.

[2] *Journ. of Egypt. Arch.*, x. p. 87.

[3] Josephus, *Contra Apion.*, i. 26, 27.

There is a similar dubiety as to the site of Pithom or Pi-Tūm (" the House of Tūm," an ancient sun-god of Heliopolis). The name is first found in records of the age of the XIXth Dynasty. In the Egyptian papyrus, for example, known as Anastasi VI., there is a letter dated in the eighth year of Merenptah (*i.e.* about 1225 B.C.), the son and successor of Ramesses II., which speaks of the eastern bedouin tribes being allowed to pass the *khetam* or " fortress of Merenptah, belonging to Theku," which protected the eastern frontier of Egypt, and to feed their flocks near " the pools of Pi-Tūm of Merenptah, belonging to Theku." [1] The city is known by scholars to be identical with Heroonpolis, spoken of so often by the later Greeks, and abbreviated by the Romans into Ero.[2] The site, however, has been the subject of much controversy. It is believed by many experts to have been discovered by Naville. While this well-known explorer was excavating, in 1883, at a modern village called Tell el-Maskûta (" The mound of the Image "), in the Wady Tumîlât, on the line of railway from Zagazig to Suez, and in close proximity to the ancient sweet-water canal, he unearthed sphinxes, naos, statues, and steles, which were evidently part of a temple of Tūm, some of which were of the age of Ramesses II. He also discovered two Latin inscriptions mentioning Hero or Ero, the one at the side of a doorway and the other close by on a small slab or milestone of date A.D. 306. The former inscription reads (in four lines), " *Loero* | *polis* | *ero* | *castra*," where *Lo* is believed to stand for *locus*. The latter is, " *Ab Ero in Klysma M. VIIII.* –*Θ*." Klysma is the Clesma mentioned by the abbess Ætheria (*c.* 533–40 A.D.), and by Petrus Diaconus, as being at the head of the Red Sea (as its northern limit then was). Further excavations by Naville led to the discovery of a temple, private

[1] *Select Papyri in the Hieratic Character*, British Museum Collections, plates cxxv.–vi.

[2] This explains the reading of the Septuagint A in Gen. xlvi. 28, " He sent Judah before him unto Joseph to meet him at Heroonpolis in the land of Rameses," where the Coptic version substitutes " Pithom, the city," for Heroonpolis. In the inscription on the obelisk of Hermapion, quoted by Ammianus Marcellinus (Champollion, *Grammaire*, p. 361), the " son of Heron " (or " Hero ") is substituted in the translation for " the son of Tūm."

habitations, some brick buildings supposed to be storehouses, extensive city walls some 18 feet thick in the form of a square (containing about 55,000 square yards), and various inscriptions. The temple occupied only a small space in the angle of the enclosure, and seems to have remained unfinished. The chambers composing the supposed storehouses had brick walls from 8 to 10 feet thick, and were without communication with each other, the only access to them being from above.[1] The fact that the whole city seems to have been ruthlessly levelled would accord with the Romans having formed their camp on the site of it and founded the later Heroonpolis on the north-eastern edge. The site of the excavations also agrees with the statement of Herodotus, who informs us that Pithom lay somewhere on the canal made by Necho (610–594 B.C.), which led from the Nile to the Red Sea.[2] The canal, he tells us, started "a little above Bubastis" (now Zagazig), and passed by the side of "Patumos, a city in the Arabian nome." Long ago, in 1864, Chabas pointed out that the site of Pithom should be sought at Tell el-Maskûta, and D'Anville placed Heroonpolis there,[3] a suggestion which was adopted by Quatremère, Champollion, and many other Egyptologists. When, therefore, Naville announced the results of his excavations, the discovery of Pithom was regarded as settled.

Of late years, however, doubts have been thrown on the matter. Peet, Gardiner, and others are not inclined to admit Naville's conclusions.[4] They lay weight on the fact that Pithom is found only on two hieroglyphic inscriptions found there, while the name most often found is Theku, showing in their opinion that the place with its thick surrounding walls is the fortress of Theku mentioned in the Egyptian papyrus Anastasi VI., already referred to. The supposed 'store-chambers,' Peet says,

[1] For further information, see Naville, *The Store City of Pithom and the Route of the Exodus* (Egypt Exploration Society, 1883), pp. 9, 21 ff., and plate xi.

[2] Herodotus, ii. 158.

[3] *Mémoires sur l'Égypte*, pp. 122 ff.

[4] Peet, *Egypt and the Old Testament*, p. 86; Gardiner, *Journ. of Egypt. Arch.*, v. pp. 267 ff., x. pp. 95 ff.

"are probably nothing more than the foundation walls of a fortress, precisely similar to those found at Naukratis and Daphnæ. These late Egyptian fortresses were built up on massive brick platforms, containing hollow compartments. No one who examines Naville's plan can remain in doubt as to the real nature of what he found." [1] These Egyptologists prefer to place Pithom at the modern Tell er-Retâbeh, 8½ miles farther west, the very place that Petrie has taken for Rameses, and they explain the milestone inscription as meaning "Nine miles on the road from Ero to Klysma." It is quite possible, however, in spite of these views, that Naville may be right. The fact that Ero was a Roman town seems to support Naville's identification,[2] for according to Petrie Tell er-Retâbeh shows no signs of having been occupied by the Romans. "The work of the first winter," says Petrie, "has shown that, so far from being a Roman camp, this is the oldest site known east of Bubastis, and that it has not had any Roman occupation." [3] On the whole, therefore, Naville seems to be right, although there is an element of doubt which can only be settled by further archæology.

But wherever Pithom and Rameses may have been, it is clearly incorrect to say that the founder of them must have been Ramesses II., and that because the Israelites are stated to have built them the Exodus cannot have taken place till after the reign of this monarch. The fact that, of all the inscriptions discovered in Pithom, there was none bearing the name of any king earlier than Ramesses II. does not prove that this king was the original founder and builder of the city, especially when we reflect that he habitually erased or destroyed the names of his predecessors and put his own name in their place; and it must be remembered that Naville "never had the good fortune to find the king's name stamped on any of the bricks." [4] In the case of the city of Rameses, too, unless the

[1] *Egypt and the Old Testament*, p. 86 n.

[2] Naville, *Journ. of Egypt. Arch.*, x. (1924), pp. 32 ff.

[3] *Hyksos and Israelite Cities*, p. 28.

[4] Report, July 1883.

name be of possible greater antiquity than we think,[1] there is reason to believe that the Biblical writer is giving the more modern appellation current in his own time. Where a modern editor would append a footnote, the Jewish writers or redactors substituted the better-known name in the text.

[1] On this point see Canon Cook, *Speaker's Commentary, Exodus*, pp. 466, 486, where he shows that Rameses may have been an old name, dating from the reign of Ahmose I. (*c.* 1580 B.C.).

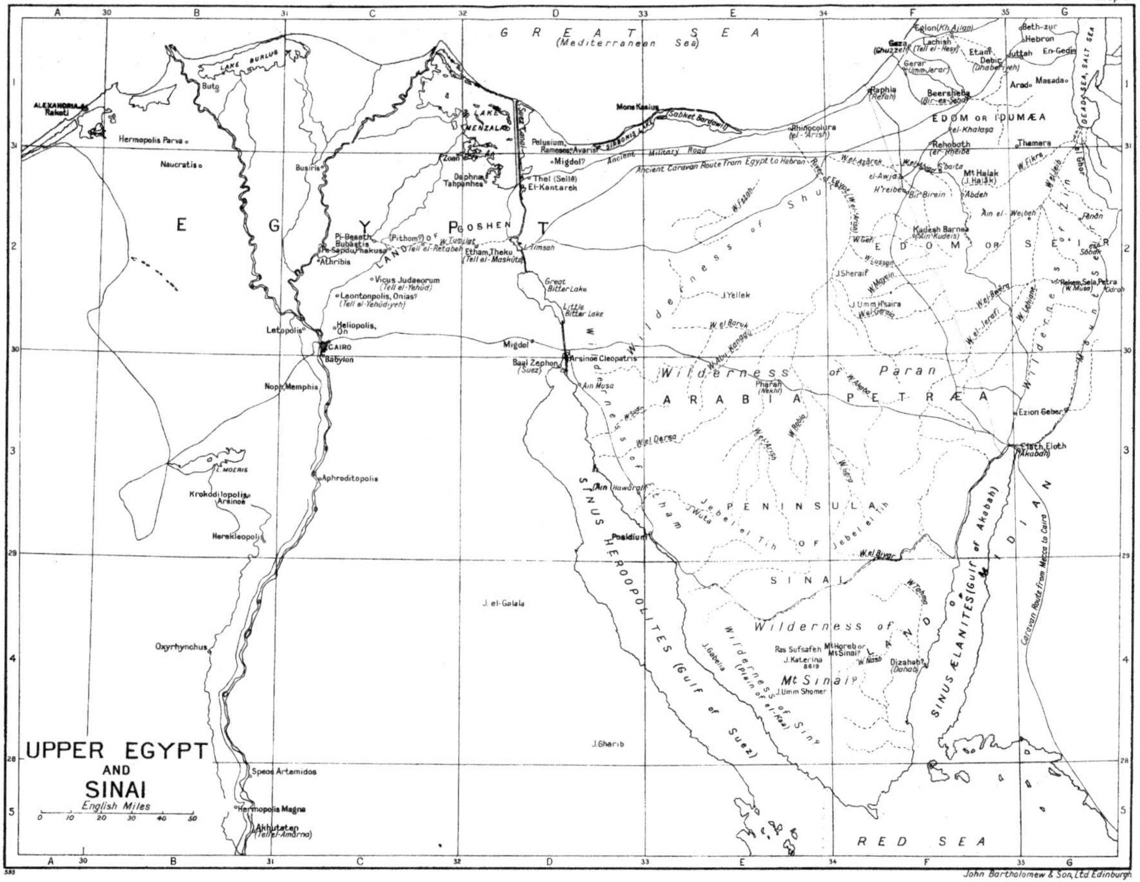
UPPER EGYPT
AND
SINAI
English Miles
0 10 20 30 40 50
GREAT SEA
(Mediterranean Sea)
RED SEA
EGYPT
GOSHEN
LAND OF
ARABIA PETRÆA
Wilderness of Paran
PENINSULA OF SINAI
Wilderness of Shur
Wilderness of Sinai
Wilderness of Zin
Wilderness of Sin
(Plain of el-Kaa)
EDOM OR IDUMÆA
EDOM OR SEIR
LAND OF MIDIAN
SINUS HEROOPOLITES (Gulf of Suez)
SINUS ÆLANITES (Gulf of Akabah)
Lake Burlus
Lake Menzaleh
Sirbonis Lake
Sabket Bardawil
Suez Canal
Great Bitter Lake
Little Bitter Lake
L. Timsah
L. Moeris
DEAD SEA, SALT SEA
Alexandria
Rakoti
Buto
Hermopolis Parva
Naucratis
Busiris
Zoan
Daphnæ
Tahpanhes
Pelusium
Rameses, Avaris?
Migdol?
Thel (Sellē)
El-Kantareh
Mons Kasius
Pi-Beseth
Bubastis
Pe-Sapdu, Phakussa
Athribis
(Pithom?)
W. Tumilat
Tell el-Retabeh
Etham, Theku
(Tell el-Maskuta)
Vicus Judaeorum
(Tell el-Yehud)
Leontonpolis, Onias?
(Tell el-Yehudiyeh)
Heliopolis, On
Letopolis
CAIRO
Babylon
Noph, Memphis
Migdol
Baal Zephon
(Suez)
Arsinoe Cleopatris
Ain Musa
Aphroditopolis
Krokodilopolis
Arsinoe
Herakleopolis
Oxyrhynchus
Speos Artemidos
Hermopolis Magna
Akhutaten
(Tell el-Amarna)
J. el-Galala
J. Gharib
Ain Hawarah
Poseidium
Rhinocolura
(el-'Arish)
River of Egypt (W. el-'Arish)
Ancient Military Road
Ancient Caravan Route from Egypt to Hebron
J. Yellek
J. Sheraif
J. Umm Hsaira
W. el Baruk
W. Abu Kanagu
Pharan
(Nekhl)
Jebel el Tih
J. Wuta
W. el-'Arish
W. el Biyar
W. Tahmo
Ras Sufsafeh
J. Katerina
8619
Mt Horeb or Mt Sinai?
Mt Sinai?
J. Umm Shomer
W. Nasb
Dizahab?
(Dahab)
J. Gabelia
Ezion Geber
Elath, Eloth
(Akabah)
Caravan Route from Mecca to Cairo
Gaza
(Ghuzzeh)
Eglon (Kh. Ajlan)
Lachish
(Tell el-Hesy)
Gerar
(Umm Jerar)
Etam
Debir
(Dhaheriyeh)
Beth-zur
Hebron
Juttah
En-Gedi
Arad
Masada
Raphia
(Refah)
Beersheba
(Bir-es-Seba)
el-Khalasa
Rehoboth
(er-Rheibe)
Thamara
el-Awja
S'baita
Mt Halak
(J. Halak)
H'reibe
Bir Birein
'Abdeh
Ain el-Weibeh
Kadesh Barnea
('Ain Kudeis)
Fenan
Sobak
Rekem, Sela, Petra
(W. Musa)
'Odroh
el Ghor
W. Fikre
W. el-Jerafi
W. Lehiane
John Bartholomew & Son, Ltd Edinburgh

CHAPTER III

EGYPTIAN CONTROL OF PALESTINE: THE AMARNA AGE

THE second argument in support of the late-date theory is that Palestine was so effectually controlled as an Egyptian province, until at least the reign of Ramesses III., that it was impossible or at least very improbable that the Israelites could have taken possession until some time after the beginning of that monarch's reign (*c.* 1204–1172 B.C.), which means that, if we allow for the generation of nomadic life in the wilderness, the Exodus cannot be dated before about 1225 B.C. at the earliest.

Certainly, in this matter, scholars are on much surer ground when they consider the historical question as to when Palestine ceased to be an Egyptian province under the strict control of the Pharaohs, for it is evident that no outside people could have taken possession of the province, unless Egyptian control had been sufficiently relaxed to permit of this. If we can discover, as we are able to do, from Egyptian history, the date or approximate date of this weakening or relaxation, we may be certain that the entry into the land could not have been anterior to it.

Egypt's control of Palestine and Syria, as dependent provinces of the Pharaoh, began far back in the early dynasties. She invaded these countries again later on, to glut her wrath on the Semites, who, as the Hyksos, had kept her in vassalage for so long. She thus became supreme ruler over the whole territory stretching from the Nile right up through Palestine to the land of the Hittites. This control lasted till near the end of the XVIIIth Dynasty, when it gradually weakened and was practically lost under Amenhotep IV., known better as Akhenaten (*c.* 1383–1366 B.C.). Let us look into the matter from the beginning of the XVIIIth Dynasty.

Invasion of Palestine took place under Ahmose I. (*c.* 1580–1558 B.C.), the founder of that Dynasty, who had expelled the Hyksos from the land, and who had ascended the throne of a united Egypt. The invasion was carried further by subsequent kings. Thutmose I. (*c.* 1545–1514 B.C.) advanced victoriously through Syria as far as Naharin, *i.e.* the district lying between the rivers Orontes and Upper Euphrates, and set up a boundary monument on the bank of the latter river, to mark the northern extent of Egyptian dominion. Thutmose III. (*c.* 1501–1447 B.C.) —the king who made the obelisk commonly known as Cleopatra's Needle, which now stands on the Thames Embankment—though only thirty years of age when he ascended the throne, commenced a huge campaign in Syria and defeated the confederated princes at Megiddo, compelling them to recognize him as overlord.[1] From the capture of the city of Megiddo alone he carried away 924 splendid chariots, 2238 horses, 2400 cattle of various kinds, 200 shining suits of armour, including those of two kings, large quantities of gold and silver, a royal sceptre, the valuable tent of one of the kings, and many other articles. Wherever he went, the cities hastened to submit to him and pay tribute; any that would not do so were ignominiously overcome. In his twenty-third year, he records a victory over the Phœnicians and Syrians; in his twenty-ninth year, a campaign to Retenu (Syria), Tunip, Arvad, and Phœnicia, with much spoil; in his thirtieth year, a campaign to Kadesh on the Orontes, and neighbouring places; and in his thirty-fourth year, a campaign which brought tribute from Phœnicia, Syria, and Arasa or A(ra)siy (? Cyprus). During twenty years, indeed, this great Egyptian ruler led some seventeen expeditions through Palestine to Syria,[2] clearing the country of most of

[1] Megiddo is the modern *Tell el-Mutesellim* ("The mound of the governor"), in the Plain of Esdraelon. For a plan of the battle of Megiddo, see H. H. Nelson, *The Battle of Megiddo*, Map IV.; *Cambridge Ancient History*, ii. p. 69.

[2] Cf. Breasted, *Ancient Records of Egypt*, ii. 391 ff.

the valuables and a large part of the crops. In one of his campaigns he captured the great Hittite fortress of Carchemish on the Upper Euphrates, and crossing this river set up a boundary tablet on the eastern bank, beside that of Thutmose I. One of the bravest of his captains tells us on the walls of his tomb how he had waded through the waters of the Euphrates when his master conquered the land. Some historians are of the view that Thutmose III. received presents even from Babylon, for we find allusion to the tribute he received from the chief of Shinʿar (*i.e.* Sumer or Babylonia).[1] He was suzerain of all Palestine, Syria, the territory around Kadesh on the Orontes, and the countries eastward to the Euphrates, and his sway extended to the distant Amanus Mountains (in the extreme north of Syria) and to the kingdom of Mitanni. He thus exercised sway over a great mixture of chiefs and peoples, including a native Semitic element, west Aryan and east Aryan groups, and intrusive elements from the far north. The Egyptian treasuries were full to overflowing, and the altars of Egypt groaned under the weight of the offerings. Even Cyprus, Crete, and perhaps the islands of the Ægean sent a yearly tribute. The streets of Thebes were thronged with foreigners—long-robed Asiatics adorned with jewels from Syria, Phœnician merchants in charge of precious wares, and vassals from all parts bearing their treasures to the palace. The Egyptian armies were feared by all the world. Everywhere the talk was of conquest, numberless war-songs were composed, and battle hymns were inscribed on the temple walls. Thutmose III., whose great empire stretched from the Sudan to the Euphrates, was sought as a friend and ally by kings on all sides. He was regarded as the mightiest of the Pharaohs, against whose authority no enemy, however powerful, would venture to lift a finger. We hope to show later on that he was the Pharaoh of the Oppression.

[1] Some scholars, however, take the allusion as applying to Sengara, the modern *Ǵebel Sinǵar*, west of Nineveh. See Burney, *Israel's Settlement in Canaan*, p. 61 n.; and cf. Breasted, *Ancient Records of Egypt*, ii. 484 n.; Hall, *Ancient History*, p. 242.

As for Palestine, the whole country on both sides of the Jordan was made into an Egyptian province, much as Germany and Thrace were by the Romans, or as India is by Britain to-day. The whole land was controlled by means of commissioners or travelling inspectors (*rabisu*) appointed by the Pharaoh. These officials had their regular circuits, in which they collected tribute, advised the vassals, assisted the friends of the king, and punished his enemies; and they had the help of Egyptian garrisons, installed in the chief cities, to keep watch upon recalcitrant regions and preserve the *pax Ægyptica*. Some of the cities were allowed to retain their Canaanitish princes, on condition that they furnished tribute to the Egyptian treasury and recruits to the Egyptian army; and in these cases an Egyptian Resident was sometimes appointed to act along with the native prince, as was done, for example, at Sidon and Hazor. If a city, however, was of political or strategical importance, it was generally incorporated into the Egyptian empire, and placed under the direct rule of an Egyptian governor, as at Megiddo, Gaza, Byblus, Gezer, Tyre, and numerous other places.[1] The extent of the conquests made by Thutmose III. may be gathered from the list which he engraved on the temple walls at Karnak. This list, which is of great geographical interest, is the oldest record of a war that history possesses. It contains the names of 119 towns or districts which had submitted to his arms, and among them we read the names of many that were afterwards conquered by the Israelites. The list was, no doubt, compiled from memoranda made on the spot by the scribes who accompanied the armies. Among the names is one which is read as Jacob-el, and another (rather doubtfully) as Joseph-el,[2]

[1] Cf. Sayce, *Patriarchal Palestine*, pp. 81 f.

[2] Nos. 102 and 78 in list, Egyptian *Y-ʿ-k-b-'ā-ra*, and *Y-ša-p-'ā-ra*. The names (the *r* standing for *l*, for which there was no sign in Egyptian) are regarded by scholars as the equivalents of יעקבאל (*Jacob-'ēl*) and יוספאל (*Joseph-'ēl*), though the latter equivalence is doubtful, as the Egyptian sibilant used does not correspond with that of יוֹסֵף. The form of the names was not uncommon. Thus we find *Jezre'ēl*, *Jabne'ēl* (Josh. xv. 11 = *Jabneh*, 2 Chron. xxvi. 6), *Yiphtah'ēl* (Josh. xix. 14, 27 = *Yiphtah*, Judg. xi. 1 ff.), *Yekabze'ēl* (Neh. xi. 25), *Yirpe'ēl* (Josh. xviii. 27), etc. Such constructions make it

showing that some Israelites perhaps had given their names to sites in southern or central Canaan (*c.* 1479 B.C.).[1]

The vast Asiatic empire thus founded remained intact, more or less, through the reigns of his immediate successors, Amenhotep II. and Thutmose IV., though both these monarchs had to quell rebellions in northern Syria and Naharin, as soon as they ascended the throne. Egyptian control, however, continued to be effectively maintained by official envoys and garrisons, or by Egyptian Residents. Thutmose IV. gained a powerful ally on the north-eastern limit of his Asiatic dominions by judiciously marrying the daughter of Artatama, king of Mitanni. In the first few years of the reign of his immediate successor, Amenhotep III. (*c.* 1419–1383 B.C.), Egyptian power in Palestine was as high as ever. Canaan, Phœnicia, Syria, and other parts of Asia continued to be subject and tributary provinces, in the fullest sense of the word. The luxury and magnificence of the kingdom had never been greater, and the splendour and gaiety of the court at Thebes remind one of some Eastern fables. The wealth of Egypt was so enormous that golden vases in vast quantities adorned the palace and the noblemen's houses, and hundreds of golden vessels were used in the temples.[2] For a few years it was a period of unexampled splendour. Amenhotep III. caused his own name and titles, and the name of his queen Ti or Teī, to be cut on a group of scarabs, and these are followed by the statement, "[She is] the wife of the victorious king whose territory in the south reaches to Karei [*i.e.* Napata, just below the fourth cataract] and in the north to Naharin." [3]

This supremacy of Egypt during the early reign of Amenhotep III. was not due, however, to this king himself, but was inherited from his warlike ancestors and resulted from their

probable that the names *Jacob* and *Joseph* are elliptical forms of a more original *Jacob-el*, *Joseph-el*, which had reference to God (*El*). There is evidence that the two names were in existence long before these patriarchs were born (see p. 232).

[1] For a translation of the list, see Breasted, *Ancient Records*, ii. 163 ff.; Petrie, *History of Egypt*, ii. pp. 323 ff.; W. M. Müller, *Mitteil. der Vorderasiat. Gesellschaft*, 1907, p. 1; *Asien und Europa*, pp. 157 ff.

[2] Cf. Weigall, *Life and Times of Akhnaton*, p. 30.

[3] As quoted by Budge, *Tutankhamen*, p. 67.

continuous efforts. He himself was content to enjoy the fruits of past achievement, and was not greatly concerned about empire-building or maintaining control over his foreign provinces. Hence it was that after a few years of his reign, certain movements began here and there in Palestine, Syria, and elsewhere, which led to the gradual weakening of Egypt's hold upon her outside possessions. The later years of his reign indeed (from about 1410 B.C. onward) were marked by ominous indications of coming trouble—signs of that ebb which soon set in, and which became swift and strong after his death. He enjoyed peace during his long reign of thirty-six years, but powerful forces were silently and surely working, which quickly culminated in the decline of his suzerainty over these provinces. He has been fitly called by Breasted "the last of the great Egyptian emperors." [1]

Under Amenhotep IV. (Akhenaten), his immediate successor, who began to reign about 1383 B.C., the crisis became acute. This great internal idealist and reformer, who attempted to introduce a new form of religion, Atenism (the worship of Aten, the solar disk), was the son of his predecessor on the throne and Queen Ti. He was a visionary—a man evidently of many lovable qualities, and with lofty conceptions of religion; but although he reigned for some seventeen years, there is little recorded of him but his religious activities. His ideals of foreign policy gave scope for rebellion to Egypt's turbulent subject races. Apart from such ideals, he was too fully engrossed at home in religious reconstruction to spend time or money on foreign affairs or political matters. While this young Pharaoh was chanting his psalms to the Aten, in his new capital at Tell el-Amarna, dreaming of peace and home, and caring little for worldly interests, the princes of Palestine and Syria were singing revolutionary songs and threatening the isolated Egyptian garrisons. They cared little for his religion—their idea of God was a vanquisher of other gods, a stern leader in battle, a relentless avenger, some one like the furious Baal or the terrible Ishtar. We need not wonder that they took advantage of his

[1] *Cambridge Ancient History*, ii. p. 93.

weakness and peaceful idealism. "He never realized," as Budge says,[1] "the true nature of the duties which as a king he owed to his country and people, and he never understood the realities of life. He never learned the kingcraft of the Pharaohs, and he failed to see that only a warrior could hold what warriors had won for him. Instead of associating himself with men of action, he sat at the feet of Ai the priest, and occupied his mind with religious speculations; and so, helped by his adoring mother and kinswomen, he gradually became the courageous fanatic that the tombs and monuments of Egypt show him to have been." Thus it was that he allowed Palestine and the Syrian lands to slip from his grasp. The whole foreign empire began to totter. In the north of Palestine the Hittites and Amorites were restlessly intriguing and fomenting rebellion, and hordes of armed invaders were pressing into the land from all sides. What was needed was a man of resolute action, a great soldier to stamp out revolution and drive back invasion, but Pharaoh Akhenaten was dreaming of Aten's world-wide beneficence rather than of Egyptian empire, and the revolutionaries and invaders proved stronger in their generation than this visionary. He was no fighter, but rather "a pacifist who lost Egypt's Asiatic empire."[2] Long before his death in 1366 B.C., Palestine had practically fallen away from Egypt. It remained in this condition for about three-quarters of a century, and was never completely recovered by any of the Pharaohs.

Our knowledge and confirmation of all this has been immensely strengthened by the discovery of the large collection of Tell el-Amarna Tablets, which formed the archives of Akhenaten's Foreign Office. We see from these records that Egyptian control of Palestine became so weakened and relaxed from about 1400 B.C. onwards that any well-disciplined organized forces could take possession of the land; and that the Israelites did actually take possession at this time we hope to show later on from the Ḫabiru (Hebrew) invasion described in the tablets. Meantime, let us be clear as to what the tablets tell us. It was in 1887 that a peasant woman, searching at

[1] *Tutankhamen*, p. 77. [2] Budge, *op. cit.*, p. xiv.

Tell el-Amarna (between Memphis and Thebes), among the ruins of king Akhenaten's palace, unearthed these tablets (made of baked clay) from what had once been a small room. Unhappily, the value of this discovery was not realized at the time, and a number were broken or damaged by being carried in sacks to Luxor, where they were hawked about among the dealers. The tablets which survived, some 350 in number, are now in museums and private collections. Most of them are in Berlin Museum, though a good many are in the British Museum, and a few in Cairo. They have all been fully translated, published, and annotated.[1] They are inscribed almost without exception in the cuneiform or arrow-headed writing of Babylonia, although only one or two of the writers were Babylonians.[2] They proved on examination to form part of the actual diplomatic correspondence from the various rulers in Asia, including the kings of Karduniash (the Kassite name for Babylonia), Assyria, Mitanni, Arzawa, and Ḫatti (the Hittites), as well as

[1] The true story of the find has been given by Budge, *Nile and Tigris*, i. pp. 140 ff. The contents of all the tablets in the British Museum, after being summarized, were published by Budge and Bezold, *Tell el-Amarna Tablets*, London, 1892, and a transliteration was given by Bezold, *Oriental Diplomacy*, London, 1893. The texts of all the tablets in Berlin, London, and Cairo were published by Winckler, along with a translation in German, but a later edition of them is that by the Danish scholar, the late Dr. J. A. Knudtzon, assisted by the well-known German Assyriologists, Otto Weber and Erich Ebeling (*Die el-Amarna Tafeln*, 1908–15), which has now become the classical edition. A new edition of the Berlin tablets has been issued by Schroeder, *Die Tontafeln von el-Amarna*. Six tablets, found by M. Bénédite in a private collection of Egyptian antiquities, were acquired by the Louvre Museum in 1918. They are catalogued under *Antiquités Orientales* (AO), and the text of these, along with French translation by M. Fr. Thureau-Dangin, was published in *Revue d'Assyriologie*, xix. pp. 91–108, Paris, 1922. Three of these are from Palestinian governors, and two from Syrian rulers, while the sixth is from the king of Egypt to Endaruta, the governor of Achshaph. This last is evidently a copy which had been kept in the Egyptian archives. For explanations of the Louvre tablets, see Dhorme, *Revue Biblique*, 1924, pp. 5 ff.; *Recueil Champollion*, pp. 377–82. Other el-Amarna fragments have been published in *Mitteil. der deutschen Orient-Gesellschaft*, 1914, No. 55, and in *American Journal of Semitic Languages and Literatures*, xxxiii. pp. 1 ff., 89 ff.

[2] This is proof that Babylonian, which is a Semitic language allied to Hebrew, was the diplomatic language of the Near East at that epoch. At a later time its place was taken by Aramaic.

the Egyptian governors in Palestine, to the two Egyptian kings, Amenhotep III. and his son, Akhenaten. Many of the letters had been transferred by Akhenaten from the royal archives at Thebes to his new city at Tell el-Amarna; the rest had been received and stored up after the new city was built. The whole correspondence deals with the political events which were happening in Asia, and which were unloosing the bonds of the vassal provinces.

Needless to say, the letters, though difficult to interpret and of uncertain sequence, are of immense value for the history of Palestine at this epoch. They give us the most trustworthy information for determining the geographical, historical, and religious conditions of Palestine, and afford us a glimpse of the manners and ideas of the Canaanites just before the Israelites from the desert came on the scene. In reading them, we see the actions of various rival peoples, Hittites, Amorites, bedouins from the desert, and others, who were all trying to take possession of the land. Widespread internal dissensions among the rulers stand out in bold relief, mixed up with the most servile protestations of their loyalty to Pharaoh, grave denunciations of this or that individual, ever-recurring asseverations of their own uprightness, incessant demands for provisions or help, and pompous formulas of politeness. "To the king, my lord, my god, and my sun for ever," is but one sample out of many of the cringing adulation with which the Pharaoh is addressed by the native princes or governors. "Even if the king," says Labaya, one of the governors, "ordered me to put a dagger of bronze into my heart and die, would I not carry out the order?"[1] Each of the rulers was appointed by and subject to Egypt. He is sometimes called *amêlu*, 'man' of such-and-such a city, in contrast to Pharaoh, who was *ilu*, or 'God'; sometimes *ḫazanu*, 'officer,' an expression which allowed the full dignity to Pharaoh; and occasionally *šarru*, 'king,' especially when spoken of by outsiders (cf. this title applied to rulers in the Old Testament). Each was under the control of the

[1] Knudtzon, *Die el-Amarna Tafeln*, No. 254, ll. 40 ff. Hereafter, Knudtzon's translation of the tablets will be cited simply as Knudtzon.

rabisu, 'commissioner' or 'inspector,' who was usually of Egyptian race. The importance of the tablets is so exceptional that the history of Palestine at this epoch has had to be rewritten. The date of the letters has been determined from the mention in them, not only of Amenhotep III. and Akhenaten, but of certain kings of Babylonia and Assyria contemporary with these Egyptian monarchs. As the letters clearly do not begin till some time after the accession of Amenhotep III. (*c.* 1419 B.C.), and cannot be placed later than Akhenaten's reign (seeing that they were discovered in his palace), they may be accurately dated from about 1400 to 1366 B.C. (the date of Akhenaten's death).[1]

One point which they clearly prove is that there was a paramount Egyptian authority, generally recognized by most of the chiefs. The people were regarded as subjects of Pharaoh. The rulers were aided by Egyptian or Ethiopian troops, with forces of chariots. One of the letters [2] is from Burna-buriash, king of Babylon, to Amenhotep IV., complaining of outrages committed upon his traders at the town of Ḫinnatuni (the Hannathon of Zebulun, about 12 miles south-east of Accho), the feet of one being cut off and the face of another trampled on, and some being killed. As Canaan belonged to Egypt and its rulers were Egyptian vassals, Burna-buriash calls upon Pharaoh to punish the assailants and restore the silver they had stolen, otherwise amicable relations between Babylonia and Egypt would be cut off. "Kinaḫḫi (Canaan) is thy land," he writes, "and its kings are thy servants. In thy land violence has been done me. Chastise them, and the money which they have taken away restore! And the men who have slain my servants, slay them, and avenge their blood! But if thou dost not slay these people, they will on another occasion slay my caravans or thy messengers, and then messengers will cease to

[1] Amenhotep III. is addressed in the letters under his name of accession, *Nb-ma't-r'*, which the scribes transformed in cuneiform into *Nibmuaria*, *Nimutria*, *Nimmuria*, etc. Similarly, Akhenaten, whose accession name was *Nfr-ḫprw-r'*, appears as *Napḫururia*, *Nipḫuriria*, etc.

[2] Knudtzon, No. 8.

pass between us." If for nothing else than the safeguarding of merchants and caravans passing between Egypt and Asia Minor or Babylonia, the Pharaohs were always anxious to maintain their authority firmly over Canaan. This same Burnaburiash in another letter [1] states that in the time of Kurigalzu, his father, the Canaanites wished to separate themselves from Egypt and join the Babylonian empire, but that Kurigalzu had rejected their request. "My father sent them this message: Abandon [the idea] of making a league with me. If you commence hostilities against the king of Egypt, my brother, I shall not help you." Another letter [2] of curious character, and sealed with a Babylonian cylinder signet, is from some unknown authority, "the great king," [3] addressed to "the kings of Canaan, servants of my brother" (*i.e.* the king of Egypt), and served as a passport for an envoy, Akiya, to the Egyptian court. "Let none detain him. Swiftly to Egypt bring him, and to the hand of the prefect of Egypt you shall bring him in haste." The whole correspondence thus shows that, during the first years of Amenhotep III., the relations of Palestine to Egypt were those of a subject province, paying tribute regularly, and showing little sign of disaffection or rebellion. Egypt occupied the proud position of authority and supremacy. All this is corroborated by the cuneiform tablets discovered several years ago in the Canaanite fortress of Taanach (modern *Tell el-Taʿanuk,* in Plain of Esdraelon) by Dr. Sellin, which date from the period between Thutmose III. and Akhenaten, and some of which are dispatches from the Egyptian travelling inspector, Amān-khashir, whose headquarters were at Gaza.

But the point of importance for our argument is that nearly all the letters dating from the latter part of the reign of Amenhotep III., and onwards through Akhenaten's time, reveal a Palestine seething with intrigue and faction, which the Egyptian government was either unwilling to suppress or the serious consequences of which it utterly failed to realize. These later letters all tell the same story of Palestinian control falling to

[1] Knudtzon, No. 9. [2] Knudtzon, No. 30.

[3] Probably the king of Mitanni (cf. Weber, in Knudtzon, pp. 1072 ff.).

pieces under attack from without and rebellion within, and prove that whether Palestine now made a stand for independence or became a prey to invading peoples, it was at this time (*c.* 1400 B.C.) passing from Egyptian dominion. The native princes and governors speak again and again of the growing spirit of disaffection towards Egypt. There was profound dissension between anti-Egyptian sections which were everywhere developing and chiefs loyal to Egypt. Brothers were divided, chiefs impeached each other, leaders frequently changed sides, while at the same time invaders were seizing the townships and lands. From one of the letters we learn that matters had been going on this way for twenty years,[1] and that no help had been sent from Egypt during all this time. It is evident that Egypt, which not long before had brought the whole world to its feet, was entering upon a stage of decline in regard to its foreign possessions, being content to rest upon the achievements of the past, and not even troubling to maintain these. It was the inevitable reaction from a period of conquest, and the natural result of a *laissez faire* policy, which generally follows a surfeit of luxury and magnificence.

The trouble was composed of several elements. First, the Hittites (cuneiform *Ḫatti*, Egyptian *Kheta*), who were an Anatolian people in Asia Minor,[2] were pouring south and encroaching upon Syria. The fortunate discovery at Boghaz Keui of the archives of the Hittite empire has given us excellent information on this matter. We now know that the Hittites held the key to the Near East in those days, and their history gives us a new perspective of the period from the sixteenth to the eleventh centuries B.C. At first they were only a collection of semi-independent tribes, loosely united by their common lineage, but about the time of Amenhotep III. there arose among them

[1] See letter from the governor of Tunip, quoted below.

[2] Cf. Hogarth, *Cambridge Ancient History*, ii. pp. 252 ff.; *Hittite Monuments of Eastern Asia Minor*, 1923; Contenau, *Éléments de Bibliographie Hittite*, 1922 (gives also history of Hittite research); G. Roeder, *Ägypter und Hethiter, Der Alte Orient*, xx. (Leipzig, 1919); Cowley, *The Hittites* (Schweich Lectures, 1918); W. Otto, "Die Hethiter," *Hist. Zeit.*, cxvii. (1917), pp. 189 ff., 465 ff.; Hall, *Ancient History*, chap. viii.; etc.

a powerful leader named Shuppiluliu,[1] son of the king of Kussar (the classical Garsaüra). This leader, who probably reigned from about 1400 to 1365 B.C., succeeded in binding the Hittite clans into a great confederation, and after many victories founded an empire which lasted for nearly 200 years under the one dynasty. His capital city, the site of which is now marked by the modern village of Boghaz Keui, was called Ḫattushash, and lay east of the river Halys, in the district known afterwards as Cappadocia ; and here the Hittite archives, written in cuneiform (some in Babylonian, and others in Hittite languages), were discovered by Professor Winckler in 1907. This powerful Hittite empire gradually expanded its territory, until in the later years of Amenhotep III. we find Shuppiluliu crossing the Taurus Mountains and marching to the attack of Syria. His huge forces invaded Katna, which lay on the farther side of the Euphrates, in the valley of the lower Khabur River, and was probably a Semitic state. Its chief, named Aki-izzi, reported the depredations to Pharaoh and appealed for support. Matters were made worse by the actions of Itakama, the prince of Kinza,[2] who along with his father Shutatarra had been taken into captivity by the Hittites, but had been allowed to return as their vassal.[3] While protesting loyalty to the Pharaoh, this prince led an army of Hittite troops into the Amki region of Syria (the *Bekâʿ* Valley of the Orontes), where he captured and burned several loyal cities. Complaints of his depredations came from Eshazi, Ḫashabu, Ḫazi,[4] and another city the name of which has become obliterated, all four of which seem to have

[1] This is the cuneiform name (in Egyptian it was Sapalel(e) or Sapelul(u)). The name has generally been transcribed 'Shubbiluliuma,' but the correct form seems to be Shuppiluliu (cf. Sidney Smith, *Journ. of Egypt. Arch.*, x. p. 109 ; Hall, *op. cit.*, viii. pp. 220 f.).

[2] Kinza is believed by some scholars to be the Biblical Kadesh on the Orontes (now *Tell Nebi Mindu* ; cf. Weber, in Knudtzon, pp. 1118 ff.), but Dr. Hogarth rather regards it as a Semitic trans-Euphratean state, lying in the district where the river Belikh joins the Euphrates (*Cambridge Ancient History*, ii. p. 263). The fact that it was able to make a direct attack on Mitanni seems to favour this view.

[3] Thureau-Dangin, *Revue d'Assyriologie*, 1921, p. 94.

[4] On the location of these towns, cf. *Revue Biblique*, 1908, p. 505, 1924, p. 9.

united to write the king, each of them in identical terms, pleading for help against this rebel leader.[1] A similar invasion was inflicted by the Hittites on Nuḫashshi, a state which has been placed by scholars, conjecturally at least, in the Killis district, north-west of Aleppo, and seems to have included much of north-west Syria. Numerous vassals of the Egyptian king were cut off throughout Syria and neighbouring parts, in spite of despairing appeals for help against the invaders. Letter after letter to the Pharaoh speaks of the growing danger, but the writers receive no response.

Second, away farther south trouble was being caused by the armies of Amurru, under their great chieftain, Abd-Ashirta. Amurru (the land of the Amorites) was the region immediately south of Naharin, and occupied the tract east of the Lebanon—the district over which the short route ran from Syria to the east. It covered almost as great a territory as the Hittites. The documents found at Boghaz Keui go to prove that the Amorites had control of the whole Syrian desert and its surrounding regions, as far as the borders of Babylonia.[2] Abd-Ashirta, with his Amorite armies, made common cause with the Hittites, as a policy best serving his own interests, while all the time he managed with great astuteness to represent himself as a faithful servant of Egypt. He and his son Aziru wrote several ingenious and entertaining letters to Pharaoh, which show them to have been very plausible rascals. They had the assistance of hordes of Aramæan nomads from the north-eastern desert, who included the SA-GAZ,[3] the Aḫlamû,

[1] Cf. Louvre Letter, AO 7097, with Knudtzon, Nos. 174, 175, 176.

[2] Cf. Professor Albert T. Clay, *The Empire of the Amorites* (Yale University Press, Newhaven, 1919); Winckler, *Mitteil. der deutschen Orient-Gesellschaft*, xxxv. pp. 24 ff.

[3] The word SA-GAZ, in the original writing of the tablets, is an ideogram, and it has become customary in translating these phonetically to put them in capitals. An ideogram is a character representing an *idea*, and not a character like an ordinary word having syllables and sounds. Babylonian writing in early times was all ideograms or pictures of objects, but afterwards developed into groups of wedges which form syllables. The ideogram SA-GAZ is known to express the idea 'fighting man' or 'plunderer' (see Chapter X.). The SA-GAZ people, whose home was the north Syrian desert, east of Palestine,

and the Sûtû. Marching westward, Aziru attacked the Phœnician and north Syrian cities on the coast, which he captured as far as Ugarit, at the mouth of the Orontes, slaying their rulers and seizing their wealth. He co-operated with the Hittites in their advance southward, and captured Niy,[1] whose king he also slew. After this had gone on for some time, the governor of Tunip [2] wrote a pathetic appeal to Akhenaten, asking for help. The letter runs : [3]

To the king of Egypt, my lord. The inhabitants of Tunip, thy servant. May it be well with thee, and at the feet of our lord we fall. My lord, Tunip, thy servant, speaks, saying : Who formerly could have plundered Tunip without being plundered by Thutmose III. ? . . . Now, however, we belong no more to our lord, the king of Egypt. . . . If his soldiers and chariots come too late, Aziru will make us like the city of Niy. If, however, we have to mourn, then the king of Egypt will mourn over these things which Aziru has done. . . . And when Aziru enters Simyra,[4] Aziru will do as he pleases in the territory of our lord the king. . . . And now Tunip, thy city, weeps, and her tears are flowing, and there is no help for us. For twenty years we have been sending to our lord the king, the king of Egypt, but there has not come to us a word—no, not one.

belonged mostly to the wide Hebrew race, which embraced not only the Israelites, but many clans or bodies of people between the Euphrates and the Mediterranean ; and on this ground the ideogram, wherever it occurs, may be taken as equivalent to the Babylonian word Ḫabiru (Hebrews), as we know also from the Boghaz Keui documents. Hence, the SA-GAZ were kinsmen of the Israelites at Kadesh Barnea, and many of these ‘ fighting men ’ were no doubt found among the latter people, or at least in close connection with them in the desert.

[1] This town is believed to have lain on the eastern edge of Syria, on or near the right bank of the Euphrates, below Carchemish. Under Thutmose III. it is referred to as at the extreme limit of Egyptian rule.

[2] Tunip (or Dunip) is placed by most authorities in the far north of Syria. It is mentioned in Egyptian and Assyrian annals as in or near Naharin, and must almost certainly have been in the lower valley of the Sajur (a tributary of the Euphrates), where its name is still attached to a Tell (cf. *Cambridge Ancient History*, p. 263).

[3] Knudtzon, No. 59.

[4] Simyra (cuneiform, *Sumur*) was a Phœnician trading port, almost due west from Kadesh on the Orontes. It was from Simyra that Thutmose III. disembarked his army when attacking Kadesh.

Meantime, Rib-Addi, the governor of Gebal, which was an Egyptian centre, with a well-known temple,[1] was displaying the utmost fidelity on behalf of Egypt. From his fifty-three letters to the Pharaoh,[2] we have the best idea of how the northern part of Palestine gradually fell to pieces while Akhenaten was singing hymns to the sun's disk in his new capital. In his earlier letters this Syrian governor, while realizing the gravity of the situation, was not without hope that a successful resistance might yet be made. Repeatedly he besought the Pharaoh to send small detachments of Sherden troops,[3] or some soldiers from Meluḫḫa or from Kash (Nubia) to help the weak native garrisons. In the Louvre letter (ll. 18 ff.), he reminds the Pharaoh that troops had been sent once before by request, when a rebel (Abashunu) had been taken prisoner. If troops could only be sent now, the rebel chiefs Abd-Ashirta and Aziru might be captured and the situation saved:

Let the king, my lord, know that Gebal, the true handmaid of the king, is safe, but very strong is the hostility of the SA-GAZ warriors against me, and may the king, my lord, not hold back from Simyra, lest it entirely join the SA-GAZ warriors! . . . From Yarimuta[4] have we procured the means of existence. Very powerful has been the hostility against us. Therefore, may the king not hold back from his city![5]

[1] Gebal (cuneiform, *Gubli* or *Kubli*), better known as Byblus from its Greek name, is the modern *Jebeil*, on the coast of Phœnicia, about 20 miles north of Beirût. If not actually an Egyptian colony, it had owned allegiance to Egypt from the time of the Pyramid builders. It was a well-known port for Egyptian vessels in quest of wine, olive oil, cedar trees, and spruce firs. A systematic exploration of the site has been made by the French, who have discovered numerous Egyptian statues, vases, etc. See *Syria*, ii. pp. 263 ff. (*Byblos et l'Égypte*), where Montet gives an account of the earlier work. The discovery of an important cave-tomb of the XIIth Dynasty is described by Virolleaud and Naville in *Comptes Rendus*, 1922, and further researches by Montet are described in later volumes.

[2] See also letter in the Louvre Collection (AO 7093).

[3] Predatory bands of sea-robbers, perhaps the ancestors of the Sardinians.

[4] Yarimuta was not in the Shephelah, as some think, but on the Syrian coast. See note 6, p. 123.

[5] Knudtzon, No. 68.

Gradually, however, the situation became worse. Aziru slew the Egyptian deputy resident in Simyra, and having destroyed the place, was free to move against Gebal. When ordered to come to Egypt and give an account of himself, he skilfully explained that he could not leave the district, because the Hittites were in Nuḫashshi, and he feared that Tunip would not be able to resist them! And when ordered immediately to rebuild Simyra, he replied that he was too hard pressed in defending the king's interests, but that he would do so within a year. Ultimately, Rib-Addi sent his son to Tell el-Amarna, to expose Aziru's perfidy and plead for assistance. At the same time, he wrote to the Pharaoh most pathetic accounts of his misfortunes. All his possessions had been taken from him and his lands devastated. He had been reduced by famine and privation to a state of destitution, and was unable to hold out much longer. His enemies had sought to prevent help reaching him by saying to Pharaoh that the plague (*mûtu*, 'death') was in the land. "It is false," wrote Rib-Addi, "the country is healthier than ever."[1] His letters increased in eloquent pleading as the great catastrophe approached. In the following despairing lines we read his fears for the future, as well as his disappointment at the abandonment of a loyal town:

Listen to me! Why hast thou so held back that thy land should be taken? Let it not be said, "In the days of the inspectors (*rabisi*) the GAZ-people have taken all lands." Let it not be said in those days, "Art thou not able to take them again?" Further, I have written for garrison troops and for horses, but they were not granted. Send a reply to me! Otherwise I shall make alliance with Abd-Ashirta, like Yapa-Addi[2] and Zimrida,[3] and I shall be saved."[4]

What befell Rib-Addi is unknown. He fled from Byblus to Beirût, and from there to Sidon, and probably was

[1] Louvre Tablet, AO 7093, ll. 45 ff.

[2] Believed to be an official at Yarimuta.

[3] The chief of Sidon.

[4] Knudtzon, No. 83, ll. 14 ff.

captured and slain at last—a man who deserved a better fate, but whose misfortune it was to be a loyal soldier of Pharaoh.

The letters of Abimilki, governor of Tyre, tell the same story of attack by invaders, and plead in vain for a small body of troops. His position in his island city soon became untenable. It is not surprising that in such circumstances his loyalty did not prove quite as strong as Rib-Addi's, and ultimately he appears to have gone over to the enemy.

Amenhotep III. seems at last to have been convinced of the true state of affairs and to have dispatched troops. In this Pharaoh's letter to Endaruta, governor of Achshaph,[1] he gives orders to prepare for an army which it was arranged to send under Ḫanni, an Egyptian commissioner, and we know from a letter in Knudtzon (No. 162) that he directed this same messenger to demand from Aziru a list of the king's enemies. We also read of troops being dispatched under Amanappa, another commissioner, which retook Simyra, and apparently marched as far as Naharin.[2] Various prisoners were, no doubt, handed over to Egypt, and the tension was partly relieved for a short time. The southern advance, however, of the Hittites continued, and these warriors were able to secure a strong footing in Naharin, which was of prime importance in their further plans for invading Syria and Palestine. Under the next Pharaoh, Akhenaten, no help of any kind was forthcoming, in spite of eloquent appeals from every part of Syria and Phœnicia. This Pharaoh seems to have exhibited astonishing leniency, and an opposition to all measures of force. The helpless cities fell one after another into the hands of the Amorites, and the whole north of Palestine was lost to Egypt. Aziru, who had certainly had some pro-Egyptian tendencies, eventually renounced them openly and became a Hittite vassal. He entered into a treaty with the Hittites, which lasted at least through the reigns of the next Hittite kings,

[1] Louvre Tablet, AO 7095.

[2] Cf. Knudtzon, No. 117, ll. 21 ff.; Breasted, *Cambridge Ancient History* ii. p. 107.

up to the reign of Hattushilish III. (*c.* 1290 B.C.).[1] The Amorite and Hittite connection, indeed, became traditional in Palestine (cf. Ezek. xvi. 3).[2]

It is impossible to say how long the northern revolt lasted before Palestine was finally abandoned by Egypt. In a letter (probably to Amenhotep III.) written before Aziru's capture of Simyra, Rib-Addi speaks of the struggle as having already lasted five years.[3] We know it continued many years after that, for there were successive Hittite and Amorite invasions, and some cities were besieged and captured more than once. Meantime, many changes took place which must have extended over many years. The expedition under Amanappa arrived. Abd-Ashirta died, as well as Amenhotep III., and still the fighting continued even more vigorously than before. We may not be far wrong in regarding the struggle as covering about twenty years (*c.* 1400–1380 B.C.).

Third, in the south, affairs were equally serious. There had arisen local dissensions among the Canaanite princes, with active intrigue against Egypt as the suzerain power. At the same time, these southern rulers, like the northern ones, were sending letters to the Pharaoh full of protestations of loyalty and accusations against others. Practically all of them appeal for help against invading armies. In particular, the governor of Jerusalem, Abdi-Ḫiba (or Arta-Ḫiba),[4] who appears to have stood faithfully for the interests of Egypt, though practically alone in his loyalty, makes urgent and repeated requests for Egyptian troops, stating that unless they can be speedily sent, the whole country will be lost to Egypt. The garrison at Jerusalem seems to have been withdrawn, and Abdi-Ḫiba complains of the entire destruction of "all the rulers" which

[1] *Keilschrifttexte aus Boghazköi*, i. 8; cf. Luckenbill, *American Journal of Semitic Languages and Literatures*, xxxvii. p. 197. The *-ish* in Hittite names is a case ending, and is sometimes omitted in English, or the Semitic ending *-i* used in its place.

[2] Cf. *Cambridge Ancient History*, i. pp. 233 ff.

[3] Knudtzon, No. 106.

[4] We adopt the form Abdi-Ḫiba as the one generally used, although we think there is little doubt that the proper translation is Arta-Ḫiba. See p. 160.

followed. His letters imply that the invaders in this part of Canaan came from the south (" the land of Seir "). He does not call them SA-GAZ, but Ḫabiru (or ' Hebrews '), a term not used in the letters from the north. As the governors, however, of cities near Jerusalem, such as Gezer, plead for help against the SA-GAZ, it is likely that large numbers of these ' fighting men ' had penetrated southward by the coast road, or had entered these central regions from across the Jordan, and were probably helping their Ḫabiru kinsmen from the south. Abd-Ashirta seems to have had enough to do among the Phœnician cities, and the Hittite monarch was too busy consolidating his power beyond the Lebanons. In the southern letters there is no mention of Aziru or Abd-Ashirta or of the Hittites: here in the south it was the Ḫabiru-SA-GAZ who were attacking the land, unchecked by any effective Egyptian control. These invaders, whom we hope in a future chapter to identify with the Israelites from Kadesh-Barnea,[1] are stated to have seized all the strongholds and to have received help from Gezer, Ashkelon, and Lachish. Many cities and rulers were in dread of them. Even Yanḫamu, Pharaoh's High Commissioner,[2] was suspected of playing into their hands and opposing the local rulers, who represented the delegated authority of Egypt.[3] Interesting information on the matter is contained in Abdi-Ḫiba's letters to the Pharaoh.[4] In one he says:

Behold the territory of Gazri (Gezer), the territory of Ashkaluna (Ashkelon), and the city of Lakisi (Lachish) have given them oil, food, and all their necessaries. Let the king therefore take care for the troops! Let him send troops against the

[1] The suggestion that the Ḫabiru were the Hebrews who had left Egypt was first made by Dr. H. Zimmern. It was also made independently by Conder in the *Quarterly Statement of the Palestine Exploration Fund*, June 1891, although his derivation of the word from Mt. Abarim, east of the Jordan, was incorrect (cf. Conder, *Tell el-Amarna Tablets*, p. 141).

[2] See note 6, p. 123.

[3] Knudtzon, No. 286, ll. 16 ff.

[4] Abdi-Ḫiba's letters will be found in English in the Appendix, p. 265. Cf. also Ball, *Light from the East*, pp. 89 ff.; Rogers, *Cuneiform Parallels to the Old Testament*, pp. 26 ff.; Sayce, *Patriarchal Palestine*, pp. 119 ff.; Percy Handcock, *Selections from the Tell el-Amarna Tablets* (S.P.C.K.).

people who have committed a crime against the king, my lord! If in this year there are troops here, then will the land and the local rulers remain to the king, my lord; but if there are no troops here, then there will remain no lands and no local rulers to the king. Behold this land of Jerusalem—neither my father nor my mother gave it to me; the mighty hand of the king gave it to me. Behold, this deed is the deed of Milki-ili, and the deed of the sons of Labaya, who have given the land of the king to the Ḫabiru . . . Adaja is in revolt, together with the garrison, the officer. . . . I sent to the king, my lord, 5000 *asiru* (prisoners?) . . . 318 (?) bearers for the caravans of the king; they were taken in the fields of Ialuna (Aijalon). Let the king, my lord, know that I am unable to send caravans to the king, my lord—this for thy information. Behold, the king has set his name in the land of Jerusalem for ever, therefore he cannot leave the land of Jerusalem in the lurch.[1]

Exasperated by the king's inaction and by the fall of so many cities, Abdi-Ḫiba wrote again and again for help:

The whole king's land, which has begun hostilities against me, will be lost. Behold the land of Seir, as far as Gath-Carmel, its princes are wholly lost; and hostility prevails against me. . . . As sure as there is a ship in the midst of the sea, the strong arm of the king will seize Naḫrima (Naharin) and Kapasi, but now the Ḫabiru are seizing the cities of the king. There remains not one prince to my lord, the king; every one is ruined. . . . Let the king take care of his land, and . . . let him send troops. . . . For if no troops come this year, the whole territory of my lord, the king, will perish. . . . If there are no troops in this year, let the king send his officer to fetch me and my brothers, that we may die with our lord, the king.[2]

A touch of vivid pleading is given to the letters by Abdi-Ḫiba's frequent postscripts addressed to the king's scribe who translated the cuneiform correspondence at the Egyptian court. One postscript says, "To the scribe of the king, my lord. Bring clearly before the king these words, 'The whole territory of the king, my lord, is going to ruin.'"

The same story of attack and helplessness is told by other

[1] Knudtzon, No. 287. [2] Knudtzon, No. 288.

native rulers or resident governors of southern Palestine. Thus Dagantakala writes imploring the king to deliver him from the hand of the SA-GAZ.[1] A chieftainess, who calls herself the 'king's handmaid,' entreats him to send help to her. The SA-GAZ, she states, had taken the city of Sabuma, and had "sent word" to Aijalon and Zorah.[2] So the letters run on, each telling the same story of successful attack and disaster to the Egyptian cause—the same tale of capture and plundering of towns and villages by the Ḫabiru-SA-GAZ. The appeals for help are worded much the same all over the land, for the language of the ancient scribes was very limited—it could not be otherwise. In many of the letters it is couched in almost identical terms, and exhibits a close similarity of style, although emanating from different chiefs.[3] The four appeals already referred to from widely separated places in North Palestine, asking help against the Hittites under Itakama, are practically identical except for the name of the sender and his city. There was evidently a standard type of style among the scribes, combined with a limited vocabulary. Consequently, the danger arising from the presence of such a multitude of invaders could only be stated in almost similar words, whether written from the north of the land or the south, "If no help comes, the lands of the Pharaoh are lost."[4] The tone of many of the letters is a despairing cry for help, but none of them records that any help was forthcoming, though eagerly expected, and few of them relate any victories over the invaders. The letters grow more and more desperate, as the danger waxes more widespread and imminent, and as the enemies close in more thickly. The whole correspondence breaks off suddenly in the midst of a falling empire, with its governors in Canaan fighting for Pharaoh, and appealing for help that never came, while Hittites, Amorites, and Ḫabiru-SA-GAZ were attack-

[1] Knudtzon, No. 318. [2] Knudtzon, Nos. 273, 274.

[3] Cf. Knudtzon, Nos. 177–183, and 203–206.

[4] It is necessary to state this fact, for some scholars have used the similarity of appeal to prove that the SA-GAZ in the north and the Ḫabiru from the south were the same invading force in every respect. The relationship between the two peoples was racial only.

ing the distracted province. The hills of Jerusalem, the fair Jordan, the cities of the coast, and away to the great Orontes and the distant Kadesh, the whole land was being lost to Egypt. To Pharaoh, dwelling in seclusion on the Nile, amid ease and luxury, the letters must have formed a disagreeable collection, which he hardly cared to read. Though written with blood and tears, they seem to have been pigeon-holed in the city archives and probably forgotten. The magnificence around Amenhotep III. may have blinded his eyes to the danger, or perhaps the carelessness of age was creeping over his life which had never been one of military ambition; while, as for the Pharaoh Akhenaten, his doctrine of Atenism, combined with his principles of peace and goodwill, had crushed nearly all his interest in foreign affairs. We need scarcely wonder that most of the Palestinian princes fell away from Egypt and made terms with the invaders. "Both in Syria and Palestine," says Breasted, "the provinces of the Pharaoh had gradually passed entirely out of Egyptian control, and in the south a state of complete anarchy had resulted, in which the hopeless Egyptian party at last gave up any attempt to maintain the authority of the Pharaoh, and those who had not perished joined the enemy. . . . At Akhetaton, the new and beautiful capital, the splendid temple of Aton resounded with hymns to the new god of the empire, while the empire itself was no more." [1]

It is worth noting that the letters in this interesting collection that belong to the first part of the reign of Amenhotep III. show a condition still of somewhat peaceful allegiance to Egypt and respect for the Pharaoh. A number of the vassal kings were loyal or at least wished to be thought so. But as time went on and the invasion became bolder and more dangerous, the faithful vassals, finding that Egypt could not help them, went over one by one to the enemy, so as to share in the plunder or save themselves from an evil fate. Hence it is specially the letters dating from the later years of Amenhotep III. and from the time of Akhenaten that bear witness to the defection of the people and the gradual loss of Palestine, Syria, and the other

[1] *Cambridge Ancient History*, ii. p. 125.

Asiatic possessions. This disastrous state of matters was undoubtedly due to the internal dissensions of Egypt, the incapacity of its central government, and in particular the religious changes brought about by Atenism, all of which things tended to weaken the morale of the officials and armies abroad and decrease their loyalty. Collectors of tribute returned to Thebes empty-handed, because foreign tribes would not pay it. The national stability had received a severe shock morally, as well as materially, and its very foundations were shaken. While Akhenaten was taken up with religious reforms, perfecting his doctrines, and playing and singing to the new deity he had introduced, the foreign empire which Thutmose III. had built up with so much military glory was tottering to its downfall. Within seventeen years from Akhenaten's accession, Egypt had scarcely a city in Palestine she could call her own. Her dominion collapsed in the time of her weakness and indecision.

It is necessary now that we should return to our main argument. The assertion of the late-date theorists that Palestine was so effectively controlled as an Egyptian province that it was impossible for the Israelites or any other invaders to have taken possession of it before the reign of Ramesses III. (*c.* 1204–1172 B.C.) is clearly not in accord with historical fact. From what we have said in this chapter, it is apparent that we have most trustworthy evidence as to Egyptian control of Palestine being weakened and the province invaded and captured by outsiders about two centuries earlier than the period referred to. The time when the weakness commenced must be placed towards the middle or end of the reign of Amenhotep III. (*i.e.* about 1400 B.C.); and this weakness developed to such an alarming extent during the reign of his successor, Akhenaten, that the country, from the Negeb in the south to the Lebanon in the north, practically fell away from the grasp of the Pharaohs. It was during this period of weakness, as we have seen—probably about the commencement of it—that invaders poured into the land, and there is good ground for the view that the southern ones, the Ḫabiru, were the Hebrews making an entry from Kadesh Barnea. We have evidence that the weakness continued for about three-quarters of a century, giving ample time to the invaders. Little or nothing in the way of reconquest was attempted by Akhenaten's immediate successors, Sʿakere, Tutankhamūn, Ai, and Harmhab, the last-named of whom ended the XVIIIth Dynasty about 1324 B.C.; nor by the next Pharaoh, Ramesses I., who headed the XIXth Dynasty. Tutankhamūn, who found Egypt in a state of chaos when he ascended the throne, tells us that if an envoy were sent to Tchah (Syria), for instance, to enlarge the frontiers of Egypt, his mission did not prosper.[1] It is possible that raids may have been made into some parts of Syria, but any tribute from such outlying provinces was so trivial as to be presented by the viceroys of the south. It was found to be impossible to re-establish in any way the old imperial control of the Asiatic provinces. As for Harmhab, his reign was a period of internal consolidation and reconstruction, during which Egypt had neither the desire nor the power for foreign expansion. We hear of one Asiatic war in which the enemy was the Hittite power, which was advancing still farther southward and making havoc among the cities of Northern Syria; but Harmhab seems to have been content to make a treaty with Murshilish II. (or III. ?), the king of these powerful foes.[2] On his temple wall, near his great code of laws, there is a list of foreign countries said to have been conquered, but this is the usual conventional enumeration and must not be taken seriously, for later conditions show that there could have been no reconquest of the land. Palestine, indeed, was left to itself, for it was no easy matter to regain control over a land which had been successfully invaded sixty or more years previously.

[1] Budge, *Tutankhamen*, p. 5; Hall, *Ancient History*, p. 354 n.

[2] Langdon-Gardiner, *Journ. of Egypt. Arch.*, vi. (1920), p. 203.

CHAPTER IV

LATER EGYPTIAN CONTROL

THE late-date theorists, while admitting the serious loss of control referred to, as well as the duration of it, hold that the land was reconquered by Egypt in numerous powerful campaigns during the XIXth Dynasty, and that the period of permanent weakness, and consequently of the Israelitish conquest, must therefore be placed about two centuries later, when the country is known to have been finally and irremediably lost. This would place the entrance of the Israelites into the land sometime during the reign of Ramesses III. (*c.* 1204–1172 B.C.), and the Exodus during the reign of Merenptah, about 1225 B.C., or later. This, as we have said, is the view of Flinders Petrie and many other Egyptologists. Thus Naville writes: "I still adhere to the view advocated first by Lepsius, and still held by most Egyptologists, that the persecutor of the Jews was Ramesses II., whose very long reign was the beginning of the decay for the Egyptian empire, and that the king of the Exodus was his son Merenptah."[1] But it seems to the writer that a proper understanding of these later campaigns, taking into account the Biblical as well as the Egyptological facts concerned, affords no historical basis for such a view. Let us first examine the nature and extent of the campaigns, and then realize their true significance.

After a lapse of about three-quarters of a century or more, the Egyptian rulers tried to recover from the *bouleversement* produced by Akhenaten. They began to turn their eyes again towards Palestine. We find Seti I. (*c.* 1322–1301 B.C.), the second king of the XIXth Dynasty, attempting measures for

[1] *Archæology of the Old Testament*, 1913, p. 93.

the restoration of Egypt's suzerainty there. This would be about sixty or seventy years after the Ḫabiru had entered the land. One of the first efforts he made was to drive the Shōsu, or bedouins,[1] before him from the frontiers of Egypt to Kana'ana,[2] and to establish a line of fortresses and wells along the shore road as far as Gaza. The way being now open for a northward move, he led his armies up the coast of Palestine, capturing the towns of the plain of Megiddo; he then seems to have turned eastward with part of his army at least, and passed through Beth-shean (the modern Beisân), which was an Egyptian fortress of the XIXth and XXth Dynasties. Dr. Fisher, and other members of the University Museum of Philadelphia, excavating at Beisân in 1923, unearthed more than one well-preserved stele of local basalt engraved by him.[3] One of the steles, the inscription on which unfortunately is largely illegible, gives the names of several of the local tribes whom he had overcome, mention being made of the Retenu (Syrians), Aamu (Canaanites), Sûtû (bedouin tribes), 'Aperu, and Tuirsha. There is no mention of the Israelites, unless the 'Aperu ('Hebrews,' see Chapter XIII.) be taken to refer to them, which is not improbable. The context implies that these 'Aperu were in possession of the citadel of Beth-shean at the time of Seti's expedition.[4] This is significant, and if we regard these people as Israelites, we have a strong argument in favour of the early date of the Exodus. Another stele describes the disposition of Seti's various forces in the campaign, from which it appears that he had come to the help of the chief of Beth-shean against a hostile league composed of the "vile one" of Hamath (now *Tell el-Hammi*, at the entrance of the Yarmuk Pass) and the

[1] The word *Shōsu* was the name of the Semitic nomads of the Arabian desert. It seems to be connected with the Hebrew root שָׁסָה, *šāsā*, 'to spoil or plunder.'

[2] *Kana'ana* is the name applied on Egyptian monuments to the whole of west Palestine (cf. Böhl, *Kanaanäer und Hebräer*, pp. 1–11; Gardiner, *Journ. of Egypt. Arch.*, vi. (1920), p. 100; Breasted, *Ancient Records of Egypt*, iii. 87; *Cambridge Ancient History*, ii. p. 135).

[3] Cf. *The Museum Journal*, Philadelphia, xiv. (1923), No. 4 ff.

[4] Cf. *Palestine Exploration Fund Quarterly*, 1923, p. 149.

men of Pella (*Pahel*), a city just across the Jordan from Beth-shean. Already these enemies had shut up the chief of Rehob (*Tell es-Sârem*) in his city, which lay a few miles to the south of Beth-shean, and was one of its 'sister' cities. The division of Re was sent to occupy Beth-shean itself, that of Amūn proceeded to take active operations against Hamath, while that of Sutekh was dispatched on an expedition north-west (probably to make some demonstration against the Hittites while the main army was engaged eastward). Seti and his forces seem then to have crossed the valley of the Jordan, for he erected a tablet of victory at *Tell esh-Shihâb* in the Decapolis, where it still stands.[1] Passing westward to the southern slopes of the Lebanon, he took the city of Yenoam, which had been captured by Thutmose III. about one hundred and fifty years before.[2] Perhaps it was in this campaign that he erected a monument at *Tell Nebi Mindu*, about the southern end of the Lake of Homs, adjoining the spot where Kadesh on the Orontes is believed to have been.[3] This appears to have been the northern limit of his first campaign; and at a spot which seems to have been near the waters of Merom he had the satisfaction of receiving the submission of the chiefs of the Lebanon, who had not seen a Pharaoh at the head of his army in Asia for over seventy years—not since Amenhotep had visited Sidon. He also requisitioned a supply of cedar logs for the bark of Amūn and the flag-staves of the temple at Karnak. He marched back by the coast, taking with him a number of captives and some booty in the shape of vessels of gold and silver. Egypt had thus assumed once more the rôle of a conquering power, and this first campaign, though not extensive, bore witness to the new spirit that was rising up in the nation.

[1] Smith, "Notes of a Journey through Hauran," *Palestine Exploration Fund Quarterly Statement*, 1901, pp. 347 f., 1904, pp. 78 ff.; H. Gressmann, *Altorientalische Texte und Bilder*, 1909, Bd. ii. p. 247. The monument is twenty-two miles east of the Lake of Tiberias, or about one hour's journey from Muzeirib, the juncture of roads from Damascus, Nawa, Edrei, Jebel, 'Ajlun, and Gadara (cf. *Cambridge Ancient History*, ii., p. 312).

[2] Yenoam is supposed to have lain about twenty miles north-east of Tyre.

[3] This stele, which is of grey-black basalt stone, and was discovered in 1921, is described in *Syria*, iii. (1922), by M. Pézard, head of the French Archæological Mission, and in *Ancient Egypt*, 1924, p. 101, by M. Grégoire Loukianoff.

In his second campaign, which is undated, Seti appears to have directed his forces upon the Amorites in the north, where he probably avenged the perfidy of Abd-Ashirta and Aziru. He seems also to have advanced to the land of the Hittites, for his reliefs at Karnak, if we can accept them, show him driving the Hittite chariots in headlong flight before him and leading crowds of captive Hittites in triumph. From his list of towns, he must have made his way along the coast as far as the Gulf of Antioch and Cilicia, overrunning districts of which we know little more than the names.

It is more than probable, however, that Seti's conquests were not nearly so complete as his reliefs would lead us to imagine. In the case of the Pharaohs of the XIXth and XXth Dynasties, it is believed by Egyptologists that several towns mentioned as captured by them are merely drawn from older lists, or are the empty fictions of flattering chroniclers; and this fact must be kept in mind in forming our judgment as to whether Egyptian control of Palestine was re-established. In his lists, Seti claims towns which would lead us to conclude that the Egyptian empire extended again practically as far north as it did in its palmiest days; but when we remember what battles his successor had to fight in these same regions, it is almost impossible to believe that Seti's statements are in accordance with actual fact. It cannot be supposed that what cost Thutmose III. an almost continuous war of seventeen campaigns was accomplished in one or two by Seti, after seventy-five years of Palestinian freedom from the Egyptian yoke, and against such powerful enemies as the Amorites and Hittites, the latter of whom were certainly one of the leading nations of the world at that epoch. At all events, although he may have succeeded in overawing the dwellers in these northern regions of Palestine and Syria, he made no lasting conquests. He finally came to terms with the Hittite king,[1] by which the latter became suzerain as far south as the Lebanon. Seti I. reigned for over twenty

[1] Probably Muwattalish (sometimes written Mutallu, Egyptian Metella), the eldest son of Murshilish II. (or III. ?), and grandson of Shuppiluliu. Muwattalish ascended the throne *c.* 1330 B.C. (or according to Weidner, 1347 B.C.).

years, but he seems to have made no further campaigns in Palestine. Probably he had come to see that it was useless to dream of reviving the great ambitions of Egypt for foreign dominion. One thing of prime importance is that there is no trace in his campaigns of any occupation of central or southern Palestine, which would be the territory in which the Hebrews of the Exodus were settled at this particular time. This is a significant fact, which we merely mention here in passing, but to which we shall direct further attention directly.

Seti's famous son and successor, Ramesses II. (*c.* 1301–1234 B.C.), the Sesostris of the Greeks, carried on war on a large scale. It is believed that countries where the Egyptians had never trod learned to know them by the soldiers of Ramesses. He established a line of Egyptian fortresses along the coast, as far as Damascus, and battled for long years against the Hittites on the northern coast plains of Syria. The tablets which he engraved on the rock at the mouth of the Dog River (*Nahr el-Kelb*), just north of Beirût, still remain to testify to his efforts in these regions. As early as the fourth year of his reign he mustered all his forces and marched northward by the coast road, as his predecessors had done. Moving with considerable rapidity, his army encamped, on the twenty-ninth day after leaving Egypt, on the high lands near Kadesh on the Orontes, from which they could see the distant walls of the town, the objective of their long march. According to a fragmentary tablet from Boghaz Keui, the Hittite king himself appears to have been at the head of his forces against Ramesses. He had by this time turned the town into a frontier fortress and made it a very formidable place. At the great battle which ensued, the Egyptian army only escaped absolute annihilation by a fortunate accident, which enabled Ramesses to extricate himself and his troops from a desperate situation.[1] There is

[1] Accounts of the battle, with plans of the positions, are found in the University of Chicago's *Decennial Publications*, 1904; Breasted, *Ancient Records of Egypt*, iii. 298 ff.; Petrie, *History of Egypt*, iii. pp. 47 f.; *Cambridge Ancient History*, ii. p. 145; and numerous stray publications within recent years.

no indication that he made any attempt upon the town, and there is no word of any tribute from the Hittites. The campaign ended in nothing, and indeed only missed serious disaster. Altogether, the net result was that both sides stood pretty much where they were. Ramesses, however, caused the battle scenes to be engraved on his temple walls in Egypt—the camp near Kadesh, the charge upon the Hittites, and the fugitives swimming across the river. The incidents were used as the subject of an epic poem by one of the court poets. A copy of this composition was made by a scribe named Pentewere (Pentaur), who has thus handed it down to future generations. In spite of the poet's exaggerated eulogies, the campaign was a failure, for the next few years showed that Palestine was still in revolt, and the flame of insurrection was felt as far south as Ashkelon.

In his eighth year, Ramesses marched north again, and proceeded to 'reconquer' the whole coast and northern regions, town by town. Perhaps it was during this expedition that he erected his stele at Beth-shean, on which he refers to the employment of Semites in the building of his name-city in the Delta (*vide* p. 22). He seems to have invaded the Lebanon district, for among the cities mentioned as captured is Dapur or Deper "in the land of Amor" (Amurru), a city which was held by Hittites.[1] But he did not succeed in winning back more than his father had held, and made no impression on the powerful Hittite nation. The chief result of his wars in Palestine and Syria was to bring ruin and disaster to the cities on or near the coast. Their land was devastated by the hostile armies which traversed it, and their towns were sacked, at one time by the Hittite invaders from the north, at another by the soldiers of Ramesses from the south. But the king of Egypt was never able to secure the mastery. These northern mountaineers had established themselves too firmly in Syria to be dislodged. All he could do was to stop their further progress

[1] This city has been identified by some scholars with Tabor of Hebrew history, in the plain of Megiddo, but the philological arguments are against this. It is generally associated elsewhere with Kadesh on the Orontes (cf. Burney, *Judges*, xc, n.).

towards the south. His campaigns in Palestine and the north were at last ended through exhaustion. In the twenty-first year of his reign he was compelled to conclude a treaty, offensive and defensive, with the powerful Hittite king, Ḫattushilish III. (Egyptian Khetasil), the treaty being engraved on a silver plate and brought to Egypt by Hittite ambassadors.[1] No boundary is mentioned, but the language implies that henceforth Egypt was bound not to disturb this strong northern empire by marching farther than the Syrian Kadesh. The treaty was faithfully kept, being cemented thirteen years later by the marriage of Ramesses to the daughter of the Hittite king, as recorded in the Abu Simbel stele of the thirty-fourth year. It finally put a stop to the warlike ambitions of Ramesses, and for the rest of his long reign of sixty-six years we hear no more of any campaigns into Palestine or Syria.

The names of some of the cities which he captured may still be read on the walls of the Ramesseum at Thebes, and others figure at Luxor in a catalogue of vanquished places. His inordinate vanity and his ambitious desire to be remembered as a great conqueror have led some Egyptologists to regard many of these conquests as due to the imagination of the scribe. In this respect they may be like his monuments, too many of which really belong to his predecessors, though bearing his own name. The geographical lists of Thutmose III. generally served as a model for the Pharaohs who followed, and when a large space had to be filled, names of cities from these lists were sometimes appropriated, although the Egyptian armies had not come within a hundred miles of them. Even places quite independent of Egyptian rule were sometimes included. An instance of this occurs in the list of captive districts which decorates a column

[1] Two copies of the treaty have been found in Egypt, the one engraved at Karnak, and the other at the Ramesseum, although the latter is no longer in existence; and fragmentary copies have been found at Boghaz Keui among the Hittite archives. Translations are numerous. For the Hittite copy, see especially Langdon-Gardiner, *Journ. of Egypt. Arch.*, vi. (1920), pp. 179 ff. Weidner has an excellent annotated translation of the Hittite copy in *Politische Documente aus Kleinasien* (*Boghazköi-Studien*, 9 Heft), Leipzig, 1923. Cf. also the usual histories of Egypt for the Egyptian copies.

in the Soleb temple of Amenhotep III. According to this list, the king of Egypt ruled over Mesopotamia, whereas we know from the Amarna Letters that the Egyptian empire never included this country. The climax of such empty claims was reached at Kom Ombo, where Ptolemy Lathyrus, a prince who actually lost what he inherited, credits himself with the conquest of several nations, which, like the Hittites, had vanished from existence many centuries before.[1] Whether the alleged conquests of Ramesses II. are genuine or not, it is difficult to say. Certainly, his boastful vanity encourages our disbelief in them. But while we cannot regard him as the ancient Greek writers did, as a universal conqueror who carried his arms into Europe and even to the confines of the Caucasus—in this respect his reputation has nothing to support it—we cannot deny that his armies really marched on several occasions into northern Syria and probably made their way to the banks of the Euphrates, and that he re-established authority in many a Palestinian city. But it should be noted that this does not affect the argument under consideration in this chapter, for practically all the places taken possession of were located either in the far north, including distant Syria, or in the Maritime Plain and Shephelah, which were not actual Hebrew territory at the time, or at least not continuously held by the Israelites till long afterwards.

"The travels of a *Maher*," which is the sarcastic account of the misadventures of a trained scribe in Palestine, written about the time of Ramesses II., is regarded by Professor Sayce and others [2] as an evidence of the complete occupation of the country by Egypt during this reign. But the argument has little to support it. All parts of Palestine, principally Syria, are no doubt mentioned in it; but it is clear that the writer, who admits that he had never visited the land himself, had simply studied the town lists of the Pharaohs, which formed an atlas of Canaanitish geography in his day, and had received additional information as to the cities and roads of Palestine from Egyptian soldiers who had been there, and from the numerous Asiatics who thronged into the valley of the Nile. As for

[1] Sayce, *Patriarchal Palestine*, p. 201.

[2] Sayce, *op. cit.*, p. 138.

Egyptian control of the central and southern regions, there is nothing in the *maher's* account to substantiate it.[1]

After Ramesses II., the hold of each successive Pharaoh, even upon Syria and the coast territories, became weaker, owing to the great movements of peoples which set the Mediterranean in a turmoil about this time, and which did not leave Egypt unscathed. In spite of the vainglorious records of Ramesses, the Egyptians found it a heavy task to retain their own borders. Merenptah (*c.* 1233–1223 B.C.), his immediate successor and his thirteenth son, found widespread revolt in Asia. Ashkelon, Gezer, Aijalon, Yenoam, and indeed all western Syria-Palestine rose against their Egyptian overlord. He seems to have undertaken a campaign against these places in his third year. In an inscription on his victory stele in Egypt, he claims also to have come up against "Israel" and "destroyed" it, but he gives no names of any Israelite towns as having been captured or sacked, which seems to show that he, no more than Ramesses, penetrated into what was Israelite territory. The fact, however, that he refers to Israel as being in Palestine is proof that the Exodus had taken place long before his day, although the upholders of the late-date theory try to explain the matter away.[2] Having overawed the revolting cities, he seems to have been content to undertake no further campaigns. He maintained intercourse with Syria by means of letters and messengers; and the treaty of peace with the Hittites was duly observed, the friendly relations established with his father being kept in force. Early in his reign he had sent corn by sea to these old enemies of Egypt at a time when there was famine in their land. In his fifth year, Egypt was invaded by a confederacy of white-skinned tribes from Libya and the shores of Asia Minor, who overran the Delta and threatened the very existence of the Egyptian monarchy. The marauders from Asia Minor were the 'Peoples of the Sea,' whom the Greeks called Pelasgians. They were wandering

[1] The document has been edited by Gardiner, *Egyptian Hieratic Texts*, Series I., Part 1, *The Papyrus Anastasi*, Leipzig, 1911.

[2] The subject of Merenptah's stele is discussed in Chapter XII.

tribes, some of them Greeks from the Ægean, who ranged the Mediterranean at this epoch in quest of plunder, "fighting to fill their bellies daily," as the Egyptian records pithily put it. It was they who brought about the collapse of the Minoan culture in a welter of piracy, folk-wandering, and barbarism.[1] Egypt was saved by a battle in which the invading armies were almost annihilated, but not before it had been weakened and drained of its resources. It almost collapsed, worn-out and overtaxed, never again able to rise to its previous splendour. The XIXth Dynasty thus ended in exhaustion.

With the rise of the XXth Dynasty and the accession of Ramesses III. (*c.* 1204–1172 B.C.), there came further invasion of the 'Sea Peoples,' who swept down on Egypt. Partly by land through Syria and Palestine, and partly by sea, they made their way southward, destroying everything as they advanced. For a time they encamped in "the land of the Amorites" (Amurru), and then pursued their onward march. Ramesses III. met them in battle in his third year, on the north-eastern frontier of his kingdom, and in a fiercely contested struggle overthrew them. The ships of the invaders were captured or sunk, and their forces on land were decimated. The Pharaoh pursued the retreating enemy into Syria. He found no difficulty in marching along the Mediterranean coast, like the conquering Pharaohs who had preceded him. North of Beirût, his army struck eastward and took the city of Kumidi (probably to the north of Hermon). Then it made its way to Hamath, which surrendered, and from there still farther north to the plains of Aleppo. In his temple palace at Medînet Habû (Thebes), he has left a record of his Syrian conquests. He seems to have made no attempt, however, to capture the cities of the coast, and re-establish Egyptian power in them. His army passed them by without any effort to reduce them. Gaza alone, so far

[1] Cf. Hall, "The Peoples of the Sea," *Recueil Champollion*, pp. 297–330; *Cambridge Ancient History*, ii. pp. 275 ff.; Smolenski, "Les Peuples Septentrionaux de la Mer," *Ann. Serv.*, xv. (1915), p. 49; Wooley, "La Phénicie et les Peuples égéens," *Syria*, 1921; Wooley, "Asia Minor, Syria, and the Ægean," *Liverpool Annals of Archæology*, ix. (1922), pp. 41 ff.

as we know, fell into his hands. Possibly the Philistines had now arrived in force on the coast and shown themselves too strong to be meddled with. These powerful fighters were probably Mediterraneans of Lycian-Carian origin, who had occupied eastern Crete (Kaphtor, Deut. ii. 23 ; Amos ix. 7) for a time, and then joined in the regular folk-wandering (due to the Phrygian invasion), until they reached western Palestine, where they settled down in the Maritime Plain, about the time of Ramesses III. or a little earlier perhaps. They were known under the name of Pulesati and Zakkal (or Thekel), and appear to have come in successive waves and not all at once. The mention of them in Genesis[1] is probably an anachronism, although there may have been an earlier settlement of them along the coast, just as there was an earlier Danauna settlement in Syria 200 years before the time of Ramesses III.[2] The arrival of all these new elements made it a very difficult matter for Ramesses to hold any part of Palestine. There could not possibly have been any reconquest of the land. The idea that there was such a thing is quite incorrect. "Ramesses," says Breasted, "places in his lists of conquered regions the cities of northern Syria to the Euphrates, including all that the empire had ever ruled in its greatest days. These lists, however, are largely copied from those of his great predecessors, and we can place no confidence in them."[3] The fact is, that Palestine, which had learned the meaning of freedom in the Amarna days and had now become independent, would no longer suffer the Egyptian yoke. Before Ramesses III. had passed away, the land of the Pharaohs was compelled to abandon the whole of her Asiatic dependencies. From this time her story is one of swift and irretrievable decline. A number of *rois fainéants*, each bearing the famous name of Ramesses and none of them

[1] Gen. xxi. 32 ff., xxvi. 1, 8, 14 f., 18.

[2] Cf. Hall, *Cambridge Ancient History*, ii. pp. 283 ff. ; *The Hittites and Egypt*, 1923, p. 165 ; Macalister, *The Philistines* (Schweich Lectures, 1911) ; Burney, *Judges*, p. xciv ; Noordtzij, *De Filistijnen* (Kampden, 1905), p. 59 ; Böhl, *Het Oude Testament*, 1919, p. 107 ; Chadwick, *The Heroic Age*, pp. 178 ff., 188 ff., 454 ff. ; etc.

[3] *Cambridge Ancient History*, ii. p. 177.

worthy of the honour, succeeded one another, until under Ramesses XII. the high priest of Amūn at Thebes, Hrihor by name, usurped the throne about 1100 B.C., and founded the XXIst Dynasty.

If further evidence were needed of the total loss of Egyptian power in Palestine, it may be found in the Gólenischeff papyrus, discovered in 1891 at El-Khibeh, in Upper Egypt. It is dated the fifth year of the reign of Ramesses XII., and consists of the report of an Egyptian commissioner, Unamūn, who was dispatched to Phœnicia in order to procure timber from the Lebanon for the sacred barge of Amūn. He was received with scant courtesy, finding nothing but hostile words and ill success. The story has been pretty fully told by Burney, Maspéro, and others.[1]

The brief historical sketch which we have now given of the later Egyptian campaigns shows that these afford little ground for the contentions of the traditional school. The upholders of this school assert that Palestine was reconquered by these Pharaohs, and again became so thoroughly an Egyptian province that the conquest by the Israelites could not well have begun until the middle or close of the reign of Ramesses III. They assert also that, as the Hebrew records bear no trace of any collision with the Egyptian armies, the only possible explanation is that the Israelites were not yet in the land. "The Egyptians," says Petrie, "were incessantly raiding Palestine down to 1194 B.C., and yet there is absolutely no trace of Egyptian action in the whole period of the Judges, which shows that the entry into Canaan must be after that date."[2] These assertions are not well founded, as we hope to show in the rest of this chapter. They are not justified by the history of the campaigns, when properly regarded, and are based upon an incorrect understanding of what is meant by the Hebrew settlement in the land. Let the following facts be remembered:

In the first place, full weight is not given by the upholders

[1] Burney, *Judges*, pp. xcvi ff.; Maspéro, *Contes populaires de l'Égypte* (4e édition, 1911), pp. 214–230.

[2] *Egypt and Israel*, p. 37.

of the late-date theory to the fact that the settlement took place only slowly and gradually. Consequently, it involved at first only a limited territory in actual victorious possession, and it was not until long afterwards—probably two or three hundred years—that the wider territory came to be under Hebrew rule. To realize this, it is necessary to understand the Biblical description of the settlement. It is well known to Biblical scholars that, in the Book of Joshua, we have two different conceptions of how the conquest was achieved.[1] One is that shared by the Deuteronomic and Priestly redactors (D and P)—that the whole land was taken possession of by Joshua and all enemies were exterminated, the conquest extending to all southern Canaan except the Philistine plain, and that the various territories were thereupon occupied by the tribes to which he allotted them. The conquest is represented as being a thorough one, effected in one generation by all the tribes acting together. The narrative (D and P), giving this picture, contains all the well-known features, such as the reception of the spies by Rahab, the drying up of the waters of Jordan, the capture of Jericho, the trespass of Achan, the two attacks on Ai, the treaty with the Gibeonites, and the battles of Beth-horon and of the Waters of Merom. Joshua appears as the successor of Moses, and as the leader of the whole people. The conquest is represented as the work of united Israel, and its course, except for the repulse at Ai, is uniformly successful. The narrative contains many generalizing features and sweeping passages, *e.g.* "All these kings and their land did Joshua take at one time" (Josh. x. 42), "So Joshua took the whole land . . . and the land rested from war" (Josh. xi. 23).

The other conception, an older one, contained in fragments of J in the second part of the Book of Joshua, regards the conquest as taking place gradually and partially, and being in the end far from complete—the slow, patient work indeed of individual tribes, who in most cases settled down side by side with races which they failed to drive out. This latter concep-

[1] On this matter, see Burney's excellent sifting of the evidence (*Israel's Settlement in Canaan*, Lecture I.).

tion is the one which is in harmony with the subsequent history of Israel, and is supported by the Book of Judges (chs. i.–ii. 5). In this opening part of Judges we have a fragmentary account of a very gradual incomplete conquest, an account which an editor has found irreconcilable with the conception that dominates the first part of the Book of Joshua, and which he has therefore, by an introductory clause (Judg. i. 1*a*), transferred to the days *after* Joshua's death. This, however, is impossible. We cannot conceive that the Israelites, having gained complete possession of the land and exterminated their enemies, were after Joshua's death driven back upon Jericho and began a second series of campaigns which restored the country by degrees to them. In itself this is impossible; and that the campaigns in Judg. i. happened in Joshua's lifetime is not only implied by the account of his death which follows them in Judg. ii., but is proved by the fact that the same episodes (*e.g.* those of Caleb and Hebron, Othniel and Debir) which are related in Judg. i. as happening after Joshua's death, are in the Book of Joshua itself related as happening while he still directed the allotment of the territories. If we omit Judg. i. 1*a* and several other verses in the chapter which are obviously inserted by an editor, what is left affords an account of the Conquest which is in harmony (as already said) with the older of the two conceptions contained in the Book of Joshua, and which is of the greatest importance in connection with the Israelite settlement in Canaan. If we compare these two conceptions of the settlement and make our choice between them, we must reasonably attach less weight to the one which pictures the occupation of the land as complete from the beginning than to the one which describes it as a gradual process. For the former theory is in conflict with the results of modern excavations in Palestine, which do not reveal any sudden changes or break in cultural conditions at the period of the Israelite invasion, such as there would have been had the invasion taken a complete and sweeping form. This is true of any period at which the invasion may be placed. Besides, as Burney has pointed out,[1] if we assume that the whole

[1] *Israel's Settlement in Canaan*, p. 25.

of Palestine, with the exception of the Maritime Plain, fell completely and at once into the hands of the Israelites as a result of Joshua's victories, we cannot account for the other conception which seems to contradict it; whereas if we accept the latter one, we can explain the former as the reading of later conditions (those of the monarchy) into the narrative describing Israel's first settlement. It was very natural that in later times there should be a disposition to represent the success of Joshua's invasion as thorough and absolute. For this reason alone, the narratives which record the defeats and failures sustained by the Israelites in their attacks on the Canaanites must be regarded as genuine and as bearing the stamp of greater antiquity.

This being so, we are thrown back upon the older account in Joshua and Judges, if we wish a true Biblical picture of the settlement. According to this account, the Hebrew tribes appear in numerous cases to have been unable to eradicate or drive out the other races and to have left them in possession of their cities. The expression, "did not utterly drive them out" (Judg. i. 28), which suggests that there was a partial expulsion, is incorrect. The Hebrew, which contains the Infinitive Absolute, implies that the expulsion was left totally unaccomplished. "Did not dispossess them at all" is a truer rendering.[1] They seem to have been content to settle down beside them, and to have gained the victory or superiority only after many generations and largely by a process of more or less peaceful penetration. The conception, indeed, which the older document gives us may be summarized as follows: (1) We see Judah and Simeon, with certain nomad tribes of the Sinaitic peninsula, such as the Kenites (Judg. i. 16), the Calibbites (Josh. xv. 13), and the Kenizzites (Josh. xv. 17), all of whom were subsequently reckoned as part of Judah, making their way by gradual conquest in the southern hill-country, especially the Negeb, but unable to settle in the western Maritime Plain owing to the iron chariots of the Canaanites, and unable to capture the Jebusite stronghold of Jerusalem to the north and probably

[1] Cf. Burney, *Judges*, p. 25.

the district around, which was dominated by it. It is apparent that a belt of cities, including Gezer, Jerusalem, and many others, connecting the Maritime Plain with the eastern routes, lay outside of their hands. (2) We see the Joseph tribes establishing themselves on the central ridge at Bethel (Judg. i. 32), being shut off from the south-west plains by Canaanite strongholds, such as Gezer, which they were unable to reduce (Judg. i. 29; cf. Josh. xvi. 10), and having their progress barred by the chariots of iron which the Canaanites had in the valley of Jezreel (Josh. xvii. 14 ff.). Even the main part of Dan and possibly Naphtali also, who had taken up their position in the Shephelah or low hill-country adjoining the Maritime Plain, were ousted from there and were compelled to seek fresh territory somewhere in the extreme north. (3) We see a belt of Canaanite cities (Dor, Ibleam, Megiddo, Achshaph, Taanach, Jezreel, Beth-shean, etc.), extending from the Maritime Plain south of Mount Carmel right across the land where the hill-country falls to the great Plain of Esdraelon. The Joseph tribes settle down south of this belt, while the rest of the west Jordan tribes (Zebulun, Naphtali, Dan, and Asher) live to the north of it as best they can among the Canaanites, who continue to hold their strong cities unreduced (Josh. i. 30–34). Dan, indeed, finds a footing at Leshem (Laish) by means of conquest (Josh. xix. 47; Judg. xviii. 27 ff.), but the others eventually gain a position of predominance, not so much by forcible means as by a gradual peaceful penetration.

This summarized conception from the old document referred to gives us a picture of possession by degrees, extending doubtless over two or three centuries. It shows us that only a small amount of territory was under Israelite control for many ages, and that the Israelites were only a handful in many places in comparison with the Canaanites. A mere list of cities which could not be conquered and were consequently left for a very long period in the hands of the Canaanites is surprising. The list in Judg. i. includes Jerusalem, Beth-shean, Taanach, Dor, Ibleam, Megiddo, Gezer, Kitron, Nahalol, Accho, Zidon, Ahlab, Achzib, Helbah, Aphik, Rehob, Beth-shemesh, Beth-anoth,

Aijalon, and Shaalbim; and there were in all likelihood numerous others whose names are not given.

Gardiner seems to have overlooked the fact that, according to the Biblical record, Beth-shean (Beisân) remained outside Israelite possession for several centuries (till the time of king David), for he uses the fact of its being under Egyptian control till the end of the reign of Ramesses III. as an argument against what he calls "an Exodus of the traditional kind."[1] The discoveries by the Pennsylvania Museum of steles of Seti I., Ramesses II., and Ramesses III. at Beisân[2] only prove that the town continued in Egyptian hands till about 1172 B.C., which is not inconsistent with the Biblical record, and forms no argument against the Israelites being settled in the land during this time. Even as late as Saul's reign (*c.* 1010 B.C.), the Philistines, who succeeded the Egyptians in the possession of the town, were able to cope with the Israelite army, for they inflicted a memorable defeat upon it on the slopes of Mount Gilboa, and then hung the bodies of Saul and his sons on the walls of the town (1 Sam. xxxi. 10). It was probably David who captured the place (*c.* 1000 B.C.); and later, in the days of Solomon, it became subject to tribute. The signs of David's attack, with the accompanying conflagration of the town, have been discovered by the members of the Pennsylvania Museum.[3]

The fact that Beth-shean was not in Israelite hands till the time of David suggests the possibility that all the cities across the Plain of Esdraelon were still outside Israelite territory at that late date. The same is known to have been the case with many other cities which were left unreduced. Gezer, for instance, was independent till Solomon's time, and was only made Israelite then because it was received as the dower of the daughter of Pharaoh (1 Kings ix. 16). Jerusalem remained for nearly four centuries in the hands of the Jebusites, "the city of a stranger that is not of the children of Israel"

[1] *Journ. of Egypt. Arch.*, x. (1924), p. 88.

[2] *The Museum Journal*, Philadelphia, 1923, p. 236.

[3] *The Museum Journal*, 1923, p. 237.

(Judg. xix. 12). Judah attacked it (Josh. xv. 63), but could not succeed in driving out the original inhabitants. It was not until about 1000 B.C., when David's men scaled the 'gutter' or 'water-channel' and took the citadel, that the place fell to the Israelites.[1] In fact, most if not the whole of the lowlands was held by the Amorites and Philistines till David's time. "It becomes exceedingly significant," says Dr. S. A. Cook, "that . . . when both Saul and David began to set up a monarchy, all Israel was practically under alien domination."[2]

We thus see that, in spite of the initial victories gained at the entry, a long time, probably a period of some centuries, was still needed to make the Israelites masters of Canaan. This is generally admitted now by Biblical scholars. For many long generations the Israelites only occupied, for all practical purposes, the central range, which was always regarded—and which we still regard—as their particular home. They settled in the heart of the land, and along its heights clustered all their historical towns. On their lofty watch-tower, 2500 feet above the Mediterranean, they looked out upon a world from which they were separated. Here their disciplined armies, fighting on foot with bow and spear, could defy the Egyptian troops whose chariots would almost have annihilated them on the plains below. For two or three centuries at least, after entering the land, they were really highlanders, forced to a life of isolation and independence on the mountain-tops, and avoiding the valleys and plains. The Maritime Plain, for instance, and to a large extent the Shephelah to the east of it, came to be in the hands of the Philistines. It was for this reason that the Israelites never had a stock of corn, famine being a frequent feature in their history,[3] and the name of Baal, not that of Yahweh, crossed the Mediterranean in early times. It was

[1] The breach made by David in the wall is believed to have been unearthed by Professor Macalister, who has found the stones at one place cast down inward in wild confusion. Cf. *Palestine Exploration Fund Quarterly*, 1924, p. 63, where a photograph of the breach is given.

[2] *Cambridge Ancient History*, p. 381.

[3] Cf. 2 Sam. xxi. 1; 1 Kings xvii. 1 ff.; 2 Kings iv. 38 ff.; Hag. i. 6 ff.; Neh. v. 3.

only ages afterwards that the Israelites managed to take possession of the land as described in Josh. i.–xii., where a picture is given of what really represents the state of conquest in the days of David.

A realization of these Biblical facts leads us to see that the military campaigns of Seti I., Ramesses II., and Ramesses III. must have left the Israelites practically untouched in the narrow highland territory which they occupied at first. They had found it easy, as the Tell el-Armana Tablets show, to enter the land during the later years of Amenhotep III., when the Egyptian weakness and incapacity first manifested itself, and when widespread invasion from all sides was taking place. They were able to continue without molestation from outside during three-quarters of a century of Egyptian inaction and pacificism. They had thus abundant time to settle down in their own towns and among outlying Canaanites. They had just as little difficulty also, as far as Egyptian power affected them, in remaining in possession during the later military campaigns of the Pharaohs, for there is no conclusive evidence that the part of the land mainly occupied by them at the time (central and southern Palestine) was ever retaken and held again by Egyptian governors as a dependent tributary province.

In the second place, it must be remembered that the campaigns of these later Pharaohs were directed almost entirely against the Syrians and Hittites in the north. This is quite apparent from a study of the campaigns. The issue always lay between Egypt struggling to maintain her power in south-western Asia, and Hittite movements from the north sweeping down and endeavouring to secure a place at her gates. The fact that the fleet was also used and that a base for it was kept in the Phœnician harbours corroborates this, for the co-operation of the fleet could only be intended to enable the armies to reach Syria and the Phœnician *hinterland* with as little difficulty and delay as possible. There is no record of any war or military campaigns launched against the central and southern regions. In the case of Merenptah's conflict with Israel, if it actually happened and if it does not refer to the oppression under Midian, when Israel's crops are known to have been destroyed (Judg. vi. 3–6, 11),[1] the probability is that some of the tribes descended from their hill-country to help the Canaanites in the Shephelah or in the Plain of Esdraelon, and were overpowered and pursued inland with disastrous results, men, women, and children being slaughtered. The Israelites were no doubt the aggressors, and their action must have been a flagrant breach of confidence. We know that the Ḫabiru were allowed to settle down with the consent of the Egyptian High Commissioner, Yanḫamu, who showed himself friendly to them or even in league with them.[2] Consequently they were never harried with fire and sword, as revolting Amorites and others were. This action of the High Commissioner, which has been largely overlooked by critics, seems to show that the Egyptian government, including Pharaoh, perhaps acquiesced in or connived at the settlement of the Israelites in the land. For Yanḫamu, it must not be forgotten, was in close touch with the Pharaoh as a trusted official, and was constantly in Egypt.[3] It is significant that the Israelites did not proceed to elect a king of their own till the legitimate overlordship of Egypt had ceased with the passing away, about 1050 B.C., of the last remnant of Egyptian empire in Asia and the division of Egypt into two opposing dynasties. If this view be correct, the main argument against the early-date theory vanishes at once, for recognition by the Israelites of Egypt's suzerainty, even though they may have paid little attention to it, would account for a good deal.

At all events, the campaigns were undoubtedly directed in the main against the Hittites and other people in the north. From the names of towns and districts mentioned in the marches, we gather that the Egyptian armies kept as far as possible to

[1] See Chapter XII. The date of Midian's attack, on the system of chronology we suggest in Chapter XI., would coincide with the beginning of Merenptah's reign.

[2] See Abdi-Ḫiba's letter, Knudtzon, No. 286.

[3] See note 6, p. 123, and the references to him in Knudtzon, pp. 1169 ff.

the coast plains west of the Palestine mountains. Troops could easily march from Egypt to the north of Syria and to the land of the Hittites without penetrating inland. The great military and commercial road ran along the shore of the Mediterranean, and is probably identical with the present caravan road which leads past El-Kantareh.[1] This is probably the oldest road in the world. It had a line of fortresses on the borders of Egypt, as a defence against invading Shōsu (bedouins) from the east. The most important of these fortresses was Thel, the Sellê of the classical writers, situated at *Tell Abu Sêfeh*, 2 miles east of El-Kantareh. This fortress formed an excellent starting-point for any expedition eastward. Necho, king of Egypt (609 B.C.), doubtless availed himself of this road, when he set out to march through Palestine (2 Kings xxiii. 29). At a later period, Titus made his way from Egypt to Judæa along this road, his halting-places being Ostrakine, Rhinocolura, Raphia, Gaza, Ashkelon, Jamnia, Joppa, and Cæsarea, all of which are coast towns. Along this Maritime Plain the great nations of antiquity passed on their way to victory or defeat. It was the bridge between Africa and Asia, and this coast road has been tramped again and again by armed hosts. "There can be little or no doubt," says Gardiner, "that the road from El-Kantareh to Gaza *via* Rafa has witnessed the marches of nine-tenths of the armies that have sought to invade Palestine from Egypt, or Egypt from Palestine, along the land route."[2] It was always the main route for military operations, until the Romans in the second century laid out roads, marked with milestones, all over both eastern and western Palestine.

Facts go to show that the armies of the Pharaohs who succeeded Akhenaten did not venture far from this coast road in their marches northward. After the decline of Egyptian

[1] Cf. Professor Buhl, "Roads and Travel in Old Testament," in *Hastings' Dictionary*, v. p. 368; A. R. Guest, *Geographical Journal*, xiii. (1899), pp. 281 ff.; Griffith, *The Mound of the Jew*, pp. 35 ff.; Martin S. Briggs, *Through Egypt in War Time*, pp. 190 ff.

[2] *Journ. of Egypt. Arch.*, vi. (1920), p. 116.

power in the later years of Amenhotep III., the Egyptians probably had no stations in the high central regions, and there is no evidence that the armies of Seti I., Ramesses II., or Ramesses III. marched into them. None of the Egyptian records of the XIXth Dynasty speaks of such a thing. The chariots which formed the basis of Egyptian power were not capable of being driven over the mountains. The land east of Jordan, the Plain of Esdraelon, and the Maritime Plain were open to the march of conquering armies, but the hills of Benjamin and the hill-country of Judah together formed a Montenegro which a resolute race could easily defend against the expeditionary forces of Egypt. The ruggedness of the approaches to this district, especially from the coast road, can hardly be exaggerated. Egyptians, Hittites, Assyrians, Babylonians, and others all came and went along the coast road, but the Israelites could watch their pomp and terror, their gorgeous pageantry and merciless cruelty, without being touched. Unless the Israelites were foolish enough to provoke attack, not one of the passing armies would risk marching inland to do battle with them. The coast towns were highly civilized and had close connection with Egypt, while the hill-tribes of the interior were regarded as a kind of bedouins, whom it was safest to leave alone. Egypt knew well that the Ḫabiru-SA-GAZ were not to be meddled with. There is excellent truth in Dr. Hall's statement that "the Egyptian reoccupation of Palestine was probably no more than a securing of the *Heerstrasse* from the Shephelah to the Plain of Jezreel and thence to the valley of the Orontes." [1]

If the Egyptian armies wanted to attack the central or southern regions of Palestine, they could of course take the caravan route which led up the centre of the Negeb (the waterless district south of Judah) to Beersheba and Hebron.[2] There was nothing to hinder them invading actual Israelite territory

[1] *Ancient History*, p. 412.

[2] For this road, cf. *Proceedings of Royal Geographical Society*, xxii. pp. 455 f.; Trumbull, *Kadesh Barnea*, pp. 349 f.; Guthe, *Zeitschrift des Deutschen Palästina-Vereins*, viii. p. 217.

from this direction, if they cared to take the risk of entering the difficult hill-country with its narrow defiles, its facility for ambush, its unsuitability for chariots, its highland clans of Ḫabiru-SA-GAZ warriors, and its other dangers. But there is no real evidence that the armies of the XIXth Dynasty did so. There may have been raids or incursions of a rapid nature into the central regions by this southern route, but these could not have touched the Israelites to any real extent. There are no records of any battles fought or war undertaken in this direction. Two or three names of towns supposed to lie in the Negeb and central regions are mentioned in the Pharaohs' lists as having been recaptured, but we must not lay too much weight on this when we remember how these lists were framed. Besides, the location of these towns is largely conjecture, and they are differently placed by different authorities. Many of the identifications offered by Petrie, Sayce, Maspéro, and others [1] must be regarded as highly precarious. Identification is not solved by finding some modern name which corresponds with the ancient one. A certain amount of drifting of ancient place-names has occurred, and consequently they are often attached now to later towns and villages in other districts many miles away.[2] A number of the places in these Pharaohs' lists, supposed to lie in the central regions, were probably north of the Plain of Esdraelon, or nearer the coast than explorers imagine, or at least beyond the bounds of actual Israelite territory at that early time. It has been said by some scholars that Seti I., in his campaign against the Shōsu, captured a fortress-town near Hebron, but this is not the case. Kanaʿana, to the frontiers of which he pushed forward, is the name applied by the Egyptians to western Palestine or the Maritime Plain, and the walled town referred to ("*the* or *a* town of Kanaʿana") must therefore have lain near the coast.

[1] Petrie, *History of Egypt*, ii. pp. 320 ff.; Sayce, *Patriarchal Palestine*, pp. 136 ff.; Maspéro, *Transactions of the Victoria Institute*, 1886, pp. 277 ff., 1888, pp. 53 ff., 1894, pp. 63 ff.

[2] Cf. *Atlas of the Historical Geography of the Holy Land*, Preface and p. xv; Macalister, *History of Civilization in Palestine*, 1912, p. 101.

All this, taken along with the Biblical interpretation which we have given of the Israelite settlement, affects considerably the weight of the argument advanced by the upholders of the late-date theory. It at least refutes the assertion that Palestine was so thoroughly reconquered in the Egyptian campaigns of the XIXth Dynasty that the Israelites could not have been settled in the land until later. It is clear that, if they could enter the land along with the SA-GAZ and other invaders, in the reign of Amenhotep III., and if their settlement was only a very gradual process extending over many generations, the campaigns referred to, directed almost entirely against the Hittites and Syrians in the far north, could have but little effect on the Israelites, whose chief centres at the time lay far away from the beaten track.

In the third place, even supposing there were attacks on Israel during these campaigns, surely the fact that the Biblical record makes no reference to such does not afford any valid argument against the early-date theory. It must be admitted that the narrative does not give us the smallest hint of any Egyptian invasion. It tells us much in the Book of Judges of the aggressions of comparatively petty antagonists, but says nothing as to any attacks by the great power of Egypt. From the time of the Exodus, indeed, whatever period we place it at, the Hebrew records mention neither Egypt nor Egyptians until the reign of Solomon. The reason, we are told, must be that the Israelites were not in the land until after the XIXth Dynasty at least.

But it must be remembered that the Hebrew records of these early times make no claim to completeness. The earliest ones were compiled, as we have said, many hundred years after the events narrated, and passed through various hands, being copied, edited, and combined into the JE forms. Much of what has been preserved, such as the Deuteronomic parts of Joshua and the middle section of Judges, is later still. At the very best, the records are mere historical fragments, and can only be a part, a small part indeed, of the historical works composed by Israelitish authors, many of which have certainly been lost. The fragments which we have bear positive testimony to the truth of this by their reference to other works quoted by name, as sources from which further information might be gained. The " Book of the Wars of Yahweh " (Num. xxi. 14) and the " Book of Jashar " (Josh. x. 13), both of which commemorated the battles and mighty deeds of the Israelites in early times, are examples of this. The want of completeness in the present records is evident from the gaps that occur here and there. There is, for instance, a chasm of thirty-seven years or more from the third year of the desert wanderings to the end of them, this long period being passed over without any reference. It is hardly conceivable that, circumstanced as the Israelites were, nothing should have happened to them which deserved to be recorded as much as many other of the events described in the Pentateuch. There must have been external wars or internal regulations which exercised an influence on the development of Israel's history, and which were therefore worthy of record. It follows that this gap can only be attributed to the inadequacy and want of completeness of the history. After the completion of the second temple, too, a break of nearly sixty years occurs in the Hebrew records, and they do not speak again until the Davidic line represented by Zerubbabel has disappeared. There is no record, moreover, in the Book of Judges of the great invasion of Palestine by the 'Sea Peoples,' who swarmed down through Syria, Amurru, and Canaan to Egypt and were defeated by Ramesses III. There is no mention of the Philistine invasion and occupation of the Shephelah, which must have been steadily going on about the same time, and which formed a more formidable oppression than ever came from the Amorites and Canaanites. It is only from a passing allusion that we gather that Egypt attacked Philistia in Solomon's time, when Gezer was burned. These great facts of history are blanks in the Hebrew records, as many others also are. In such a matter we have only to compare the present records with the elaborate treatment given by Herodotus to the Persian War, or Livy to Roman history, to notice that hundreds, even thousands, of most interesting and important items of information have been omitted, suppressed, or lost in the course of early tradition. What would we not give for more light even on the later factors in Israel's history, such as the rebellion of Absalom, the cleaving of the monarchy, the foundation and development of the prophetical schools, and innumerable others? "History might have been on a far greater scale," says Dr. S. A. Cook, "than our sources have remembered. We have only to contrast Kings and Chronicles with what we now know of the sweeping Assyrian campaigns. The Old Testament preserves the echoes, scarcely more, and one can often only guess and guess." [1]

Besides, one at least of the attacks on Israel, described in the Biblical narrative, may have been Egyptian in origin. We refer to the oppression of Israel for eight years, stated to have taken place under Jabin II., king of Hazor (Judg. iv.). The date of this oppression, on our theory of the Exodus, seems to coincide with the reign of Ramesses II. Jabin's captain, Sisera, bears a name not apparently Semitic. It has been regarded by some scholars as Hittite in origin, its termination being compared with that in Sangara (name of a Carchemish king in the time of Ashur-nasir-pal and Shalmaneser II.) and in Tarḫulara (name of a north Syrian king). Cheyne considers it a north Arabian ethnic name. Others regard it as Babylonian, deriving it from *seseru* or *sisseru*, 'child.' The name, however, may just as easily be explained as Egyptian. Budge gives the Egyptian words *šesu*, *šesut*, or *šesi* as meaning "those who follow, or are in the train of some one," and the words occur frequently in the Book of the Dead in this connection. The name may thus be *Šesi-Ra*, *i.e.* 'servant of Ra,' for although the first sibilants do not correspond, other cases of the same kind have been found. This captain, and not Jabin, is represented throughout as the actual and independent leader of the attacks —his forces were under his own control (cf. Judg. iv. 13 with iv. 3), including several hundred chariots, and to slay him was to carry off the honours of the battle. Kings of Canaan are represented as co-fighters with him, but they only receive brief

[1] In a communication to the writer, June 5, 1924.

mention, and are evidently subordinate to him. It is recognized by scholars that Jabin, king of Hazor, should really have no place in the narrative. He is a shadowy figure, stated to have been "king of Canaan," which means that he must have been superior monarch or overlord of all the other kings of the Canaanite cities. Yet we know that Canaan was not a national or political unit. It is apparent that he belongs to quite a different tradition—the one recording Joshua's victory over the northern confederation of Canaanite kings (Josh. xi. 1–9) near the waters of Merom—and this has been interwoven with the Sisera narrative. The fact that Sisera's central camp was about 35 miles from Hazor, at 'Harosheth of the Gentiles' (Judg. iv. 2), a place which has been plausibly identified with *el-Hârithiyeh* on the right bank of the lower Kishon and north-west of Megiddo, commanding the great road from the central plain to the sea, corroborates the supposition that he was an Egyptian vice-regent or general. The same name occurs in Ezra ii. 53 (= Neh. vii. 55) in a list of 'Nethinim' or foreign temple-slaves who returned to Judah after the Exile, and in this case also it may have been Egyptian.

Besides, many of the conflicts which Israel had with the people on the plains may have been inspired by Egypt, for it is well known that the Pharaohs used native levies and contingents. Egyptian raids may thus appear in the Book of Judges as those of 'Canaanites' or 'Philistines.' The struggling Israelites in the heart of the land were beneath the notice of the main Egyptian armies, and could be safely left to the soldiery of the tributary princes to deal with. In repelling these native attacks, the Israelites were actually fighting Egypt through her outposts in Canaan.

Considered, therefore, from the points of view we have expressed, the argument, urged with such plausibility by Petrie, Sayce, Burney, and others, that, had the Israelites been in Palestine during the period of the Egyptian expeditions of the XIXth Dynasty, there would have been some reference in the Hebrew writings to these expeditions, loses practically all its force, and seems a rather dubious basis on which to found such an important thing as the date of the Exodus. The argument that these scholars advance as to Egyptian control of Palestine appears just as weak as the one regarding the building of Pithom and Rameses; and as these are the two main arguments on which the late-date theory is founded, it is apparent that this theory does not have the weight usually attributed to it.

CHAPTER V

THE AKHENATEN SCHOOL: ATENISM

THE writer has endeavoured to show that the traditional or late-date theory has no substantial basis to rest on, inasmuch as it is founded on two erroneous ideas: first, that Pithom and Rameses must have been built by the Israelites in the time of Ramesses II.; and second, that no outside force could have settled in Palestine till the reign of Ramesses III. at least, as the Egyptian armies were constantly invading the land down to that time. The theory has also chronological and other objections, to which he will refer later on. Meantime, in the next two chapters, he wishes to discuss the view which has gained many adherents within recent years, including the well-known Egyptologist, Mr. Arthur Weigall, that the Exodus was connected in some way with the religious changes under Amenhotep IV. (Akhenaten).[1] The date must be looked for, we are told, sometime during the great national upheaval, social confusion, and religious persecution resulting from his policy. Moses and the Israelites, it is said, were in Goshen at the time, and would certainly be on the king's side in his efforts to abandon the old idol worship. They may even have been implicated in the movement, if indeed they were not the actual cause of it. Their own spiritual worship of Yahweh was not unlike the new religion, especially in its monotheistic ideas. They would thus set against themselves the idolatrous priesthood of Thebes, which was being overwhelmed with shame and put to silence. And when the old religion was restored under Tutankhamūn (*c.* 1365–1359 B.C.), or still more drastic-

[1] Weigall, *Tutankhamen and Other Essays*, pp. 80 ff.; *Daily Mail*, January 18, 1923.

ally and securely under Harmhab (*c.* 1358–1324 B.C.), the last king of the XVIIIth Dynasty, the Israelites would naturally be persecuted and ill-treated. Their lives would be made bitter, and ultimately they would be driven from the land (Ex. xii. 39).[1]

The Exodus, according to this theory, must be placed about the end of the XVIIIth Dynasty; in other words, somewhere between 1358 and 1324 B.C. "During the Aton heresy, as it came to be called," says Mr. Weigall, "there had been a general tolerance of foreign customs; but already, under Tutankhamen and Ay, an attack of foreigners had begun, and when Horemheb came to the throne the Egyptian armies were launched against the Asiatic frontiers, and Egypt shook herself free of Semitic influences. This reactionary 'cleansing' of the country was being carried on at just about this period (say, B.C. 1345), to which the Biblical genealogies bring us back, as stated above; and it has always seemed probable to me, therefore, that this is the real date of the Exodus."[2] Mr. Weigall thus places it about 120 years earlier than the date put forward by Petrie, Sayce, Burney, and others, though still 100 years later than the date we are advocating.

In order that the reader may understand the theory, we propose in this chapter to describe the situation within the land of Egypt at the epoch referred to.[3] In the next chapter we shall deal with the arguments advanced in favour of an Exodus at this epoch.

During the latter part of the reign of Amenhotep III. (Akhenaten's father and predecessor), who died *c.* 1383 B.C., there was a serious movement throughout the land to break

[1] The same theory is adopted by, among others, Professor S. A. B. Mercer, of Trinity College, Toronto, in his *Tutankhamen and Egyptology* (1923). Professor Mercer suggests that Tutankhamūn was "in a general sense" "*a* pharaoh of *an* exodus from Egypt."

[2] *Daily Mail*, January 18, 1923.

[3] In addition to the ordinary histories of Egypt, cf. Weigall, *Life and Times of Akhnaton*; Budge, *Tutankhamen*; recent *Journals of the Egypt Exploration Society*; Sethe, *Beiträge zur Geschichte Amenophis IV.*, 1922; H. Schafer, "Altes und Neues zur Kunst und Religion von Tell el-Amarna," *Zeitschrift für Ägyptische Sprache und Altertumskunde* (1918), pp. 1 ff. (containing also references to earlier writings on the subject).

away from the worship of the Theban god Amūn, " hidden " (one), with its priestly domination, and to bring in the worship of Aten, " the sun's disk." There was a considerable difference between these two divinities. Amūn had originally been merely a tribal god, confined to the district of Thebes, but when this city became the capital of Egypt, he was made the state god of the land, and became the most powerful of all the deities. His worship had developed slowly and surely for a thousand years or more, and had now become so engrained in the hearts of the people that any movement to destroy it and introduce a new deity was sure of widespread opposition. Aten (or Athen), on the other hand, was not an anthropomorphic form, like the other gods, but the celestial body itself, the word *aten* being an Egyptian expression for the sun's ' disk ' or ' face.' [1] Atenism was thus a form of worship connected with the sun. It was not the oldest form, as several solar gods had been worshipped in Egypt many centuries earlier. One of the first of these was Her or Horus, who was symbolized by the sparrow-hawk, and who fought daily against Set, the night sky, and triumphed over him. Another was Tem or Tūm (Atem or Atūm), who had absorbed the attributes of several indigenous gods, and had created himself the Great God. Still another was Re, whose attributes and character resemble closely those of the Babylonian god Marduk, and whose principal seat of worship was the famous city of On or Heliopolis, where a college of the sun-god existed from time immemorial, with a body of priests renowned for their wisdom and learning. Tūm claimed to dwell in the disk of the sun, as Re also did after he usurped the attributes of Tūm. The Aten or Disk was thus a recognized aspect of the sun-god in Egypt from ancient times, and in this respect there was nothing new in the movement towards Atenism which now began in the reign of Amenhotep III.,

[1] The word Aten or Aton has been erroneously regarded by some as the Semitic word '*Ādhōn* (אָרוֹן; Greek, ' Adonis '), ' lord,' but there is no connection between the two. *Adhon* was a title applied by the Canaanites to the Babylonian god Tammuz, who was addressed as *Adhonai*, ' my lord.' The name made its way from Canaan to Cyprus, and from there to Greece.

although it developed some conceptions more lofty and enlightened than those of ordinary sun-worship.

No doubt Amenhotep III. was influenced to some extent towards Atenism by his mother, Mutemuya, who was a foreign princess, the daughter of Artatama, king of Mitanni. This princess, who had been accustomed to worshipping solar and celestial deities akin to those in India, is believed to have introduced into Egypt religious views more in common with solar worship than with the worship of Amūn. Her arrival in Thebes, accompanied by a number of influential followers, was bound to involve religious changes, for her sympathy and support would naturally be given to Tūm and the other sun-gods. A further influence in the same direction came from the wives of Amenhotep III. One of these, the lady Ti or Teī, who is stated on the scarabs to have been the daughter of Iuau and Thuau,[1] was a private individual, apparently of no high rank in society. She was a very remarkable woman and wielded great power both inside the palace and in the country generally. If her parents were not foreigners from Asia, her father at least is thought by some to have been a prince of Zahi (Phœnicia).[2] What her religious views were, or what gods she worshipped, we cannot tell, but some inscriptions on large steatite scarabs suggest that she was in favour of Atenism. Being possessed of considerable ability, she would be able to impress her religious views on her husband and turn his eyes and those of the court away from the sombre worship of Amūn. Of her four daughters she named the last one Bakten-aten, in honour of the sun's disk. Later on, as we discover from the Tell el-Amarna Tablets, Amenhotep III. married Giluḫipa, a sister of Tushratta, the powerful king of Mitanni, and we know that she arrived in Egypt with a retinue of lady attendants and an escort of 317 persons. Afterwards he received a daughter of Tushratta, named Tatumḫipa, as a wife, and this lady's *entourage* was no

[1] Cf. T. M. Davis, *The Tomb of Queen Tīyi*, 1910; Newberry, *The Tomb of Iouiya and Touiyou*, 1907.

[2] Cf. S. A. Cook, *Cambridge Ancient History*, ii. p. 300; Hall, *Ancient History*, p. 256 n.

doubt equally imposing.[1] It follows that the influence of these foreign princesses on the king and his court must have been considerable, and an additional impetus was thus given to the cult of the sun. The new queens brought with them not only foreign names and customs, but their foreign faith as well.

We need not wonder, therefore, that during the latter part of the reign of Amenhotep III. the cult of Atenism began to take an influential place. Soon we find one of the Pharaoh's regiments being named after Aten, and this deity's name begins to occur on the monuments. On a block of stone found re-used in the pylon of Harmhab at Karnak there are cartouches of Akhenaten, who is represented standing before the falcon-headed sun-god Horus in his name of "Shu-who-is-in-the-Disk (Aten)," but a close examination proves that they have been altered from those of Amenhotep III. This discovery shows that Atenism was in existence during the reign of this latter Pharaoh. The court was thus bringing into prominence a deity closely related to the gods of Heliopolis. No doubt, the powerful priests of Amūn at Thebes were considerably perturbed as they watched the development. The fact that Amenhotep made a great lake, over a mile long, on Ti's estate in western Thebes, and presented her with a magnificent barge named Aten-Tehen ("Aten sparkles"), shows that both king and queen wished to pay honour to this solar deity; and Maspéro is probably correct in stating that the gorgeous opening festival on the lake was the inauguration of the worship of Aten at Thebes. It was the public commencement of the new conception, which so far was only like a cloud no bigger than a man's hand, but was destined in the next reign to spread across the whole sky and darken the national life of Egypt. The desire of the court for a change in religion is understood

[1] Tushratta's letter making arrangements for his daughter going to the Egyptian harem is marked by the Egyptian registrar as belonging to the thirty-sixth year of Amenhotep III., and as this was the year the king died, the daughter may never have become queen of Egypt. The theory that she became the wife of Akhenaten is hardly possible. Akhenaten's wife was his own sister, Nefertiti, daughter of Amenhotep III. and Ti. Cf. Hall, *Ancient story*, p. 258 n. Tushratta reigned c. 1399–1367 B.C.

when we remember that the worship of Amūn was so hedged about with regulations that freedom of thought was almost impossible; and, in addition, the priests of this worship had obtained such power and wealth through abundance of revenues that they had become a serious menace to the nation.

Ti's son, Amenhotep IV., who succeeded next to the throne (*c.* 1383–1366 B.C.), was brought up under this religious movement. His nurse's husband, Ai, was a priest of Aten, and the young king naturally absorbed his teaching, as well as that of his mother and the Mitannian ladies. As a boy, he was clever, precocious, sincere, intelligent, and of strong will and fearless nature. He had no fancy for the arts of war, but spent much time in zealously studying the problems of religion. He soon began to take a hatred to Amūn, as well as to the old gods and goddesses of Egypt, with the exception of the solar gods of Heliopolis; and he developed a thorough dislike for the arrogant priesthood at Thebes, which was usurping royal prerogatives, and was becoming the dominant power in the kingdom, from Napata in the south to Syria in the north. No doubt, his mother had the chief religious influence on him. The portraits of her which have been discovered show a face of outstanding character and great charm, and one is not surprised at the persuasive power she must have wielded over her son. Whether she actually ruled or not during his early years on the throne, she was undoubtedly the chief power behind it. The Amarna Letters and the Wady Hammamât inscription show that she was regent till his coming of age, and that she had to be consulted in affairs of state. At all events, she certainly succeeded in filling his mind with a passionate devotion to the cult of Aten, for before he was nineteen years of age, as is commonly believed,[1] he had thrown himself

[1] Möller ("Echnaton," *Zeitschrift für Ägyptische Sprache*, lvi. pp. 100 ff.) justifies the youthfulness of Akhenaten by the interesting analogy of the Moslem boy-heretic El-Hâkim (A.D. 996–1021), who began to rule at Cairo as a boy of eleven, and issued extraordinary religious decrees at the age of sixteen. Recently, however, the extreme youth of Akhenaten has been called in question. Sethe, for instance, believes him to have been between twenty and thirty years old at his accession.

with all the ardour of youth into the new movement, and had drawn to his support some of the greatest nobles in the land. According to the teaching of Heliopolis, the Aten or sun's disk had been created by Tūm or Khepera, but Akhenaten asserted its self-creation and self-subsistence. In the usual symbol of the solar gods, the disk was encircled by a serpent, but the young king abolished the serpent and treated the disk differently. He made a number of rays stream down from it towards the earth, and at the end of each ray was a hand, reaching down the signs of life and power.

In the sixth (or some think, the fourth) year of his reign, the movement came to a height. He determined that Amūn and the other gods of Egypt, with all their dogmas and priestly regulations, should be abolished, and that Aten should be proclaimed, as Sir Wallis Budge has expressed it, "the One self-created, self-subsisting, self-existing god, whose son and deputy he was."[1] For this purpose he built a temple, Gem-Aten, at Thebes, with a shrine in it containing the *ben* or 'sun-stone,' and he resolved that henceforth the worship of Aten should be the one religion of Egypt. This was equivalent to imposing the new creed on all his subjects as the state religion, and effecting a religious revolution in the land. It meant the confiscation of the revenues of Amūn, and the hostility of the powerful priesthood, whose means of livelihood would thus disappear. The young king was doing one of the greatest things any man ever put his hand to, but the blood of the sun-god was in his veins, and he was master in his own country. He changed place-names and personal names in accordance with the reformed cult. From Amenhotep, meaning 'Amūn is content,' he changed his own name to Akhenaten, generally translated 'Spirit of Aten,' the names of his wife and daughters being likewise altered; and at the same time, believing that he had found the real truth and that other religions were false, he added to his name the title Ankh-em-Mat, 'Living in Truth.'

[1] *Tutankhamen*, p. 82.

The result of all this can easily be imagined. At first, there were murmurings among the Amūnites, but these soon developed into curses and open threats, with the result that Akhenaten found residence in Thebes impossible. In his daily life there he was confronted with symbols of Amūn's power, and cramped and thwarted by hostile influences. He decided, therefore, to abandon Thebes, which had been the capital of Egypt for many centuries, and build a new city far away from all contamination, so that he could develop his religious schemes in peace and worship his god as he chose. Accordingly, in the sixth year of his reign, he moved his court 300 miles farther down the Nile to an isolated spot on the east side, where the cliffs recede from the river and leave a stretch of plain about 5 miles long and 3 miles across at the widest part. The site is near the modern village of At-Til, about 190 miles south of Cairo and 50 miles north of Asyût, and is known to Europeans as Tell el-Amarna. Here on virgin soil, which had never been defiled with the worship of Amūn, he founded his City of God, extending nearly 2 miles in length along the river bank, and called it Akhut-Aten, 'The horizon of Aten.' To him and his followers this new capital was the visible symbol of the glory and magnificence of Aten, and the one place in which the new god was to be found. Here he built a superb palace, covering a space of 1500 by 500 feet, and in about two years' time took up his residence in it. With the help of one of his devoted followers, named Bek, an architect and master-builder, he erected a splendid temple to Aten, 250 feet square, making it brilliant with painting and sculpture, and inlaying it in many parts with precious stones and gold. He built a second temple for the queen-mother, Ti, a third for the princess, Baktenaten, and probably others throughout the land.[1] The boundary around the new capital was marked out by great steles, and formed a district of 8 miles in length, and not less than 12 miles in width from the eastern to the western cliffs. This was the domain of the new god, enclosing, as Mai, one of Akhenaten's nobles, described it, "the mighty City of the Horizon of Aten,

[1] We know from the Amarna Tablets that he erected one in Syria.

great in loveliness, . . . rich in possessions, . . . like a glimpse of heaven."[1] The new city was soon filled with adherents of the Aten worship. Their tombs, which are yet to be seen in the cliffs that encircle the desert on the east, are quite different from all others in Egypt. On the walls there are hymns to Aten, as well as texts containing much adulation of the king for his goodness, and pictures representing him and his mother worshipping.[2]

But not even Pharaoh could change the whole religious outlook of Egypt without exciting bitter opposition. The national mind was not ready for these new ideas, and it was inevitable that a struggle should come. The priesthood of Amūn, especially, who owed their occupation and daily bread to the old stereotyped form of worship, strongly resented the changes. To them the new religious thought was heretical, and the new art which accompanied it was distasteful. Their organization was one of enormous power and wealth. The high priest at Thebes was one of the most influential personages in the land, frequently acting in a civil capacity as Grand Vizier, and the other priests were usually nobles of the highest rank. By degrees, practically everything connected with the civil administration had fallen into their hands. In their hostility to the new religion, they had behind them also multitudes of people who were determined to abide by the old worship. To these people, Aten was a strange deity, who did not sit with them at their hearth, nor bathe in the

[1] Weigall, *Life and Times of Akhnaton*, p. 176; cf. Breasted, *Cambridge Ancient History*, p. 115.

[2] For an account of the tombs and of the excavations at Tell el-Amarna, see the series of volumes issued by the Egypt Exploration Society, London, particularly N. de G. Davies, *The Rock Tombs of Tell el-Amarna*, six vols., 1903–1908. See also the recent issues of the *Journ. of Egypt. Arch.*, and the Journal's illustrated brochure, *The Proposed Excavations at Tell el-Amarna*, which contains an account of the great significance of the site and a *résumé* of previous work done there by Professor Petrie and the German Orient-Gesellschaft. Further interesting information is found in *The City of Akhenaten*, by Eric Peet, Leonard Wooley, Battiscombe Gunn, and P. L. O. Guy (Egypt Exploration Society, 1923); *Mitteil. der deutschen Orient-Gesellschaft*, Nos. 34, 46, 50, 52, 55, 57; Petrie, *Tell el-Amarna*, 1894.

Nile waters, but reigned in the distant sky, in solitary isolation. Thus, between the priests and the people, the king came in for a large amount of ill-will and enmity, which must have embittered his days.

No doubt, it was this hatred and opposition that led him to take drastic action. Being persecuted, he became a fanatical persecutor of the old priests and Amūn worshippers, and indeed of all the old gods. Perhaps the death of Ti, who must have had a kindly restraining influence on him, had something to do with this fiercer chapter in his life. At all events, he seems to have made the attempt not only to suppress the old gods or at least relegate them to a secondary place, but to destroy their names in the inscriptions and literature of the country. The priests were driven out and their rights abolished, the great temples of the land were closed, the sculptures of Amūn and the other gods on the walls were mutilated, and all the temple properties were confiscated and their proceeds applied to the cult of Aten. The names of the hated gods were everywhere erased, and their figures battered out. Even his own father's name was ruthlessly destroyed, wherever possible, that the title of Amūn should nowhere be seen. The evidence of all this is still visible to-day in temple after temple throughout the land. What was at first mere enthusiasm on the part of the king seems to have developed into spiritual arrogance, self-sufficiency, and religious madness. Professor Breasted has described him as "a God-intoxicated man, whose mind responded with marvellous sensitiveness and discernment to the visible evidences of God about him."[1] This may be so, but facts go to show that he was obstinate, intolerant, fanatical, considering himself an incarnation of God, usurping the attributes of Deity, and substituting for the worship of Amūn something that was merely a form of sun-worship, different no doubt from previous forms, but still replete with pagan crudities.

For several years he dwelt and reigned at Tell el-Amarna, but he could not stave off the impending crash. He gradually

[1] *Religion and Thought in Ancient Egypt*, as quoted by Weigall, *Life and Times of Akhnaton*, p. 99.

lost his Asiatic empire, as we have seen, and alienated his subjects. His government became weak and chaotic, the foreign tribute practically ceased, the treasury was rapidly emptying, and he was always being menaced by the anger and scheming of the priests. At last his whole policy tumbled in ruins about his head. He was never a strong man physically, and he found it necessary during the last year or two to associate with him as co-regent his son-in-law Sʿakere, who had married his eldest daughter Merit-aten, and who is supposed to have been an influential noble at the court. Akhenaten, after reigning seventeen years, died at the early age of about thirty (*c.* 1366 B.C.), leaving several daughters, but no male issue. He was buried in a rock-hewn tomb 5 miles away, on the eastern bank of the Nile, and not in the western hills, where the other kings of the XVIIIth Dynasty were buried.

It was soon evident that the revolution had depended on the energies of Akhenaten, for on the death of this originator of the upheaval, the ancient religion quickly reasserted itself. Sʿakere was succeeded by Tutankhamūn, who had married Akhenaten's third daughter, Ankhsenpa-aten, a girl hardly twelve years old. This Pharaoh, whose tomb, with all its magnificent furniture and equipment, was discovered in 1922 by Lord Carnarvon and Mr. Howard Carter, is believed to have been one of Akhenaten's greatest nobles, Tutu. Inscriptions at Tell el-Amarna show him to have been Foreign Secretary, Lord High Treasurer, and Lord Chamberlain, as well as the holder of other important offices. He was probably the highest official in the realm.[1] When he ascended the throne, he professed to be an adherent of the Aten-worship, and to hold Akhenaten's doctrines of the solar disk. Evidence of this is found in the fact that he is described as 'Tutankh-Aten' on a stele preserved at Berlin, and he is known to have commenced work on some building to the honour of Aten at Thebes. But he was not the man to resist the reaction that was setting in.

[1] Cf. G. Elliot-Smith, *Tutankhamen and the Discovery of his Tomb*, 1923 Carter and Mace, *The Tomb of Tut-ankh-Amen*, 1924.

Finding the hostility of priests and people too strong for him, he broke with Atenism to some extent, and endeavoured to steer a middle course between the two factions, giving freedom of action to both. In a short time, however, he found it necessary to relinquish the worship of the sun's disk, and returned to the orthodox cult, substituting the title of Amūn for that of Aten in his own name and that of his wife. After residing for a time at a palace near Memphis, he was forced to bring the court back to Thebes, and to restore the government there. He also caused the name of Amūn to be re-engraved on the monuments, and made the Atenites give up their hold on the sacred revenues. Ultimately he did more than any of his predecessors to enhance the power and splendour of Amūn and the other Egyptian gods. He rebuilt the desolate temples from one end of the country to another, and endowed them richly, so that there would be no lack of daily offerings. Whatever sympathy he may have had for the cult of Aten during the lifetime of Akhenaten entirely disappeared before he erected his great stele at Karnak,[1] which shows that his reign had the approval of the ancient priesthoods of Heliopolis, Memphis, Hermopolis, and Thebes, as well as of the whole nation.

After a reign of six or seven years, so far as we can gather, he was succeeded by Ai, who had married the nurse of Akhenaten and was Master of the Horse. This king only reigned a year or two, by which time the reaction to the old gods was complete. Tell el-Amarna lost all its importance and became a deserted city, while a deluge of hatred descended on the memory of Akhenaten. He was rarely named again in Egypt, except as a villain and heretic, who had brought the empire to the verge of ruin. His mummy, which is thought to have been discovered at Thebes, in 1907, in the tomb of Queen Ti, by an American explorer, Mr. Theodore M. Davis, showed that his name had been mutilated in all the inscriptions. If the mummy, which Dr. Elliot-Smith believes is that of a young man, be really Akhenaten's, it must have been removed from

[1] Discovered by Legrain, in 1905. See *Annales du Service*, v. (1905), p. 192; *Recueil de Travaux*, 1907, xxix. pp. 162–173.

Tell el-Amarna in mistake for Ti's, and buried in Thebes as her mummy.[1]

It was the next king, however, Harmhab, who firmly established the old polytheism and initiated a completely new epoch. He had been Tutankhamūn's Commander-in-Chief and the virtual dictator of Egypt. His sympathies lay with the priesthoods of Ptah of Memphis, and Re of Heliopolis, and he had been one of the leaders in the movement back to the old gods. As soon as he ascended the throne, he completed and made secure the restoration of Amūn-worship, which had been begun by Tutankhamūn. Realizing that the disturbance for which Akhenaten had become responsible could not be remedied except by vigorous reorganization and strong measures, he set himself to work with great energy, assisted by his patrons, the priests of Thebes. He cleared the country of those Aten worshippers who appeared rebellious, deleting their names from the archives, and driving some of them from the land. During the reigns of Tutankhamūn and Ai, there had been some toleration of the new worship and of foreign habits, but under Harmhab the Egyptian armies were strengthened, and fear took hold of all rebels, political and religious. The result was that Aten-worship was practically wiped out. The great shrine which had been made by Akhenaten at Thebes was demolished, and its blocks of stone, bearing fragments of prayers addressed to the disk, were used for two great pylons which Harmhab added to the temple of Amūn at Karnak. Soon the worship of Aten survived only in a few isolated places, and even there only to an insignificant extent. The last traces of it were merged into the Heliopolitan system of sun-worship, from which it had emanated. Within forty years after Akhenaten's death, the old order was as firmly re-established as if no revolution had taken place.

[1] Cf. Budge, *Tutankhamen*, p. 75; Davis, *The Tomb of Queen Tīyi*. Sethe, on the other hand, gives weighty reasons for rejecting the identification, and holds that Akhenaten was not less than forty-three years of age when he died. (Cf. *Nachrichten der Gesell. der Wiss. zu Göttingen, Phil-hist. Klasse*, 1921, Heft 2, pp. 122 ff.)

CHAPTER VI

YAHWISM AND ATENISM

IT has been said by those who connect the Exodus with Akhenaten's movement that there may have been some relation between the faith of the Israelites and the worship of Aten. In some respects, we are assured, there was a wonderful similarity between the two. Both of them were concerned with one God only, both condemned graven images and other superstitions, and both had spiritual characteristics of a high order. Akhenaten, according to Mr. Weigall, was directing men's eyes to "the worship of the true God, almost as we understand Him now, under the name of Aton."[1] Was Moses not at the back of this attempt to establish the new religion? It is a well-known tradition that he received his education and training at Heliopolis, the city of the sun-god, to which the Aten-worship can be traced. What more probable than that he lived during this revolutionary period of Egyptian history and had something to do with the efforts to put down Amūn-worship and other false religions and introduce a purer 'monotheistic' worship? Is it not quite natural to think that the Israelites so influenced the land in this matter as to lead a large section, headed by the king himself, to abandon idolatry and worship the Being in the disk, the 'One God' who gave life and light to all men? And when Atenism fell, would not the Israelites be persecuted, maltreated, and perhaps even threatened with massacre (we read of the "slaying of the Asiatics")? We know that the Israelites could not worship their God Yahweh as they wanted without being stoned (Ex. viii. 26), and they had to request leave to go into the wilderness

[1] *Tutankhamen and Other Essays*, p. 81.

to sacrifice to Him. Was it not likely, therefore, that the persecution of them led ultimately to their being driven out of the land by Pharaoh's armies during the reign of Ai or Harmhab? In support of this theory several other details are put forward, such as the death of the first-born (none of the 'heretic' Pharaohs being succeeded by a son), and the enslavement of foreign people by Tutankhamūn in great building operations. A remarkable confirmation of the theory, it is said, is to be found in Manetho's account of the Exodus. "I think," says Mr. Weigall, "it is clear that Manetho's account of what Josephus calls 'the fatal thirteen years' is based on fact, and that it definitely tells the story of the historic thirteen years of the Aton heresy. But if he be correct in this, it may be presumed that he is also correct in speaking of Moses as being implicated in this movement, and in regarding the Exodus of the Israelites as being a forced flight in consequence of these events."[1]

The incorrectness and indeed the absurdity of this theory is apparent. Mr. Weigall holds that the Ḫabiru mentioned in Abdi-Ḫiba's letters, who invaded Canaan shortly after 1400 B.C., were Hebrews, related to the children of Israel in Egypt. Moses, who was in Midian at the time of the invasion, heard of this land 'flowing with milk and honey' which his fellow-Hebrews were conquering, and he hastened back to Egypt to urge his kinsmen there to join in the movement. In other words, the conquest of Canaan by the Ḫabiru was going on long before the Israelites left Egypt or spent a generation in the wilderness, and yet the latter were in plenty of time to join in the victory. "Indeed," says Mr. Weigall, "the leader of the Khabiri, so often referred to in these letters as 'that dog,' may be Joshua himself."[2] Surely from this point of view alone, the whole theory breaks down as quite improbable. The Ḫabiru were entering Canaan about 1390 B.C., and the letters show that they

[1] *Daily Mail*, January 18, 1923; cf. *Tutankhamen and Other Essays*, pp. 87 f.

[2] *Tutankhamen and Other Essays*, p. 93.

managed to take possession, whereas the Israelites, according to Mr. Weigall, did not leave Egypt till about 1350, and if we allow for the wilderness period, they could not have entered Canaan till about 1310 at the earliest, being eighty years later than their fellow-kinsmen, the Ḫabiru. That is to say, the invasion of Canaan mentioned in the Amarna Letters was either a movement continuing for nearly a century after the letters were written, and of such a slow kind that the invaders who entered last were able to be the leaders—an idea which is contradictory to the history of the land—or else there were two separate invasions by Hebrew people, the one following the other nearly a century later. Mr. Weigall thus lands himself in a remarkably inconsistent jumble of history.

Further, he makes an extraordinary mistake. "We read in the Book of Exodus," he says, "that the whole period of the sojourn of the Israelites in Egypt was 430 years, and a rabbinical tradition states that 190 years of this period were passed before the Oppression and 240 years after it. In the Book of Genesis the prophecy is made that the Israelites shall pass 200 years in bondage; but as there is no means of saying whether this 200 years or the 240 years is the correct figure, we may as well split the difference and reckon that the bondage lasted somewhere about 220 years."[1] He then deducts 220 from 1570 B.C., which he gives as the date of the expulsion of the Hyksos and therefore of the beginning of the Oppression, and arrives at 1350 B.C. for the Exodus! But it is nowhere stated in Genesis or in any of the Hebrew records that the years of bondage would be 200. It is said (Gen. xv. 13) that the Israelites would be afflicted for 400 years, and this is no doubt the Biblical statement Mr. Weigall is referring to. Yet on this false basis and by unwarrantably altering the figures of a rabbinical tradition (untrustworthy enough in itself) to suit his view, he succeeds in placing the Exodus where he does, at the end of Tutankhamūn's reign.

[1] *Tutankhamen and Other Essays*, p. 91.

His conception also of the nature of the priestly genealogies in 1 Chronicles, on which he bases an argument for eleven or twelve generations between the Exodus and Solomon, is erroneous. These genealogies are purely artificial, and do not contain generations in single natural descent from father to son, as we hope to show in the chapter on Chronology. Mr. Weigall, unfortunately, is not the only Egyptologist who has erred on this point.

The main absurdity, however, of his theory is seen at once by comparing the religion of Akhenaten with that of the Hebrews. There could have been no relation between them such as he imagines, except the common one which existed between all ancient religions at that epoch. Atenism, whichever way we regard it, was simply the sun-worship of Heliopolis, modified by the religion of Mitanni and the philosophical conceptions of Akhenaten. It was when Mutemuya, the daughter of Artatama, king of Mitanni, arrived in Egypt to become the wife of Thutmose IV. that the first influences were introduced towards Atenism. This foreign princess, who undoubtedly worshipped the sun-gods of her native land, became the mother of the next king, Amenhotep III., and her religious views must naturally have made some impression on him. These influences would be considerably increased by Amenhotep III. taking Mitannian princesses himself for wives, and by the numerous retinue of ladies and high officials that accompanied them. The kingdom of Mitanni appears to have been formed sometime about or before 1500 B.C. by a group of warriors of Iran, who had pushed westward to the Upper Euphrates, where they established a dynasty in the great western bend of the river. Their influence and language extended westward to the Orontes valley and eastward to Nineveh. They appear to have lived alongside another invading race, the Ḫarri (or Murri, according to Sayce), perhaps of Turkic stock from Central Asia. We know little of the Mitannian race, but a treaty discovered at Boghaz Keui mentions the names of four Mitannian gods, which have been clearly shown to be the Indian solar and celestial gods Mîtra (Mithras), Varuna, Indra, and the heavenly twins, the Nâsatyâs.[1] All these were primitive gods in India under the Vedic religion, before its development into Brahminism and Buddhism. The fact that their names occur in tablets 2500 miles from the nearest point of India is not due to Indian princes carrying their conquests so far afield, but to the records of the Aryan people not yet being differentiated into Iranians and Indians. All these four gods had common characteristics with Re and the solar gods of Heliopolis. They were personifications of the sun and the other forces and elements of nature. Varuna was a sun-god who had a moral character. Like Aten, he was an inspector and judge of men's actions, seeing all and knowing all, an omniscient being. Like Aten, he made the forces of nature—sun, winds, seas, rivers ; and like him too, he dwelt remote in the heavens, but was omnipresent on earth. Mîtra, another form of the sun, was worshipped as his brother. Indra was the god of fertility, watering the earth from above and sending down all good things (reminding us of much of the language in Akhenaten's hymns). He is also represented as 'holding the sun in the sky,' and transporting it from east to west. In some parts of the Rig-Veda he is spoken of as one with the sun, 'lord of the sky.'[2] According to the Vedic cult, sacrifice had to be offered to these solar gods every morning, and was accompanied by the recitation or singing of hymns, exactly as we find Akhenaten and his supporters doing. Facts go to show that the princesses of Mitanni who married into the Egyptian Royal family carried this native worship with them and preferred it to the worship of Amūn at Thebes, with its arrogant priesthood. It is thus easy to see how the cult of the sun's disk developed in Egypt as it did towards the end of the

[1] The names in the Hittite text are : Mittraššil, Uruwanaššel, Indar, and Našattijanna (cf. *Politische Documente aus Kleinasien*, Heft 8, i. Rv., 55 f.). On the question of their identity, see Winckler, *Mitteilungen der deutschen Orient-Gesellschaft*, No. 35, p. 51 ; *Mitteilungen der Vorderasiatisch-ägyptischen Gesellschaft*, 1913, No. 4, p. 76 ; A. Cuny, *Rev. des Ét. Anc.*, x. 1908, pp. 279 f. ; Jacobi, *Journal of the Royal Asiatic Society*, 1909, p. 723 ; Oldenberg, *ibid.*, p. 1097 ; Keith, *ibid.*, p. 1104 ; Sayce, *ibid.*, p. 1106 ; Konow, *The Aryan Gods of the Mitanni People*, Christiania, 1921 ; and numerous other publications.

[2] On these points, cf. Professor Washburn Hopkins, *Journal of the American Oriental Society*, No. 36, pp. 250 ff.

reign of Amenhotep III. With these foreign ladies there came an influence that was subversive of Amūn-worship and in favour of sun-worship.

Amenhotep IV., who was a mere boy when he succeeded to the throne, would soon imbibe these religious views; and his antipathy to Amūn and the priesthood of Thebes, together with his determination to set up the worship of the disk, can be dated from his daily contact with the princesses of Mitanni, supported probably in their views by his mother Ti. He was an apt pupil and learned readily about these Aryan gods, whose characteristics resembled those of Horus, Tūm, Re, and the other Egyptian solar deities. There was nothing really un-Egyptian in his form of worship, for Atenism was a recognized Egyptian religion, though its cult had been non-existent for centuries; but he went farther than previous worshippers in regarding the disk not only as the abode of the sun-god ("Shu in the Disk"), but as the god himself in bodily form, who with long arms handed down light and heat from his own body to every living creature on earth. This idea of the disk, with divergent beams terminating in human hands, was a novel one, suggesting a celestial power putting unnumbered caressing hands on the affairs of the world. It was not, however, new to Egypt, for, as Breasted says, "As far back as the Pyramid Texts, the rays of the Sun-god had been likened to his arms, and had been conceived as an agency on earth."[1] The idea, too, is thoroughly Indian, for Sûrya was worshipped as a vivifier who stretched down his long arms of gold to infuse energy into all his creatures.[2] Akhenaten's religion, it is clear, was a form of very old Egyptian sun-worship evolved from the Heliopolitan system, but modified by philosophical doctrines of Mitannian and Indian origin, and it was these foreign esoteric doctrines that led his subjects to dislike the cult.

The idea that there was some connection between this pagan form of sun-worship and the higher moral and spiritual religion of the Israelites is not warranted by the facts. There is a sense,

[1] *Cambridge Ancient History*, ii. p. 112.
[2] Wilkins, *Hindu Mythology*, p. 33.

of course, in which all religions are connected and possess certain thoughts and characteristics in common, but beyond this there was no relation between the two. The latter religion, known to scholars as Yahwism (the worship of Yahweh),[1] had little in common with Atenism, and had special features which raised it far above such a pagan cult. So far from Yahwism having any connection with Heliopolis, the early Biblical records clearly show that the scene of Moses' spiritual education was the land of Midian, situated north-east of the Gulf of 'Akaba, in the neighbourhood of the hill-country of Seir; and the principal individual by whose advice he was guided in religious matters was Jethro, the 'priest of Midian,' who was a Kenite. It was here, among the bedouins of the wilderness, while he was an exile from Egypt, that Moses came into contact with those influences which shaped his subsequent teaching, and which sent him back to Egypt to rescue his people. There is good ground for believing that the God whom Jethro worshipped was Yahweh, and that the principal centre of the worship was Mount Sinai, believed by many scholars to have been among the mountains of Edom, not far from Kadesh.[2] The religion of

[1] The form of name 'Jehovah' is based upon error. The Jews, who regarded it as blasphemy to utter the Divine name, the consonants of which were JHWH (which are alone original), attached the vowels of the word *'Adōnai*, 'Lord,' to it, in order to warn readers to substitute the latter term for it. This false vocalization gave rise (first in the sixteenth century A.D.) to the word 'Jehovah,' in place of 'Yahweh.' The idea that God's name was unutterable sprang from an exaggerated fear of breaking the commandment in Ex. xx. 7.

[2] The traditional site of Sinai, viz. *Jébel Mûsâ*, in the south of the peninsula of Sinai, more than 150 miles south of Kadesh and about as far from Edom and Midian, does not go back beyond the Middle Ages, and seems to have little authenticity. It would imply that the Israelites marched from Egypt into what was virtually an Egyptian province, visited frequently by armed expeditions in connection with the mines. Mount Sinai seems rather to have been in the *Jébel el-Makrah* group of Edomite hills, south-east of *'Ain Kudeis*. This location removes many difficulties, and accords with the Hebrew parallelism of Deut. xxxiii. 2:

> Jahweh came from Sinai, and rose from Seir unto them;
> He shined forth from Mt. Paran, and came from Meribah Kadesh.

At the same time, as eleven days' journey is stated (Deut. i. 2) to have separated Sinai and Kadesh, it would be foolish to dogmatize on the matter.

Yahweh, it is true, may not have been confined to this particular district. There seems to be evidence that He was known and worshipped by the Amorites of western Syria, who probably came from the Arabian peninsula, and who founded the first dynasty at Babylon.[1] But even though the name had been known and used in earlier ages, and among a wider range of tribes, this does not lessen in the least the uniqueness of the revelation which Moses is stated to have received (Ex. iii.), and for which his mind was prepared by his association with Jethro. There is abundant evidence in support of the view that the Decalogue of Ex. xx., in its original short form, was promulgated by Moses, who in this respect was in advance of his age, as all founders of religious movements are, and that this moral element formed the background of the religion which he established. The Yahwism of Moses was thus a high form of ethical religion. It could only have arisen from a special Revelation granted to Moses, as a great leader endowed with exceptional qualifications; and apart from this fact, the history of Israel's moral and religious development, as well as the history of Christendom, must remain an insoluble mystery.

The argument for the connection between the two religions is strengthened, we are told, by the fact that Akhenaten was a monotheist, and that his Atenism was an approach to the purer monotheism of the Israelites. The movement he initiated was for the recognition of only One God, who gave life and light to all men, and was the all-loving Father. This One God was the only one that was to be worshipped. The old local or national gods, and all the gods of the dead, were to be abolished, and indeed their figures are not found in any of the Tell el-Amarna tombs. "One God, like whom there is no other," says Ai, the overseer of Akhenaten's

[1] Cf. Burney, *Judges*, pp. 196, 243 ff., 249 ff.; Sayce, *Expository Times*, xxxiii. (1921), p. 38. Luckenbill (*American Journal of Theology*, xxii. (1918), pp. 47 ff.), however, has endeavoured to show that 'Yahweh' is not found in cuneiform literature till the eighth century B.C., and so was not known by Moses. He was introduced by missionary Levites just before the time of David. Such a view, however, has no real ground to support it.

Horse, in his hymn to Aten. Eric Peet, Weigall, and some other Egyptologists have no doubt as to this question of monotheism. Eric Peet, for instance, concedes that at first Akhenaten only expunged the name Amūn from the monuments, but asserts that the rigorous erasure later on of the plural word 'gods' points distinctly to monotheism, and he is convinced that the religion of Akhenaten was a truly monotheistic one.[1]

With all deference to these Egyptologists, it requires to be said that the value of their arguments depends on the meaning attached to the term 'monotheism.' If they hold that Akhenaten believed in the existence of one God only, the great spiritual, unseen, inscrutable, infinite, supreme Being of the wide universe—the conception to which the Greek philosophers rose a thousand years later—all that can be said is that they are mistaken. The Egyptians had certainly a dim and vague idea of this great Divine Being, whom they regarded as distinct from local and national gods, for among the Moral Aphorisms of the ancient sages there are frequent allusions to an unseen power to which no personal name is given, and which is simply referred to by the word 'Neter' or 'Nether,' whose significance is unknown to us.[2] In this sense all the Egyptian priests and scholars were monotheistic. But this great unseen and unknown Being was not Akhenaten's god—his monotheism was entirely different. The nature of his god is seen from the title which he gave him, "The Living Horus of the two Horizons, exalted in the eastern Horizon in his name of Shu-who-is-in-the-Disk (Aten)." If we take Shu here to be a common noun, its meaning is 'heat' or 'light and heat,' and if we regard it as a proper name, it would signify heat personified or deified. In either case, it is clear that what Akhenaten worshipped was either the ordinary heat and light inherent in the sun's disk, or its deified form as the eternal, creative, vivifying force. But in this respect his religion was no more 'monotheistic'

[1] *Journal of the Manchester Egyptian and Oriental Society*, No. 9; cf. also Peet, *Cambridge Ancient History*, ii. p. 206.

[2] Cf. Budge, *Tutankhamen*, p. 144.

than that of Amūn or the other gods of the land. From time immemorial, even before the close of the VIth Dynasty, the worshippers of the old gods Tūm, Re, Khepera, Amūn (after his union with Re), and others, had attributed this same 'oneness' to their deities, and all the great priesthoods of the land had proclaimed it to be the chief characteristic of their gods. While Akhenaten was insisting on the 'oneness' of Aten in his new city, the priests of Re and Tūm were doing the same for their god in Heliopolis, and the priests of Amūn were doing the same in Thebes. Maspéro truly says that the Egyptians applied the epithets 'One God' and 'Only God' to several gods, even when the god was associated with others.[1] Oneness was an attribute, it would seem, "of everything that was worshipped in Egypt, just as it is in some parts of India."[2] The oneness or unity of Amūn, for instance, was absolute. The existence of other gods was admitted, but they were merely forms of him. He was the "One Image, maker of everything that is, One Alone, maker of things that are," "Chief of the Great Nine Gods, One Alone, without a second."[3] In the hymn to Aten, on the stele of Her and Suti, both Amūn and Aten are declared to be self-created and not begotten, and to each is applied the attribute 'One.' In the hymn to Re, contained in the Papyrus of Ani, we read, "O thou Only One, who didst dwell in heaven before ever the earth and the mountain came into being! O Shepherd, O Lord, O Only One, creator of what is!"

It will thus be seen that the monotheism of Akhenaten was not new, but was shared by practically all the chief gods of Egypt. Whether he actually suppressed all the other gods in an attempt to make Aten the chief national one is a different

[1] "Il est à Thèbes le *dieu unique* Amon, à Memphis le *dieu unique* Ptah, qui diffère d'Amon comme de tous les autres *dieux uniques* des nomes, et son unité, pour être absolue dans l'étendue de son domaine, n'empêchait pas l'unité de tous les autres dieux. . . . Mais ce dieu un n'est jamais *dieu* tout court" (Maspéro, *L'Égypte*, Nouveau Larousse Illustré).

[2] Budge, *Tutankhamen*, p. 79.

[3] From Hymn to Amūn in Cairo Museum, Sections xv. and xix. There is a French translation by Grébaut, *Hymne à Amon-Ra*, Paris, 1875.

question that cannot be settled with the information at our disposal, but assuming that he did so, such a 'monotheism' could not have been of a high order, being political and national rather than religious. At all events, his worship was not monotheism in the high sense in which we understand this word, but rather a humanized henotheism or monolatry. He was, as Professor Mercer has said, "a clever, self-centred, individual henotheist."[1] His worship was that of One alone, the unique One rather than the only One, and this was a common characteristic of the Babylonian and all other religions in those early times.[2] Even Yahwism was only henotheistic at the beginning, its main idea being to recognize no other gods beside Yahweh, who was God of gods and Light of lights. It was not until the age of Deuteronomy and that of Deutero-Isaiah that His sole godhead was directly expressed. In this matter of 'monotheism,' therefore, any comparison between Atenism and the religion of the Israelites is only such as can be made between all religions at this early epoch, and consequently no argument can be drawn from it for any peculiar identity between the two. As Mr. N. de G. Davies has shown, Akhenaten furnished neither a monotheistic nor an ethical system.[3] To say that Moses had something to do with the rise of Atenism, because the latter was a 'monotheistic' religion, and to base the date of the Exodus on such false premises, implies a misunderstanding of the facts.

It is further stated by the upholders of this theory that the religion of Akhenaten contained many sublime spiritual truths, superior even to any found in the Old Testament. In the Amarna tombs, we are told, have been found several "beautiful hymns," touched with spiritual feeling, in which the new deity is hailed as the beneficent star, the bringer of light and heat, the creator and nourisher of all things and beings, and the only deity that is worthy of veneration. Mr. Weigall even assures us that there is such a remarkable simi-

[1] *Journal of the Society of Oriental Research*, Chicago, October 1919.

[2] Cf. Hehn, *The Biblical and the Babylonian Idea of God*, pp. 30 ff.

[3] *Journ. of Egypt. Arch.*, ix. (1923), p. 150.

larity between what is known as Akhenaten's Hymn to Aten and the 104th Psalm that they must be regarded as one and the same composition, of which Akhenaten is probably the author.[1] He also says: "Though so remote, the Aton was the tender, loving Father of all men, ever-present and ever-mindful of his creatures. There dropped not a sigh from the lips of a babe that the intangible Aton did not hear; no lamb bleated for its mother but the remote Aton hastened to soothe it. He was the loving 'Father and Mother of all that he had made.'"[2] Such a way of describing Akhenaten's religion is totally incorrect. It has in it elements of sentiment and romance, but after all, when reduced to sober truth, Atenism becomes nothing more than a form of sun-worship, Indian in origin, and modified by heathen philosophic thought. We admit that the Atenites adopted many beautiful precepts and ideals. They refused to indulge in many of the superstitious rites and ridiculous fictions of the old priesthood, and practically abandoned the spells, incantations, and litanies contained in the Book of the Dead. Facts go to show, however, that their worship was largely material, temporal, and indeed selfish. They sang and danced to their god in the disk because he sent his heat and light down to them, but they seem to have had no spiritual worship beyond what was based on this pagan cult.

So much has been made of the supposed connection of Atenism with the Exodus, that this point as to its 'spirituality and beauty' is an important one. Apart from Akhenaten's actions, practically all that we know of the doctrines of the Aten worship is contained in two hymns found in the tombs at Tell el-Amarna. The shorter of these, of which several copies have been found, is believed to have been composed by Akhenaten himself. The longer one was discovered in the tomb of Ai, his disciple and successor, and fragments of it have

[1] *Life and Times of Akhnaton*, pp. 134 ff.; *Daily Mail*, January 18, 1923. The similarity was first pointed out by Breasted (*History of Egypt* p. 371).

[2] *Op. cit.*, p. 104.

been found in the other tombs.[1] No doubt, these were the two main psalms used in the temple worship, and from them we can form a sufficiently good estimate of what Atenism really was. They undoubtedly present an interesting picture of the pleasures received from the sun, as a vivifier and fructifier, together with a spirit of sincere appreciation and thankfulness, but to say that in sublimity of truth and purity of tone they surpass other religious poems of antiquity and even the teaching of Christ, is to misunderstand their nature.[2] The shorter one is addressed to "The Living Horus of the two Horizons, who rejoiceth in his name of Shu-who-is-in-the-Disk, the giver of life for ever and ever," and the longer one opens in almost similar language. A close examination of them shows, as Budge has pointed out,[3] that there is scarcely a doctrine or precept in them which is not taken from the older religious literature of Egypt. All the essential powers and attributes with which the Atenites endowed their god are to be found in hymns sung in praise of the other sun-gods and Egyptian deities.[4] The unity, eternity, infinity, and even loving-kindness attributed to Aten are all found in Egyptian hymns written long before Akhenaten was born. The idea that Atenism was the only Egyptian religion that made reference to the love of God is incorrect. Many hymns to other gods contain the same thought, expressed just as beautifully. From a papyrus at Leyden, for instance, consisting of some hymns to Amūn, we read (chap. xi.): "To him whom he loves he

[1] Copies of both hymns are given in the Appendix, p. 265. Versions of the shorter one have been published by Bouriant, Daressy, Piehl, and others. An excellent one is that published by Davies in his *Rock Tombs*, iv. p. 28. An English version of the longer one has been given by Breasted, *History of Egypt*, p. 315. The whole of the hymn, with a Latin translation, has been published by him, *De Hymnis in solem sub rege Amenophide IV. conceptis*, Berlin, 1894. An excellent text of the longer one has been issued by Davies, *Rock Tombs*, vi. plate xxvii., and by Bouriant, *Monuments du Culte d'Atonou*, i. plate xvi. See also Griffith, *World's Literature*, p. 5225; Hall, *Ancient History*, p. 306; and other Egyptologists.

[2] Cf. Blackman, "A Study of the Literature celebrated in the Temple of the Aton at el-Amarna," *Recueil Champollion*, pp. 505 ff.

[3] *Tutankhamen*, p. 112.

[4] Cf. Scharff, *Ägyptischer Sonnenlieder*, containing translations of the principal hymns to the sun, with notes (1922).

gives more than fate has allotted to him." In the teaching of Amenemapt, written probably in the XVIIIth Dynasty, we have the words: "The love of God is more than the respect of the Chief." [1] Take also the following beautiful thoughts from a Turin stele:

> I hymn Re when he sets,
> O august, beloved, merciful God,
> Who hearest him that prays,
> Who hearest the entreaties of him that calls upon thee,
> Who comest at the voice of him that utters thy name! [2]

The same spiritual truths were not even confined to Egypt, but are to be found in the psalms of other heathen nations. Some of the liturgies sung at that very time under the Babylonian Dynasty were equally sublime in their conceptions of God and duty. Will any one say that the two hymns to Aten are superior in spiritual tone or devout aspiration? The fact is, that they are inferior in many respects, even in phraseology, and have serious defects from a religious point of view. There is little or nothing spiritual in them. "Our surviving sources for the Aton faith," says Breasted, "do not disclose a very spiritual conception of the deity, nor any attribution to him of ethical qualities beyond those which Re had long been supposed to possess." [3] Breasted thinks this may be due to the accidents of preservation, but everything we know otherwise of Akhenaten's religion goes to show that he had not risen to the conception of a spiritual and righteous God. In none of the hymns is there any prayer for spiritual knowledge, or appeal to man's higher nature, or moral outlook, or call to purity of life, or a single word as to sin or repentance, or any evidence of a belief in a Judgment or even in a future life.[4] The gods of Babylonia and India indeed, who spied out sin and judged the

[1] Cf. Budge, *Tutankhamen*, pp. 41, 148.

[2] *Journ. of Egypt. Arch.*, 1916, p. 91.

[3] *Cambridge Ancient History*, ii. p. 120.

[4] Cf. Budge, *Tutankhamen*, p. xv, where this noted Egyptologist reduces Atenism to sane and proper proportions, in place of such romantic descriptions as those of Mr. Weigall. Cf. also Sethe, *Beiträge zur Geschichte Amenophis IV.*, and Schafer, *Die Religion und Kunst von El-Amarna*.

sinner, had divine attributes that were wanting in Akhenaten's sun-god.

It must be admitted that there is a remarkable similarity, both in thought and sequence, between parts of Akhenaten's Hymn and the 104th Psalm. The psalm, however, is believed by many modern scholars to be of much later origin; and in this case, while it may have been based upon the Egyptian hymn, its connection with so early a phenomenon as Atenism is pretty hopeless. The further view must not be overlooked that both may have been adapted from the same source, either Mitannian or Syrian. In this respect the hymn does not stand alone. Many heathen hymns might be taken as similar to the Hebrew psalms. In a papyrus at Leyden, we read that Amūn is "The One Watcher, He hates slumber. Men sleep on their beds, but His eyes watch," [1] which corresponds to part of the 121st Psalm, "He that keepeth thee will not slumber. Behold, He that keepeth Israel shall neither slumber nor sleep." In a well-known Babylonian hymn, which was chanted to the sun-god every morning in the temple of Borsippa, the sun is represented in a manner exactly similar to that of the Hebrew psalmist, as a bridegroom coming out of his chamber (Ps. xix. 5), and his bride is even conceived as going to meet him.[2] The Babylonian deities were worshipped in hymns which present striking analogies to our Hebrew psalms, not only in the thoughts expressed, but in their feature of parallelism or repetition of phrase or refrain (like that of Psalm cxviii., "For His mercy endureth for ever").[3] The apparent similarity, therefore, between Akhenaten's Hymn and the 104th Psalm does not afford any argument in favour of the supposed connection of the religion of the Israelites with that of the Atenites. They were only connected in so far as all religions were connected in a general sense.

If there be no actual similarity between the religion of the Israelites and that of Akhenaten, the whole theory of the

[1] Budge, *Tutankhamen*, p. 40.

[2] Pinches, *Hastings' Dictionary*, iv. p. 629.

[3] Cf. Zimmern, *Babylonische Hymnen u. Gebete in Auswahl* (in *Der Alte Orient* series); Whitehouse, *Expositor*, xxv. p. 329.

Exodus taking place after that Pharaoh's death, during the persecution that followed, falls to the ground. *Sublata causa, tollitur effectus.* For, if there was no such similarity or connection, why should the Israelites (assuming they were still in the land) be ill-treated at the Restoration and driven out? They had lived peaceably for many generations in a small corner of the land, and if they had no part in the movement towards Atenism, why should they be thrust out now? We know that they were by no means sun-worshippers—the law of Yahweh was stringent against this, the penalty being death by stoning [1] —but even though they were, it is difficult to see how such a mere handful of people, confined pretty much to an insignificant tract on the border, nearly 400 miles from Thebes, could have influenced Pharaoh and his court; and surely there would have been some Israelites, even Moses himself, among Akhenaten's officers in his new city, but there is absolutely no evidence of such a thing.[2]

The theory, indeed, bristles with so many difficulties that possibly it would never have suggested itself to its upholders, if it were not that Manetho, in his legendary account of the Exodus, seems in their view to connect it with the revolution under Akhenaten.[3] His account of the Exodus, quoted by Josephus, states that a certain Pharaoh Amenophis, being desirous of becoming a spectator of the gods, communicated his desire to his namesake, Amenophis-son-of-Papis, a wise, far-seeing man, who told him that he must first clear the whole country of the lepers and other unclean people. Some 80,000 such people were therefore collected and sent to the quarries on the east side of the Nile. The wise man, however, predicted that these unclean people would gain the assistance of others and would exercise dominion over Egypt for thirteen years; and he so dreaded this that he wrote a letter of warning about it to the king, and then took his own life. After these people had been working in the quarries for a long time in a miserable

[1] Cf. Deut. iv. 19, xvii. 2–5, and see also Job xxxi. 26–28; Isa. xxiv. 23, etc.

[2] For the names of Akhenaten's officials, see Budge, *Tutankhamen*, p. 92.

[3] Weigall, *Tutankhamen and Other Essays*, pp. 87 ff.

state, the king set apart the city of Avaris for their use. Once in possession of this city, they revolted against Pharaoh, and appointed for themselves a ruler out of the priests of Heliopolis. This ruler was named Osarsiph, but he afterwards changed his name to Moses. He made laws for them that they should not worship the Egyptian gods, nor have anything to do with the so-called sacred animals of the land, nor conform to the popular customs. He took into his friendship the other priests and sent to Jerusalem, inviting the shepherds there to join with the oppressed people in Avaris in a war against Egypt. As a result, 200,000 came, and this invasion put king Amenophis in great confusion when he remembered the prediction of the wise man. The king, after sending his little son, Sethos or Rameses, aged five, to a friend for safety, marched to Avaris with 300,000 picked soldiers, but being afraid to attack, in case the gods would be displeased, he proceeded instead to Memphis, took the sacred Apis bull from the temple there, and marched with his whole army and many sympathizers into Ethiopia, where he lived for a long time in exile. Meanwhile the confederacy of people located in Avaris destroyed the images of the old gods, killed the sacred animals, and committed many acts of desecration and sacrilege. But at last the king returned from Ethiopia with a large army, joined battle with the shepherds and polluted people, defeated them, and pursued them to the bounds of Syria.

Such is Manetho's account, and Weigall and others take it as referring to the Aten movement which began under Amenhotep (Amenophis) III. and culminated under his successor, and as connecting the Exodus of the Israelites with that crisis in Egyptian history.[1] But it is clear to any impartial examiner of the account that it has nothing to do with the Aten movement. The prediction that the lepers and their supporters would exercise dominion over the land for thirteen years has been connected with Akhenaten's rule, on the ground that this Pharaoh is believed to have imposed his Atenism on the land for this period of time. But the argument is weak at this

[1] *Tutankhamen and Other Essays*, p. 88.

point, as it is all through, for Akhenaten reigned over Egypt religiously as well as nationally for about seventeen years, and the fourth year of his reign does not mark the commencement of the Aten sway, but merely the time when it is believed to have come to a height. Work was probably going on at el-Amarna in the third year, and the peculiar sepulchral art displayed there was a Theban invention of the second or third year.[1] Atenism was certainly in power some time before the fourth year, and, as Mr. Davies shows, seems to have risen swiftly about the second or third. Even though the Aten sway could be limited to exactly thirteen years, this fact at the most would be no more than a mere coincidence with Manetho's statement. No amount, moreover, of fanciful explanation can spread all these events referred to by Manetho over the reigns of six Pharaohs, Amenhotep III., Akhenaten, Sʿakere, Tutankhamūn, Ai, and Harmhab, even though, as Weigall suggests, we should reckon the last-named as the real successor of the first.

The fact is that Manetho is referring to Amenhotep II. not III., for the famous adviser mentioned, Amenhotep, the son of Hapu, certainly lived through the reign of the former king as well as into that of the latter. He figures in Egyptian history as a man of extraordinary wisdom, and appears to have been born in the reign of Thutmose III.,[2] lived through that of Amenhotep II., and ultimately rose to the highest honours in the court of Amenhotep III. Add to this the fact that Breasted, Hall, and practically all modern Egyptologists identify this 'Amenophis' of Manetho with Amenhotep II. (the eighth in Manetho's list),[3] while Horos is really the name Manetho gives

[1] Cf. N. de G. Davies, *Journ. of Egypt. Arch.*, ix. (1923), pp. 147, 149.

[2] Hall, *Ancient History*, p. 297.

[3] Some of the late-date school have attempted to identify this 'Amenophis' in Manetho's account with Merenptah, but the two names cannot be regarded as the same. 'Amenophis,' it is true, occurs for Merenptah in Josephus (*Contra Apion.*, i. 15), but this is evidently a corruption, for both Africanus and Eusebius have 'Ammenephthes' ('Αμμενεφθῆς), which can only mean Menephtah, *i.e.* Merenptah (see Professor Orr, *Expositor*, 1897, p. 168). The fact that Manetho refers to the son of Hapu is proof that his story applies to the XVIIIth Dynasty, not the XIXth. Names and details appear to be

to Amenhotep III.[1] On these grounds it is apparent that Manetho's date for the Exodus, instead of supporting the theory of Weigall and others, corroborates the one we are advocating, *viz.* that the Israelites left Egypt during the reign of Amenhotep II. To that extent, at least, Manetho's account is correct, though it has in it many elements that are absurd and improbable, drawn evidently from legendary lore. Manetho wrote about 1200 years after the Exodus (according to the early-date theory); and although he must have had some Egyptian sources of information at his disposal as a priest, there is good ground for believing that not all of them were authentic, and that he frequently adapted them to his own views. His narratives, such as we have them, give a very confused idea of Egyptian history, and his royal lists are crowded with errors of detail. Even Mr. Weigall himself, in his *History of the Pharaohs*,[2] admits that Manetho's figures are "hopelessly wrong, except here and there." There are numerous inaccuracies as to date, even in the later ages of Persian and Greek monarchies. "No real historian is known to us in Pharaonic Egypt," says Dr. Hall, "nor is it likely that one will ever be discovered. The Egyptian had very little historical sense, and to him, as to his modern descendant, a popular legend was as worthy of credence as the most veracious chronicle."[3] Josephus, an historian of much greater learning, has exposed Manetho's ignorance and his inveterate prejudice against the

greatly confused, but the story, on the face of it, is an XVIIIth Dynasty one. The version given by Chœremon (Josephus, *Contra Apion.*, i. 32), in which the Israelites are led out by Joseph and Moses, also gives the king's name as 'Amenophis'; and Eusebius, although he puts the Exodus for some reason a little later, under a king 'Achencheres' (*i.e.* S'akere), still assigns it to the XVIIIth Dynasty.

[1] Cf. Hall, *Ancient History*, p. 228; see also List of Kings at commencement of this volume. Where some Egyptologists have gone wrong in Manetho's order of names is by taking his 'Misphragmouthosis' to represent Amenhotep II., whereas there can be little doubt that this name (corrupted by Josephus into 'Alisphragmouthosis') is to be identified with the cartouches of his predecessor, Thutmose III.

[2] Vol. i.—*The First Eleven Dynasties*, Butterworth, 1925.

[3] *Ancient History*, p. 12.

Jews, and has dismissed his details of the Exodus as incredible. In regard to the date of the Exodus, however, as having taken place during the reign of Amenhotep II., Manetho's account is undoubtedly correct, as it also is in a few other matters, such as the quarry work of the Israelites, their miserable existence, the setting apart of Avaris (later Rameses) for their use, and their pursuit by Pharaoh into the desert. Indeed, in Manetho's account, if it be divested of its improbable elements, we have some interesting details which may supplement the Biblical record.

Some scholars hold the view that Manetho is connecting the Exodus with the expulsion of the Hyksos, by merging the Israelites among the other nomads whom he groups under this designation elsewhere. The expulsion of the Hyksos is thought by some (see Chapter VII.) to have continued as late as Thutmose III. (*c.* 1500 B.C.), and Manetho, they think, may be regarding the Exodus of the Israelites as the last act in the expulsion. Other scholars consider his story to be a confused tradition of some purely native Egyptian event, having no connection with the Exodus at all. The awkward way in which Moses' name is brought in, by a sudden turning of Osarsiph's name into his, looks not unlike an interpolation. If the Moses-clause be removed, the whole narrative can be understood as a legendary version of some purely Egyptian affair. But whatever view we take of the story, we think there can be little doubt that it refers to the Exodus, and thus upholds the theory we are endeavouring to prove in these pages, that this event in Israel's history took place during the reign of Amenhotep II.

CHAPTER VII

THE ḪABIRU[1]

SO far we have considered the arguments of the late-date theory and the Akhenaten one, and it cannot be said that these are at all convincing. When closely examined they are found to have little or no basis to rest on. There is little to support the idea of an Exodus in the reign of Merenptah except the old popular notion (based on Ex. ii. 23, iv. 19) that Ramesses II., on account of his long reign, must have been the Pharaoh of the Oppression, and that Merenptah succeeded him. But it must not be forgotten that these special circumstances are just as applicable to Thutmose III. and his successor Amenhotep II. There is little, too, to uphold the Akhenaten theory except erroneous notions as to the meaning of Atenism, due largely to some writers' fanciful descriptions of it, combined with the apparent similarity between the 104th Psalm and one of the hymns to Aten. On the other hand, the early-date theory of an Exodus about 1445 B.C. seems to have solid

[1] The literature on this subject has become so extensive that we can only refer to the more important publications. Cf. Knudtzon, pp. 45–53, 1145 ff., 1574 f., 1336 ff.; Dhorme, *Revue Biblique*, 1908, pp. 500–519; 1909, pp. 67–73; 1924, pp. 12 ff.; F. M. T. Böhl, *Kanaanäer und Hebräer*, Leipzig, 1911, pp. 83–96; Winckler, *Geschichte Israels*, 1895, i. pp. 16–21; *Altorientalische Forschungen*, iii. pp. 90–94; *Die Keilenschriften und das Alte Testament*, pp. 196 ff.; Burney, *Israel's Settlement in Canaan*, pp. 66–81; *Judges*, pp. lxxiii–lxxxiv; Langdon, *Expository Times*, xxxi. pp. 324 ff.; Sayce, *op. cit.*, xxxiii. p. 43; Peet, *Egypt and the Old Testament*, pp. 115–120; Jirku, *Orientalistische Literatur-Zeitung*, 1921, Sp. 246 f.; 1922, Sp. 38; *Zeitschrift f. d. Alttestamentl. Wissensch.*, xxxix. (1921), pp. 156–158; Gustavs, *op. cit.*, xl. (1922), pp. 313 f.; Edelkoort, *Uittocht en Intocht: Een Geschieden van het Volk Israël*, 1924 (Utrecht), pp. 113–126. Other sources of information are referred to throughout the chapter.

ground beneath it. It has at least documentary testimony, as we hope to show in this chapter, along with chronological and other evidence of the strongest kind.

We have referred in a previous chapter to the Tell el-Amarna Letters. A large number of these are addressed to the king of Egypt, either Amenhotep III. or IV., and must be dated from *c.* 1400–1366 B.C. Nearly all of them record imminent disaster to the Egyptian power in Palestine and successful uprisings against it, coupled with urgent entreaties for help. The country at this particular time seems to have been seething with factions and plots, which the Egyptian government took no notice of, or failed to suppress. In the north, especially in Phœnicia and Syria, the Hittites and Amorites, aided by a people who are referred to ideographically as the SA-GAZ,[1] were attacking several of the cities and districts. Most graphic details of the disorganized condition that resulted may be gathered from a perusal of the dispatches from the governors of Byblus, Tyre, and other places.

In the south, Abdi-Ḫiba, the governor of Jerusalem, refers to the invaders in this part of the land as Ḫabiru.[2] He is the only governor who does so. He describes them as coming from the land of *Še-e-ri* (Seir), and as attacking districts and towns in the Negeb and south Palestine, and threatening Jerusalem itself.[3] A careful study of the letters shows that these southern invaders were a separate section and had entered the country somewhat later than the SA-GAZ in Syria and the northern parts. Shuwardata's letter, for instance, in the Louvre Museum (AO 7096), reporting to

[1] See note 3, p. 46.

[2] The term 'Ḫabiru,' which is Babylonian, is a collective noun (the 'Ḫabiru man or men'), not a gentilic expression. It is used only in the singular. Ḫabiru is the nominative, but the word only occurs in this form in two places in the letters. In the remaining six places, the form used is the genitive-accusative 'Ḫabiri,' the word being a diptote. For example, the scribe writes, "Why lovest thou the Ḫabiri (accusative)?" Many writers accordingly speak of the people as 'Ḫabiri.'

[3] Abdi-Ḫiba's letters will be found in Appendix, p. 265.

Pharaoh the aggressions of the SA-GAZ and mentioning help he had received from two northern governors, Zurata of Accho and Endaruta of Achshaph, is anterior to any of Abdi-Ḫiba's letters referring to the Ḫabiru. This is evident from the fact that it mentions Zurata as still living and ruling, whereas we know that Abdi-Ḫiba was a contemporary of Zurata's son and successor, Zatatna. This is corroborated by another Louvre letter (AO 7095), written by the Pharaoh to Endaruta, from which it is apparent that this governor also must have lived and ruled some time before the date of Abdi-Ḫiba's appeals, for the Pharaoh gives orders to prepare food, wine, and other necessaries for the advent of a large army to Achshaph, and this could only have been several years anterior to the deeply disorganized state of affairs portrayed by Abdi-Ḫiba. That the SA-GAZ, in the northern parts at least, invaded the country some time before the Ḫabiru is accepted by Knudtzon, who says: "It is deserving of note, whatever way we look at the matter, that the letters in which the Ḫabiru are referred to are certainly later than several of those in which the SA-GAZ people are mentioned."[1] This conclusion is sound, and may be arrived at by any careful reader who compares the circumstances in the one set of letters with those in the other.[2]

Abdi-Ḫiba's city, even in those early times, was one of the most important fortresses of Canaan and the capital of a large district,[3] and the governor, who realized the danger of the situation, pleads again and again for troops to be sent to ward off the invaders. He describes their attacks as widespread and powerful, and makes urgent and repeated entreaties for help, otherwise the whole country will be lost. He accuses certain native leaders or Egyptian vassals, particularly Milki-ili, Shuwar-

[1] Knudtzon, p. 52.

[2] See also note 2, p. 164.

[3] Abdi-Ḫiba insists in his letters that he was no mere *ḫazanu* (or 'governor' in the ordinary sense), but an *ú-e-ú*, which was a title meaning 'shepherd.' It was employed by Hammurabi, and by Seti I., who called himself a 'good shepherd,' as well as by Merire, Akhenaten's high priest. It is common in cuneiform annals as a title of divinity (cf. also Ps. xxiii. 1; Isa. xl. 11; Jer. xxxi. 10; Ezek. xxxiv. 11–14).

data, Ili-milki, and the sons of Labaya,[1] with aiding and abetting them, and putting them in possession of the land. We find that some time previously he had assisted Shuwardata and some other leaders (Zurata of Accho, and Endaruta of Achshaph) in their efforts against the SA-GAZ,[2] but now the situation had changed, and Shuwardata at least had become hostile. Abdi-Ḫiba states that the district of Shechem had gone over to the Ḫabiru,[3] and that the cities of Gazri (Gezer), Ashkaluna (Ashkelon),

[1] Milki-ili is the Biblical name Malchiel (מַלְכִּיאֵל, 'God is King'), which is the eponym of an Asherite family (Gen. xlvi. 17; Num. xxvi. 45; 1 Chron. vii. 31), who were known as Malchielites. The name appears to have been in early use in Canaan (cf. Gray, *Hebrew Proper Names*, p. 206; Jastrow, *Journal of Biblical Literature*, x. p. 120; Hommel, *Ancient Hebrew Tradition*, p. 231, pp. 233 ff., p. 260 n.). Milki-ili, who appears to have been governor of some city (probably Aijalon or Zorah) near Jerusalem, is the author of several letters to the Pharaoh. He was the son-in-law of Tagi, mentioned in the letters, who guarded the caravans passing through central Palestine.

Ili-milki is Elimelech (אֱלִימֶלֶךְ, 'God is King'), another Hebrew or Semitic name. In later years an individual of this name seems to have been head of a clan in the tribe of Judah (cf. Ruth ii. 1–3).

Labaya appears to have had his centre at Shechem, of which he was probably governor. As he seems also to have had connections with Gezer and Beth-shean, he may have had charge of central Palestine. Sayce (*Patriarchal Palestine*, p. 116), Luckenbill (*American Journal of Semitic Languages*, 1910, p. 100), and some others regard the name as Hittite, but in Jastrow's *Dictionary of the Targumim* (p. 689), the name Labya (לִבְיָא) is quoted as a variant reading for Levi, and the name Lebbæus (Matt. x. 3, A.V.), which the Nestorians vocalized Labbaj, is similarly regarded by Westcott and Hort, as well as Grotius (cf. Origen, *Contra Celsum*, i. 62). The name thus seems to show that Labaya may have been of Hebrew race, though the name Levi was originally Egyptian, as Moses and Phinehas ("The Negro") likewise were. It is a strange coincidence, perhaps, that Levi is associated in the Hebrew narrative with Shechem (Gen. xxxiv.).

Regarding Shuwardata, whose name is supposed to mean 'sun(*surya*)-given' (Ἡλιόδοτος), nothing is known except that he was governor of Keilah, and probably also of Ḫarabu (supposed to be Arrâbe, south of *en-Gannim* or modern *Jenin*). Like Labaya, he is the author of several letters, assuring the king of his faithful service, and he seems to have been held in favour by the Egyptian government.

[2] This piece of information is contained in a letter of Shuwardata's at the Louvre, being one of those published by Thureau-Dangin (AO 7096). We give an English translation of it in the Appendix, p. 271.

[3] There is some dubiety about the text here, but the name is (*Mâtu*) *Ša-ak-mi* in the original, according to Knudtzon (No. 289, l. 23). Shechem appears as *Ša-ka-ma* in the Papyrus Anastasi. Some scholars, however, including

and Lakisi (Lachish) had assisted them by giving them oil, food, and other necessaries.[1] The Ḫabiru were carrying on hostilities against him from the land of Seir, and from there northward to the city of Ginti-Kirmil (Gath-Carmel, about 10 miles south of Hebron) the ruling princes were "wholly lost," and all the fortresses were captured. Milki-ili and Shuwardata, along with Tagi, had hired soldiers from Gezer, Gimti (*i.e.* Gath, near Gezer),[2] and Kilti (*i.e.* Keilah), and had seized the land of Rubute,[3] and were now making determined efforts against Jerusalem. The people of Keilah had taken the town of Beth-Ninib,[4] which lay within the land of Jerusalem. The governors Turbazu, Zimrida, and Jephthah-Hadad had been slain,[5] and not a single local ruler remained to Pharaoh. Even the Egyptian commissioner (*rabisu*), who appears in this case to have been the High Commissioner Yanḫamu,[6] had such a high regard for

Winckler (No. 185) find the difficulties of transliteration too great. If Shechem had thrown in its lot with the Ḫabiru, this would be accounted for by the fact that it was connected with the history of Jacob, and some of his descendants may still have been dwelling in it. Labaya, too, seems to have had control of it.

[1] Knudtzon, No. 287. The passage does not state that it was the Ḫabiru to whom these three places had given help, but the words are preceded by a gap of several lines, and it is evident that the Ḫabiru must have been mentioned in the missing part, as they are again in the section that follows.

[2] For the identification, cf. Dhorme, *Revue Biblique*, 1908, p. 517.

[3] Rubute is probably Hebron (*vide* p. 154), although some scholars take it to be Rabbah of Judah (Josh. xv. 60).

[4] NIN-IB was a Babylonian god, usually known as *Nin-urta* (cf. Legrain, *Historical Fragments*, xiii. pp. 42, 89, 94).

[5] The news in regard to Turbazu and Jephthah-Hadad is confirmed by a mutilated fragment of a letter (Knudtzon, No. 335), the sender of which is unknown, but who cannot be Abdi-Ḫiba according to the few signs of the name which are left.

[6] Yanḫamu was vizier for all Palestine. He had control of the stores in Yarimuta, a corn-growing district which has been identified by some with Old Testament Jarmuth, in the Shephelah, but which must rather have been on the Syrian coast according to Sargon's inscriptions (Poebel, *Historical Texts*, pp. 173 ff.). It was his duty to forward supplies to the Pharaoh's towns. His power is seen in his command over the Egyptian troops, and the submissive tone of the reports addressed to him. He was *persona grata* among the population, a faithful servant of the Pharaoh, and a personage of considerable influence. His importance has led some scholars, such as Marquart, to see in him a prototype of Joseph (cf. Schrader, *Die Keilinschriften und das Alte Testament*, 3rd ed., p. 211, n. 2).

the invaders that he was taking their side and encouraging them. Abdi-Ḫiba had found it necessary to tax the commissioner with his disloyalty in the matter. "Why lovest thou the Ḫabiru," he had asked him, "and hatest the local rulers (*ḫazianuti*)?" For this remonstrance he had been slandered to the king. Matters were so serious that Abdi-Ḫiba was anxious to make them known personally to the king, but hostile chiefs and officials prevented him leaving Jerusalem, and Kashi troops (Egyptian, from Ethiopia) had even attempted to kill him. He could not send caravans any longer to Egypt, as the last ones were captured in the outskirts of Aijalon.[1] There was no longer any garrison in Jerusalem, as Yanḫamu had withdrawn it, and the troops which the king had dispatched had been held back by Addaia in Gaza. He pleads for a contingent of soldiers to protect the city. If troops should come, the danger might even yet be averted; but if none should come, the whole country would be lost. "Let the king listen to Abdi-Ḫiba, thy servant," he says, "and send troops, that I may restore the king's land to the king." The way in which he repeats his statements regarding the Ḫabiru and insists on the gravity of the situation cannot fail to be noticed by the most cursory reader:

Behold, this deed is the deed of Milki-ili, and the deed of the sons of Labaya, who have given the land of the king to the Ḫabiru (Knud., No. 287, ll. 29–31).

As sure as there is a ship in the midst of the sea, the mighty arm of the king will seize the countries of Naharîn and Kapasi, but now (meanwhile) the Ḫabiru are seizing the cities of the king (Knud., No. 288, ll. 32–36).

As for Zimrida of Lachish, his [own] servants, become Ḫabiru, have slaughtered him (Knud., No. 288, ll. 43, 44).

Labaya and the land of Shechem have given everything to the Ḫabiru (Knud., No. 289, ll. 22–24).

The land of the king is lost to the Ḫabiru (Knud., No. 290, ll. 13, 14).

[1] It is noteworthy that Tagi, Milki-ili's father-in-law and ally, was guardian of the trade-routes (cf. Knudtzon, No. 264), one of which passed through Aijalon, only about 14 miles west-north-west of Jerusalem.

If there are no troops, the land of the king will be lost to the Ḫabiru (Knud., No. 290, ll. 22–24).

Why lovest thou the Ḫabiru and hatest the local rulers? (Knud., No. 289, ll. 18–20).

The Ḫabiru are devastating all the lands of the king (Knud., No. 286, l. 56).

Letters from other correspondents or representatives of the Egyptian government in central and southern Palestine corroborate Abdi-Ḫiba's statements. Some of them do not mention the enemy by name at all, while others refer to the invaders as SA-GAZ. The term SA-GAZ is a descriptive title, representing the Babylonian word *ḫabbatu*, 'fighting man,' 'plunderer' (cf. note 3, p. 46). The SA-GAZ were plundering nomads from the north Syrian desert. They might belong to any nationality, but in general were connected with the Hebrew race. They were now invading Syria and Palestine and joining hands with their Ḫabiru kinsmen from the south. Thus, Yapaḫi, governor of Gezer, writes the Pharaoh informing him that, unless help should come, the city would be annihilated by the SA-GAZ (Knudtzon, No. 299). A chieftainess, thought to be ruler of the city of Chephirah, only about 10 miles north-west of Jerusalem, writes him that the SA-GAZ have taken Sabuma, and have been in communication with Aijalon and Zorah (Knudtzon, Nos. 273, 274). Shubandu and Dagantakala, both believed to be rulers in south Palestine, plead with him to deliver them from the SA-GAZ (Knudtzon, Nos. 305, 318). In the Louvre letter of Shuwardata's, to which we have referred, this ruler states that the SA-GAZ have invaded the 'territories' (*mâtât*) over which he has charge, and that Abdi-Ḫiba and he, along with Zurata and Endaruta, who had come to their help with fifty chariots, were making war upon them. He pleads with the Pharaoh to send the High Commissioner, Yanḫamu, to their assistance. From the fact that he does not mention Keilah, of which he was governor, and that the forces in aid came from Accho and Achshaph in the north, the reference is probably not to Keilah or any place south of Jerusalem, but to the district of Ḫarabu (near *Jenin*), of which he is known also to have had charge.[1] As the SA-GAZ had been overrunning Syria and Phœnicia, it is apparent that these more southerly groups must either have penetrated south from these regions, or must have entered the land from across the Jordan. Whichever of these alternatives we adopt, we may safely conclude that, as they were kinsmen of the Ḫabiru, they had put themselves into alliance with the latter, and were closely associated with them in the plan of campaign. Most of them at least had entered the country some time before the Ḫabiru, probably a few years before them—a fact which makes it probable that they had penetrated in course of time from the north. They were now intent on helping their fellow-Hebrews from the land of Seir. Large bodies of them certainly joined the Israelite armies, when these arrived in the land. All this accounts for the intimate connection and parallelism that exist between the actions of the two peoples, and explains their apparent identity.

Another governor or Egyptian representative, Mut-Baal by name,[2] writes a report to Yanḫamu, the High Commissioner, regarding affairs in the south, and although he does not mention the invaders by name, there can be no doubt that he refers to the Ḫabiru. He reports that all the cities of 'Gari' had become hostile or been captured. Following Niebuhr and Clauss, it used to be thought that 'Gari' represented the *Ghôr* (the plain of Jordan), but in this case the name would have been 'Ḫari' according to philological rules.[3] Gari, as Winckler suggests,[4]

[1] Accho (cuneiform *Ak-ka*, modern *'Akkâ*) is a coast town about 10 miles north of Mount Carmel. Achshaph (Jos. xi. 1, xii. 20, xix. 25) was situated somewhere in the neighbourhood of the plain of Esdraelon, for it is mentioned in the Palestinian list of Thutmose III. (under the name of *Akšp*) as evidently lying between Shunem and Taanach. This accords with Jos. xii. 20, where the king of Achshaph is placed between the king of Shimron (*i.e.* Septuagint Shimon, west of Nazareth) and Taanach.

[2] Mut-Baal is believed to be a son of Labaya, according to letter No. 255, l. 15, where he refers to himself as the son of "——*b-a-ia*," a word from which the first syllable happens to be worn away, but which is evidently meant for *La-ab-a-ia*.

[3] Cf. Dhorme, *Revue Biblique*, 1908, p. 54.

[4] Cf. also Steuernagel, *Die Einwanderung d. Israel Stämme in Kanaan*, 1901, p. 120.

is undoubtedly 'Kharu,' the Egyptian name for south Palestine (the land of the Horites), and this is corroborated by a careful reading of Mut-Baal's report, which certainly refers to cities lying to the south and south-west of Jerusalem. Among the cities mentioned as hostile or fallen are the following,[1] *viz.*:

UDUMU (the Biblical Duma, modern *ed-Dôme*, 12 miles south-west of Hebron).
ADURI (the Biblical Adoraim, modern *Dûrâ*, 4 miles south-west of Hebron).
ARARU (the Biblical Aroer, modern *'Ar'ara*, 11 miles south-east of Beersheba).
MESHTU (unidentified).
MAGDALIM (supposed by some to be the Biblical Migdal-Gad, modern *el-Mejadil*, east of Ashkelon, but more likely to be ***Tel Mejadil***, 7 miles west of Udumu).
ḪINYANABI ('well of Anab,' Biblical 'Anab, modern *'Anâb*, 14 miles south-west of Hebron).
ZARKI (modern *Bir el-Sherky*, east of Maon, and 13 miles south-east of Hebron).
ḪAWINI (Biblical 'Anim, modern *Ghuwen*, south-west of Maon, and 12 miles south of Hebron).
YABISHIBA (unidentified).

If these identifications, some of which are given by Weber and are accepted by Dr. S. A. Cook and other scholars,[2] are correct, it is evident that we have here what seems to be a valuable report of the invasion of the Ḫabiru in the southern parts. As Mut-Baal seems to have been a son of Labaya, he must have been contemporary with Abdi-Ḫiba[3] and consequently the report may be taken as referring to the same events as those mentioned in the Jerusalem letters. Dr. S. A. Cook refers the report to the activities of Abdi-Ḫiba himself, but the governor of Jerusalem, situated as he was, without troops or outside help, was quite unable to make such a widespread far-reaching movement, extending 50 miles or more from Jerusalem. According to his own statement, he was confined pretty much to his own

[1] Mut-Baal's letter (Knudtzon, No. 256) will be found in Appendix, p. 270.
[2] Cook, *Cambridge Ancient History*, ii. p. 316.
[3] See note 2, p. 164.

city. The only satisfactory explanation of the report is that it has to do with the aggression of the Ḫabiru. The fact that Labaya's sons were in league with the Ḫabiru does not affect the question.

Abdi-Ḫiba felt himself in a dangerous position, as the Ḫabiru were always creeping nearer to Jerusalem. He insisted that he was in the 'right' (*saduk*) about the situation. Matters were no doubt aggravated in his mind by the fact that Tagi, Milki-ili, and their friends were influential and powerful at court. An envoy, whom Tagi had dispatched to Egypt, had had a personal interview with the Pharaoh and had returned with sundry gifts. Milki-ili was in such favour that he could write and ask for healing myrrh.[1] Whether these supporters of the Ḫabiru gained the king's ear, we do not know. At all events, no answer seems to have been returned to all Abdi-Ḫiba's complaints and entreaties for help. There was religious war going on in Egypt, with serious national upheaval, and Akhenaten was a pacifist who had no desire to send troops. One by one, most of the cities of south Palestine, including those belonging to the territory of Jerusalem, fell into the hands of the Ḫabiru.

Who were these invaders of southern and central Palestine? We hope to deal with the SA-GAZ later, but meantime let us consider who the Ḫabiru were. Who else could they be but the Hebrews of the Exodus, and have we not here the native version of their entry into the land? The subject has been a *vexata quaestio*, the centre of one of the keenest discussions in Biblical archæology, and the best scholars, it must be said, are divided on the matter. But taking into consideration the Biblical, chronological, and other aspects of the case (see later chapters), there is good ground for believing that in these letters from Palestine, dating from between 1400 and 1370 B.C., we have the tribes of Israel entering on the Promised Land. This important and far-reaching conclusion, treated with some distrust at first, or at least with the utmost caution, is now admitted by numerous competent scholars to be the only

[1] Knudtzon, No. 269.

Map 3

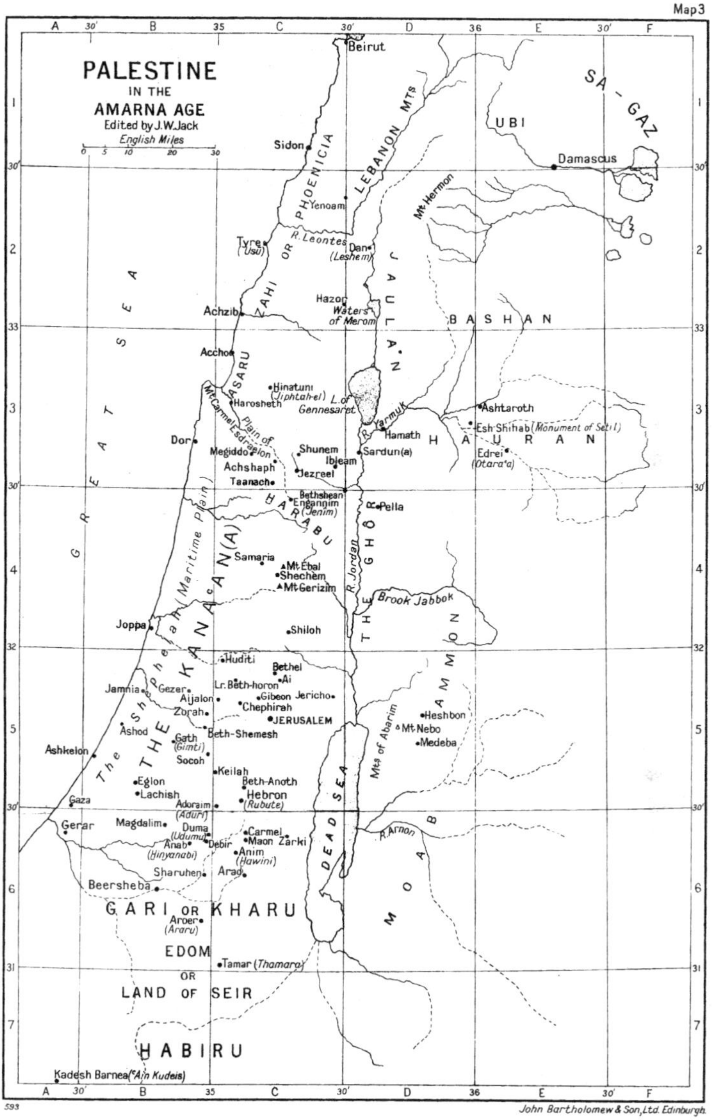

593 John Bartholomew & Son, Ltd. Edinburgh.

sound one. Many who at first doubted it have now come to accept it.

The Ḫabiru were certainly foreign invaders, in spite of the views of Eerdmans, Dhorme, and others to the contrary. Some of them may have belonged to the settled population, but the mass of them must have come from outside, probably a few years before Abdi-Ḫiba complained. Now they were advancing still farther northward and westward. The term Ḫabiru is not a mere appellative designation, for it is followed in one case at least [1] by the termination *Ki*, which denotes a people connected with some locality (Gari, or Kadesh-Barnea ?), and they seem, moreover, to be contrasted in the letters with the actual inhabitants of the land. Therefore, in general, they could not have been Hebrews already settled in Canaan and rising in rebellion, but must have been invaders. Many Assyriologists and Biblical scholars regard them as having come from the north and as being a section of the northern SA-GAZ who had penetrated southward. In this case, of course, they could not have been the Hebrews of the Exodus, located at Kadesh-Barnea. This is the view adopted by those scholars who hold the late-date theory of an Exodus under Merenptah. They have scarcely any other option, as the identification of the Ḫabiru with the Hebrews who left Egypt under Moses would involve the abandonment of their favourite theory and the placing of the Exodus over two hundred years earlier. This point of the relation of the Ḫabiru to the SA-GAZ and to these 'fighting men' in general is one with which we shall deal in another chapter. All that need be said here is that there was undoubtedly a close connection between the two peoples. Both belonged to the Hebrew stock and were desert nomads. They were tribe-companions ('Stammesgenossen,' as Knudtzon calls them, p. 32). But this does not affect our argument. The Ḫabiru of Abdi-Ḫiba's letters may still have been for all that the Hebrew tribes that formed the Exodus and invaded Canaan from their desert home around Kadesh-Barnea. There may indeed have been, as seems very probable, some kind of

[1] Knudtzon, No. 289, l. 24.

co-operation between the Ḫabiru and some of their SA-GAZ kinsmen in the Syrian desert for the invasion of Canaan. Meantime, let us look into the Ḫabiru question philologically and historically.

There are no linguistic difficulties whatever between the word Ḫabiru and the word 'Hebrew.' Whether we compare the word Ḫabiru with *'Ibhri* (עִבְרִי), which is the gentilic word for a 'Hebrew,' or with *'Ebher* (עֵבֶר, Septuagint Ἕβερ),[1] which is the word, whether taken as a proper noun or other form, from which the Hebrews are believed to have derived their name,[2] the comparison proves the two to be practically the same. Professor Langdon, Professor of Assyriology in the University of Oxford, says: "The possibility of identifying Ḫabiru with the Hebrew *'Ibhri* is philologically unquestionable."[3] Winckler has expressed the same opinion.[4] Professor Burney takes a similar view, and states that the "philological equivalence" of Ḫabiru with either *'Ibhri* or *'Ebher* is "perfect."[5] Professor Peet says: "The spelling of Ḫabiru which we find in the cuneiform letters is a perfectly sound phonetic equivalent for Hebrew."[6] A philological examination of the two words removes all doubt on the question. When Hebrew was a current language, the letter ע with which עֵבֶר (*'Ebher*) commences had two sounds, a rougher (approaching a *g* rolled in the throat), and a softer (a mild breathing, resembling somewhat *ch* in the Scotch *loch*).[7] We know that ע had the softer sound in *'Ebher* (עֵבֶר), for it has been transliterated in the Septuagint with a light breathing (Ἕβερ, Ἑβραῖος), as

[1] The term Ḫabiru does not correspond so much with *'Ibhri* as with *'Ebher*, for it is not a gentilic expression like the former, but a collective noun (a proper name) in the nominative case. The gentilic form in Babylonian would be Ḫabirâ (*i.e.* Ḫabira-a). Similarly, we find in the Amarna Letters Sûtû and Aḫlamû, which are not gentilics either, but collective nouns designating two nomad tribes in the north Syrian desert.

[2] Cf. Gen. x. 21, xi. 14, xiv. 13; Josh. xxiv. 2 (עֵבֶר הַנָּהָר), etc.

[3] *Expository Times*, xxxi. p. 324.

[4] *Geschichte Israels*, pp. 16 ff.; *Die Keilinschriften und das Alte Testament*, 3rd ed., pp. 197 f.

[5] *Israel's Settlement in Canaan*, p. 68.

[6] *Egypt and the Old Testament*, p. 115.

[7] The two sounds correspond to the two Arabic letters غ *Gain*, ع *'Ain*.

the softer sound always was.[1] Now, this soft sound of ע is frequently represented in the Amarna Letters and in the tablets of the Babylonian First Dynasty by the letter *ḫ* (*i.e.* *kh* or *ch*) as being the nearest Babylonian equivalent. Numerous examples of this could be given,[2] but there is no need for enlarging on the point. The first letter of *ʿEbher* therefore corresponds exactly with the *Ḫ* of Ḫabiru. There is no philological difficulty, moreover, as to the equivalence of the vowels in the two words. Vowels, especially short ones, vary considerably in ancient languages, and no great reliance can be placed on them. The Hebrew word Aram (אֲרָם), for instance, is found in Assyrian inscriptions as *Arma*, *Aramu*, *Arimu*, and *Arumu*; the *E* of Edom appears as *I* in Idumæa; Ethiopia appears in hieroglyphics as *Kash*, *Kaish*, *Kish*, *Keshi*, or *Kesha*, and in Hebrew as Kush (Cush); while a case corresponding exactly to the one before us is that of Eden (עֵדֶן or עֶדֶן) in Amos i. 5 (margin), which is found as *Adini* (Beth-Eden = *Bît-Adini*). Looking at *ʿEbher* and Ḫabiru (or Ḫabiri) in this light, we see that the vowels of the two words, like the consonantal sounds, may be regarded as equivalent, and that the terms Hebrew (עֵבֶר) and Ḫabiru are one and the same word. It is, of course, not impossible that two entirely different peoples may have had names as closely alike as these two, but this is very improbable, for no other people with this form of name—even taking the consonants alone without the vowels—except the Hebrews, has been discovered by historian or archæologist. If Ḫabiru does not mean Hebrew, then no name has been found in Babylonian or Assyrian to designate this important race. Besides, it would be very strange, if two different peoples bearing the same form of name should be found from history to have invaded Palestine not long after each other. We are therefore shut up to the conclusion that the Ḫabiru of the Amarna Letters were none other than Hebrews. In addition to Winckler and the other authorities whom we have quoted,

[1] Cf. עֵדֶן = Ἔδεμ, עֲרָב = Ἀραβία, etc.

[2] *E.g.* עָמְרִי (Omri) = *Ḫumri*, עַמּוּ = *Ḫa-mu*, עַזָּה (Gaza) = *Ḫaziti*, עָפָר = *ḫa-pa-ru*, כְּנַעַן = *Ki-na-aḫ-ḫi*, זְרוֹעַ = *zuruḫ*, עֵינַי = *ḫinaia*, שִׁנְעָר = *Šanḫar*, etc.

it deserves to be said that Knudtzon and a large number of noted Assyriologists take this view.[1]

The name Ḫabiru occurs in cuneiform writings outside the Amarna Letters. It has been found in tablets as far east as Babylonia, and as far west as Boghaz Keui in Asia Minor. This is due to the wideness of the Hebrew race, which had its origin farther east than Palestine. According to the Biblical records there are two variant traditions on the matter. There is one, a late one perhaps, which speaks of Abraham and 'Hebrew' and derives the people from Babylonia; and another which speaks of Jacob and 'Israel' and derives them from Aram (Mesopotamia). The two traditions are evidently independent of each other, but are not irreconcilable. According to the Abraham one, it is probably among the hordes known as Semites, which poured out of the interior of the Arabian peninsula in the direction of the Euphrates valley that we must seek for the origin of the Hebrew race.[2] The earlier Semites who left the Arabian peninsula and wandered north (before 2500 B.C.) to Sumer[3] and Akkad founded the greatest of Semitic states there, those of Babylonia and Assyria, assimilating the culture already in existence and impressing their Semitic personality on those regions. It is to them that the Semitic dynasty of Sargon (*c.* 2752 B.C.) and Narâm-Sin (*c.* 2680 B.C.) in Akkadia and northern Babylonia must be traced. About five hundred years later came the second great Semitic movement from Arabia, including this time the ancestors of the Hebrews, allured by the attractions of Babylonian civiliza-

[1] Thus Knudtzon (p. 48) says: "Dagegen lässt sich kaum etwas einwenden gegen die Ansicht, die zuerst von Conder und Zimmern ausgesprochen bezw. in Erwägung gezogen worden ist, dass die Ḫabiru mit den Hebräern (עִבְרִים) gleichzusetzen sind. Geschichtlich ist nichts dagegen einzuwenden, aber auch nicht sprachlich; denn *ḫ* vertritt oft . . . und der Vokalwechsel hat nichts zu sagen."

[2] Cf. Nöldeke, *Die semitischen Sprachen* (Leipzig, 1887), and his "Semitic Languages," in *Ency. Brit.*[9]; Brinton and Jastrow, *The Cradle of the Semites* (Philadelphia, 1891); Barton, *A Sketch of Semitic Origins* (New York, 1902), chap. i.

[3] Sumer is the Hebrew Shinar, as Schrader suggested long ago. Cf. Whitehouse, *Expositor*, xxv. (1923), p. 324.

tion and making settlements for themselves along the Euphrates, first at Ur and later farther north at Haran. It is to these people, along with the western Semites of Maer and Amurru, that we must attribute the dynasty of Isin, which lasted 281 years (*c.* 2357–2076 B.C.), and the Ist Dynasty of Babylon (*c.* 2169 B.C.).[1]

According to the other tradition, the Jacob one, the home of the Israelite section at least was in the Aramæan region (the Biblical Aram or Mesopotamia). The Aramæans were northern Semites, occupying a large range of country. Within historical times they had settlements under sheiks not only in Mesopotamia, but in Syria to the west, as well as on the banks of the Tigris and Euphrates, and the coast of the Persian Gulf. They seem to have been equally at home driving caravans along the Euphrates, bargaining in the markets of Babylon, or holding bazaars in the streets of Haran and other northern towns. The tradition that the Israelites came from Aram is generally reconciled with the Abraham one by placing it chronologically after the latter, and regarding Jacob as the grandson of Abraham. But the two traditions are so independent of each other that many scholars believe 'Hebrews' and 'Israelites' to be distinct peoples, and do not consider Jacob to be a descendant of Abraham. This may be so, but they were only distinct in the sense that they represented separate waves of Hebrew immigration into Canaan. The Israelites were a new and energetic branch of the Hebrew race which migrated from Aram and pushed forward into Canaan, probably long after the Abraham clans. There they amalgamated with the other Hebrews already on the spot, and the change of name from 'Jacob' to 'Israel' (Gen. xxxii. 28) probably points to the fusion of the two peoples. Judging from the Jacob tradition, it is not unlikely that the Hebrews belonged to the Aramæan division of Semites, and that their home, or later home at least, was in the Aramæan region.[2]

[1] Langdon's date, based on the Oxford Prism. See p. 122.

[2] Cf. Professor Clay, *The Empire of the Amorites*, where the Syro-Babylonian district is advocated.

There seems, indeed, a strong chain of evidence in support of this view (cf. Gen. xii. 1, xxiv. 4, 7, 10, J). Not only did Jacob's mother, Rebecca, come from Aram, and his wives also, but he himself is called a "wandering Aramæan" (Deut. xxvi. 5, אֲרַמִּי אֹבֵד), and Abraham's nephew, Bethuel, is also called "the Aramæan" (Gen. xxiv. 20, P, xxviii. 5, P). Abraham too, though he seems to have been connected in some way with Ur, to the west of the Lower Euphrates, probably had Aramæan associations, and it may be in accordance with this that we find him dwelling for a time in Haran, the great Aramæan centre in Mesopotamia. The testimony of history, archæology, philology, and ethnology, no less than the native traditions of the Hebrews themselves, seem to favour the theory that their principal home, after some time at least, was in the Aramæan region. It is on this account that they were so closely related to the SA-GAZ 'fighters' (Hebrews also) from the north Syrian desert.

But whatever view we take of the original home of the Hebrew race, the point we wish to emphasize is that the whole stock, with characteristic nomadic habits, spread themselves out far and wide in the course of time, throughout the whole region between the Euphrates and the Mediterranean. They were only a part of the Semitic race, but they included all the descendants of Peleg, the son of Eber (Gen. x. 25–30, J).[1] They not only founded settlements for themselves along the Euphrates and in Babylonia, but sections of them in the person of Abraham, of Isaac, and of Jacob, and other Hebrews moved along westward in successive waves from the Euphrates valley by the northern route into Palestine. Once on the west of the Jordan, they continued their wandering habits, and it was not until about 1000 B.C. that this stage in their career was definitely ended. All this goes to show us that those Hebrews who entered Palestine were not only related to the Babylonians and more

[1] The Hebrew race also embraced a branch in south Arabia, represented by the children of Joktan, the brother of Peleg, but the name 'Hebrews' is not generally applied to this section. The Joktan tribes dwelt "from Mesha to Sephar" (Gen. x. 30). Cf. Ibn Kutaibah, *Manual of History*, p. 209, ed. Cairo.

closely still to the Aramæans, but that their ancestors had moved up and down the Euphrates and along the western outskirts of Babylonia for many ages before Abraham, and must have left indelible marks on Babylonian customs and institutions.[1]

How they came to receive the name Hebrew has never been definitely determined. The most plausible explanation is that they were called after 'Eber (עֵבֶר), their famous ancestor,[2] for they are spoken of as "the children of 'Eber" (Gen. x. 21, בְּנֵי עֵבֶר). A second theory is that of Hommel and others,[3] who, basing their view on a comparison of Minæan inscriptions with cuneiform documents, hold that the region between Borsippa and Ur, *i.e.* west of the Lower Euphrates, was originally known as *'Ebir-nâri* (*'Ibr-naharân* in Minæan, and *'Eber-hannāhār* in the Bible), and that the Hebrews (*'Ibhri*) were so called because they dwelt in that land *'Eber*. The word *'Eber* in this case is not taken from the name of the great ancestor, but is a Hebrew common noun, meaning 'on the other side,' 'across,' and *'Ebir-nâri* signifies 'across the river,' or the land across the river. It was across the river to the Babylonians, who are supposed to have coined the term, for their dominion lay on the eastern side. It is the region referred to in Josh. xxiv. 2 ("Your fathers dwelt in *'Eber-hannāhār* in old time") as the home of the Hebrew race, including that of Abraham.[4] There are other theories on the question, but we need not here refer to them. That which derives the name 'Hebrew' from *'Eber*, the great ancestor of the race, seems the most satisfactory. At all events, whatever be the deriva-

[1] On the wide movements of the Hebrews in the third and second millennium B.C., cf. Professor Anton Jirku, *Die Wanderungen der Hebräer im 3 und 2 Jahrtausend v. Chr.* (1925).

[2] Gen. x. 21, 24, 25, xi. 14, 17; 1 Chron. i. 18, 19, 25.

[3] Appendix to *Ancient Hebrew Tradition.*

[4] For criticism of this theory, however, see Margoliouth, *Expository Times*, 1897, p. 500, and Langdon, *Expository Times*, xxx. p. 461. Langdon shows that the geographical expression *'Ebir-nâri* included, in later times at least, Syria and Palestine. It was so used in Assyria from at least the reign of Ashurbanipal (668–626 B.C.) onward, and in Babylonia from the time of Cyrus (538 B.C.). It seems to have been adopted, too, in this sense by the inhabitants of western Asia, including the Minæans.

tion of the word or the original home of the people, it is clear that long before 2000 B.C. there were large colonies of Hebrews in Babylonia and the districts to the north-west, who had subdued or absorbed the alien population in their midst, and were implanting their name on Babylonian institutions and history. Here they were practising their agriculture and shepherd life with large and rich results, and here they traded by river, sea, and land long before Abraham was born.

We need not be surprised, therefore, at the name Ḫabiru occurring in Babylonian and Hittite documents of those early times, in exactly the same form as it does in the Amarna Letters. The wonder would be if it did not. We find the Ḫabiru serving in the army of the Elamite Rîm-Sin, king of Larsa in the days of Abraham, 700 years before the Amarna Letters. In 1915, Père Scheil discovered on a small tablet dug up on the site of ancient Larsa (modern Senkereh) an important record which mentions them, the record being evidently from the military archives of the king: "Four flounced cloaks for the serjeants of the Ḫabiru,[1] received from Ibni-Adad the master-workman. Levied (?) on the property of the temple of Shamash by Ili-ippalzam."[2] We have here a proof that Hebrews were serving among the military forces of Larsa in the time of Abraham. Several centuries later (*c.* 1450 B.C.), we find an unnamed Kassite king[3] writing to an Assyrian ruler, and accusing him of intrigue with one *Ḫarbishipak Ḫabirâ*.[4] Ḫarbishipak is believed to be a Kassite name, and the term *Ḫabirâ* is the gentilic form of Ḫabiru, *i.e.* it means 'Habiræan.' Again,

[1] The original is *amêlu Ḫabiri,* exactly as on the Amarna Tablets. The word *amêlu,* 'man,' or plural *amêlûtu,* 'men,' was placed before the names of people or classes. It is a Determinative, *i.e.* a complement placed before a word to facilitate the reading of the text. There are various Determinatives in the Amarna Letters, the one just mentioned being very frequent.

[2] *Revue d'Assyriologie,* xii. (1915), p. 115.

[3] The Kassites were foreigners from the east (probably from Elam, which was also known as Kash) who obtained possession of the Babylonian throne and maintained their supremacy for a period of 576 years (according to Weidner, *c.* 1746–1169 B.C.). They were at last driven out, and native Babylonians, who came it is believed from Isin, mounted the throne.

[4] Rawlinson, *Cuneiform Inscriptions of Western Asia,* iv. (2), 34, No. 2, 5.

the Babylonian king Marduk-aḫî-eriba (*c.* 1061 B.C.) has left a memorial deed by which he bestowed an estate upon one Kudurra, son of a '*Ḫabirâ.*'[1] In this latter case there is no need to suppose that the man was a Kassite, as the name according to Langdon[2] was a common one in Semitic Babylonia, and Marduk-aḫî-eriba's predecessor was of Hebrew or Aramaic stock.[3] Further still, we learn from a tablet discovered by the German excavators of Ashur that there was a god 'Ḫabiru' (*ilu Ḫabiru*),[4] in whom we may probably see 'Eber, the ancestor and representative of the Hebrew race. It is known that ancestor-worship prevailed in the early Hebrew period, although no consciousness of it seems to have survived in Israel in historical times, except in regard perhaps to the use of the *teraphim* (Gen. xxxi. 19 ; 1 Sam. xix. 13, 16).

We read of the Ḫabiru, not only as far east as Babylonia, but as far west as the Hittite capital in Asia Minor. They are mentioned in some of the treaties unearthed there, in which the expression "gods of the Ḫabiru" occurs as an equivalent for "gods of the SA-GAZ."[5] In King's Hittite Texts (6, 18), we also read of "the Ḫabiru people." The connection in which they are spoken of in this particular case is not quite clear according to Weidner,[6] though Sayce associates them with the

[1] Hilprecht, *Old Babylonian Inscriptions*, No. 149, Obv. 22. See also W. J. Hinke, *A New Boundary Stone*, 190–5 (Philadelphia, 1907).

[2] *Expository Times*, xxxi. p. 324.

[3] Cf. King, *Chronicles concerning Early Babylonian Kings*, ii. 59. Knudtzon (p. 47 n.) also takes the view that the name of Kudurra's father, which is mentioned in the deed, though in a mutilated form, is not Kassite.

[4] Cf. "Keilschrifttexten aus Assur verschiedenen Inhalts" (*Veröffentlichung der Deutschen Orient-Gesellschaft*), 42, col. ii. l. 9; Sayce, *Expository Times*, xxxiii. p. 43; Jirku, "Der Stammesgott der Ḫabiru-Hebräer" (*Orientalistische Literaturzeitung*, November 1921).

[5] See p. 189.

[6] Weidner's transliteration is "LU^{meš} Ḫa-a-bi-ri-ja-aš," and he translates it "Die Ḫabiri-Leute," but in a communication to the writer adds, "in unklarem zusammenhange." The form of expression is the same as occurs in the god-list of one or two of the Hittite treaties. Thus we find:

"DINGIR^{meš} Ḫa-bi-ri-ja-aš" (*Keilschr. aus Boghazköi*, iv. 10, Rs., l. 3),
"DINGIR^{meš} Ḫa-bi-ri-e-eš" (*Keilschr. aus Boghazköi*, v. 3, col. 1, l. 56),

in both cases meaning "gods of the Ḫabiru."

soldiers, priests, and judges attached to the Hittite palace.[1] In another Hittite Text (Bo 3944), several thousand Ḫabiru soldiers or 'fighting men' are referred to as connected with the State of Burshaḫanda.[2] According to Mr. Sidney Smith, if Burshaḫanda is the same place as Burshḫatim in the Cappadocian Letters, it lay north of Ganish, which is believed to be the ancient name of Kültepe, near Cæsarea Mazæa, a few miles south of the great bend of the Halys river. This would place Burshaḫanda north of the Cicilian gates, and either in eastern Cilicia or one of the adjoining provinces. There is no doubt that numerous Hebrews, probably SA-GAZ from the Syrian desert, were enrolled in the Hittite army, as they were in the Amorite ranks of Abd-Ashirta. Being mercenary 'fighting men,' adventurers accustomed to ravage and plunder, they were easily recruited and formed excellent soldiers, especially when well paid and trained under some military power. Apart from this fact, the Boghaz Keui Tablets show that, as far back as 2300 B.C., a large number of Babylonian merchants, probably Hebrew, had penetrated to the heart of Asia Minor and created important colonies among the Hittites.[3] In the course of a few centuries there must have been a large Hebrew population there, scattered among all the cities. We are convinced that the examination of the numerous Hittite tablets, so far untranslated, will reveal the existence of large sections of Ḫabiru west of the Taurus range.

When we remember the wideness of the Hebrew race, we can only conclude that the term Ḫabiru in all such cases must refer to the Hebrews and no others. "It can now be held conclusively," says Weber,[4] "that they (the Ḫabiru) are identical with the Hebrews, which was already asserted after the first publication of the Jerusalem letters by H. Zimmern."

[1] *Expository Times*, xxxiii. p. 43; cf. also Forrer, *Zeits. der Deut. Morgenländ. Gesellschaft*, 1922, pp. 251 f.

[2] Weidner, in a communication to the writer.

[3] Cf. *Revue Biblique*, 1921, p. 627; 1922, p. 461; 1924, p. 20.

[4] Knudtzon, p. 1336.

Père Scheil, however, basing his inference on the Larsa Tablet and on the Kassite name or names just mentioned, adopts the view that the Ḫabiru were not Hebrews, but Elamites or Kassites who served among the armed forces of the Elamite Dynasty at Larsa.[1] They were employed also, he thinks, in the "far-off countries to the west," in order to maintain the supremacy there of the Babylonian kings and to support anti-Egyptian sentiments and forces, and hence their presence in Palestine at the time of the Amarna Letters. They were like the foreign auxiliaries whom the Romans used to enlist and employ so freely to assist their legions. The fact that Abdi-Ḫiba complains of outrages committed against him by the 'Kashi' people,[2] who seem on one occasion to have nearly killed him in his own house, is adduced as corroboration of this theory. There is, however, absolutely no proof that Kassite rulers maintained armed troops in Palestine at any time, as this country was under Egyptian rule from the beginning of the XVIIIth Dynasty at least. There is reason to believe that the 'Kashi' mentioned by Abdi-Ḫiba were either from the district of Kash in the land of the Hittites, as Sayce holds, or more probably were mercenary troops from Ethiopia at the service of the Egyptian High Commissioner.[3] Ethiopia occurs frequently in the hieroglyphics as Kash (Hebrew Kush, Cush), and was included in Egypt by Thutmose I. of the XVIIIth Dynasty. That the name 'Kash' in the Amarna Letters refers to this southern Egyptian province is evident from the fact that Rib-Addi of Byblus frequently pleads with the Pharaoh to send his Kashi troops to restore Egyptian prestige in Phœnicia,[4] and that in one of the passages where he mentions them[5] the

[1] Scheil, *Revue d'Assyriologie*, xii. (1915), pp. 114 ff. Practically the same theory had been put forward by Scheil in 1894 (*Recueil de Travaux*, xvi. pp. 32 f.), and by others, such as Halévy, *Journal Asiatique*, 1891, p. 547; Reisner, *Journal of Biblical Literature*, 1897, pp. 143 ff.; Hilprecht, *Assyriaca*, 1894, p. 33 n.; Lagrange, *Revue Biblique*, 1899, pp. 127 ff.

[2] Knudtzon, No. 287, ll. 32 ff., 71 ff.

[3] Cf. Weber, in Knudtzon, pp. 1100 f.; Burney, *Israel's Settlement in Canaan*, p. 78.

[4] Knudtzon, No. 131, l. 13; No. 133, l. 17.

[5] Knudtzon, No. 133, l. 17.

word Kashi occurs as a gloss on Meluḫa (*i.e.* Ethiopia).[1] Père Scheil's view has thus little or nothing to support it, and is considerably weakened now by the discovery of the Boghaz Keui Tablets, mentioning Ḫabiru as far west as the Hittite capital. There is no reason why the Ḫabiru who served in the Elamite or Kassite forces of Rîm-Sin in the time of Abraham, like those referred to in the Hittite documents, should not have been Hebrews in the widest sense of the term, *i.e.* descendants of Peleg, son of Eber. Abraham, who is called 'the Hebrew' (Gen. xiv. 13), was connected by tradition with the city of Ur (Gen. xi. 23, 31, xv. 7), immediately to the west of the lower Euphrates and not far from Larsa on the east, and Burney has pointed out that a regular part of Rîm-Sin's title was 'he that cared for Ur.'[2] As for Ḫarbishipak, he may still have been Hebrew, though bearing a Kassite name, for if Hebrews entered the service of the Kassite kings, as many no doubt did, there would be nothing unusual in their adopting Kassite names. "There is no reason," says Professor Langdon, "for assuming that the Habirites at Larsa were not a west Semitic people."[3]

Considering that the Euphrates district had been connected with the Hebrew race for many centuries, the most natural explanation is surely that Ḫabiru and its gentilic form Ḫabirâ refer to Hebrews, especially as the philological equivalence is perfect according to the highest authorities. "The evidence is conclusive," says Professor Langdon, "for the identification of the Ḫabiru at Babylon and Larsa in the twenty-second and twenty-first centuries with the Ḫabiru in Syria and Palestine six centuries later. . . . They appear, therefore, to have been a wandering people precisely as Hebrew tradition describes the '*Ibhrim*, the Israelites, and the sons of Jacob. Were their heroic deeds in the service of Larsa, Babylon, and the Hittites

[1] This is Knudtzon's view also, "Diese *Kaši*-Leute werden nichts mit den Kassiten zu tun haben, sondern vom Lande *Kuš* herrühren" (p. 47). In the case of the gloss referred to, the words Kashi and Meluḫa are unfortunately mutilated, but the syllable *Ka-* is clear, as well as the final syllable *-ḫa* of the latter word. For the occurrence of glosses in the Amarna Letters, *vide* p. 178, n. 2.

[2] *Israel's Settlement in Canaan*, p. 79 n.

[3] *Expository Times*, xxxi. p. 324.

also written in the Book of Jashar? When I first came upon the Larsa texts and discovered the undoubted identity of the Ḫabiru of the twenty-second century with those of the Amarna period, their identity with the Hebrews of the Old Testament tradition seemed impossible. The implications were so large as to be overpowering. But with what other important people can we identify them, even if we deny the perfect philological evidence?"[1]

Adopting then the view, for which there are sound philological and historical grounds, that the Ḫabiru were Hebrews, the question arises, Were the Ḫabiru of the Amarna Letters the Hebrews of the Exodus, otherwise known as the Israelites? This is the question with which we deal in the next chapter.

[1] *Expository Times*, xxxi. p. 324. This is also the view of Knudtzon (p. 48). "Hebräer kann aber sehr wohl, wie Winckler und andere meinen, mehr umfasst haben als im Alten Testament."

CHAPTER VIII

THE ISRAELITE INVASION OF CANAAN

IF we accept the Abraham tradition, to which we referred in last chapter, the history of the Hebrews, according to the Old Testament records, begins with the journey taken by Abraham, 'the Hebrew,'[1] and his nephew Lot, from Ur-Casdim (Gen. xi. 31), which has been identified by Assyriologists with Uru, the modern Mugheir, in south Babylonia. The movement was not, of course, confined to Abraham and Lot: it was a great tribal movement. It was not a single migration, occupying a few months, but consisted of a series of waves which went on from southern Babylonia to Haran in the Aramæan region (Aram or Mesopotamia), and thence by the northern route into Canaan. These early Hebrews gradually separated into little groups, and as these groups grew, rivalry and opposition ensued, which led to further separation. This is partly represented in the quarrel between Abraham's 'men' and the followers of Lot, which is a common occurrence among nomads. Hence we have the Moabites, Ammonites, and other clans or tribes which were at one time not differentiated from the Hebrews proper. The Moabites and Ammonites remained on the east of the Jordan, while the Hebrews moved to the west. Many generations afterwards, other Hebrews, represented by the Jacob clans, pushed westward from their home in Aram and settled down in Canaan beside their kinsmen who were already there. In virtue of their superior practical abilities, the Jacob section, now known as 'Israel,' gradually

[1] For the historical reality of Abraham, cf. Dhorme, *Revue Biblique*, 1910, p. 156; Jirku, *Die Wanderungen der Hebräer im 3 und 2 Jahrtausend v. Ch.* (1925).

acquired the supremacy, not only over the northern Hebrews, as represented by the Laban tribes, but over the other Hebrews in Canaan. They managed to throw off the Edomite section, represented by 'Esau,' which was driven to settle in the south and south-east of the land. Though they gained the upper hand and became the leading people, there were still numerous Hebrews in Canaan who were not absorbed by them, and hence it is that while 'Hebrew' and 'Israelite' are practically synonymous in the Old Testament, they are sometimes distinguished from each other, and there are sporadic traces of this distinction as late as the time of Saul (cf. 1 Sam. xiii. 6 ff., xiv. 21).

By and by, about 1875 B.C., the Jacob tribes (the 'children of Israel'), or some of them, fell under the spell of Egyptian influence and migrated south, where they were given a home in the land of Goshen. They were only a branch of the great Hebrew race, though the most outstanding one, but they took the name 'Hebrew' with them. It was the one used as a rule when Egyptians spoke of them, or whenever they spoke of themselves to the Egyptians,[1] and was the chief name by which, during their sojourn in Egypt, they were generally known to the Pharaoh and his government. Pharaoh's daughter is represented, for instance, as saying of Moses, "This is one of the Hebrews' children." Moses is stated to have said to Pharaoh, "The Lord God of the Hebrews hath sent me unto thee."

When, therefore, we find the name Ḫabiru (Hebrew) in the Amarna Letters about 1400–1370 B.C., as the designation of a large body of people invading Palestine from the south, attacking and capturing the cities, and taking possession of the land, and when we remember on Biblical grounds that the date coincides with the entry of the Israelites who proceeded north from Kadesh-Barnea and overran the land, we can have no difficulty in concluding who these invaders were. The parallel is just about perfect, especially if we remember the

[1] Cf. Gen. xxxix. 14–17, J; xli. 12, E; Ex. i. 15 ff., ii. 6 ff., E; iii. 18, v. 3, J; vii. 16, ix. 1, J.

evidence of the Israel stele of Merenptah (see Chapter XII.). They could have been none other than the Hebrews from Egypt. Abdi-Ḫiba's letters were addressed to the Pharaoh, and no explanation of the term Ḫabiru is given in them, from which we infer that it represented a people well known in Egypt. Who would the king or his scribe naturally understand by the term? They could only take it to mean the people who had been in Goshen a generation ago, and were already known in Egypt under that name. Abdi-Ḫiba, who came in constant contact with Egyptian officials and was himself a high governor under Pharaoh, must have been aware of the existence of this large body of Hebrews, and of their being known under that name to the officials, yet he does not gloss the word Ḫabiru, as we would expect him to do if he intended some other people, nor does he distinguish the word in any way from the particular meaning of it which must have been in the mind of the Pharaoh and his advisers. Besides, if Abdi-Ḫiba wished to say that the Hebrew tribes which had been in Goshen and latterly at Kadesh-Barnea were invading and attacking south Palestine, how better could he express the fact in Babylonian than by using the term Ḫabiru, the cuneiform equivalent of 'Hebrew'? It was the best word he could use if he wished the Pharaoh to understand who the invaders were. Perhaps the main reason why he carefully avoided the ideogram SA-GAZ and invariably spoke of the Ḫabiru was that he did not want the king to conclude that the invaders were from the north Syrian desert and had penetrated the country from the north, but wished him to understand that they were the well-known Hebrews from the south. There can, we think, be little doubt on the matter, although the upholders of the late-date theory endeavour to identify the Ḫabiru of Abdi-Ḫiba's letters with SA-GAZ mercenaries in the Hittite army, Aramæans from the north-east, Kassites, or some other people, rather than give up the theory of an Exodus in the reign of Merenptah, over two hundred years later.

Burney, while admitting that the southern invaders were Hebrews, connects them with the re-entry of Jacob into the land, and makes them come from the north-east as part of the SA-GAZ invasion from that direction. They were *included* in the SA-GAZ, like a single clan in a larger body.[1] Owing to the disagreement that had taken place between the two tribal groups, Esau-Edom and Jacob, the latter had crossed the Jordan to the ancestral home in Aram, but having been reinforced by the Leah, Rachel, Bilhah, and Zilpah tribes, the enlarged group was now entering Canaan, borne along on the stream of the immigration of the Aramæan SA-GAZ, to whom they were related.[2] The fact that Jacob, in re-entering Canaan, was being pressed by the Aramæan Laban (Gen. xxxi. 22 ff.) is regarded by Burney as corroboration of this theory. But in reply to this, it is sufficient to say that, while the Ḫabiru of Abdi-Ḫiba's letters were not unconnected with the widespread movement into Canaan as represented by the northern SA-GAZ and the Sûtû, the letters go to show that the Ḫabiru section of invaders came from the south, not the north or north-east. There is nothing in Abdi-Ḫiba's presentation of their movements to suggest that they entered the land from the direction of Aram, but there is everything to lead us to conclude that they came from the opposite direction, or had their territorial connection in the south. According to Burney's theory, too, the Jacob tribes would be entering Canaan at the date of the Amarna Letters, *i.e.* about 1400 B.C., or nearly 700 years after Abraham's entry (*c.* 2090 B.C.), and during the time when the Israelite tribes (or Joseph tribes at least) are admitted according to his own theory to have been dwelling in Goshen. Besides, it is difficult to see how Abdi-Ḫiba, if he were referring to some Hebrew invaders from the direction of Aram-Naharaim, should have called them Ḫabiru rather than SA-GAZ, or how he should not at least have used the two names as variants of each other. The Pharaoh could never have understood the term Ḫabiru in these letters as pointing to a people from the distant north, the

[1] This, too, is the view expressed at one time by Père Dhorme (*Revue Biblique*, 1909, p. 69), although he has since adopted the theory of the complete identification of the Ḫabiru with the SA-GAZ (*Revue Biblique*, 1924, pp. 12 ff.).

[2] *Israel's Settlement in Canaan*, pp. 77, 86.

other side probably of the Euphrates: he could only have understood it in the sense already well known to him.

The view of Sayce and others, that the Ḫabiru were "mercenaries who served as a bodyguard to the Hittite governors of the Canaanite cities,"[1] has no foundation in fact. He translates the word as 'Allies,' 'Companions,' or 'Confederates,' and makes Hebron (meaning, he thinks, 'Confederate City') their centre. "Their representatives," he states, "continued to exist in Asia Minor down to the Roman age. In Lydia they were called Tralleis or Astrallia, which according to Hesychius was the name given to the royal mercenaries." He identifies them with the Kashi people mentioned in Abdi-Ḫiba's letters, and regards Kash as a name for the land of the Hittites, or part of it. It is clear, however, that, whoever the Kashi people were, whether Ethiopians, Babylonians, or Hittites, they were certainly a different people from the Ḫabiru. Abdi-Ḫiba says: "Behold this deed is the deed of Milki-ili and the deed of the sons of Labaya, who have given the land of the king to the Ḫabiru. Behold, O king, my lord, I am innocent as regards the Kashi," etc.[2] Surely the two peoples are here distinguished from each other, for if they were identical, why should Abdi-Ḫiba apply different names to them in successive sentences? The fact is, the Kashi were not like the Ḫabiru, foreign invaders: they were evidently royal servants or troops who had made accusations against him to the Pharaoh, and he found it necessary to defend himself in his letter by stating that they had nearly killed him in his own house.

Sayce's idea, too, that the word Ḫabiru is an Assyrian word borrowed from 'Amorite' or west Semitic,[3] and meaning 'Allies' (cf. Hebrew חָבֵר, *habher*, an 'ally or companion'),[4]

[1] *Expository Times*, xv. pp. 282 ff.; cf. also Sayce, *Proceedings of the Society of Biblical Archæology*, 1887–8, p. 496; 1888–9, p. 347; W. Max Müller, *Asien und Europa*, p. 396.

[2] Knudtzon, No. 287.

[3] *Ancient Egypt*, 1923, p. 100.

[4] Dhorme adopts the same view, making both Ḫabiru and SA-GAZ to mean 'Allies' or 'Confederates' (*Revue Biblique*, 1924, p. 15); cf. Forrer also (*Zeitschr. der Deutsch. Morgenländ. Gesellschaft*, 76 (1922), p. 252), who takes the word Ḫabiru in the sense of 'friends.'

seems to be the weakest of all the Ḫabiru theories. It is precluded by the fact that the word is not an appellative designation, but a proper name, since it has a gentilic form '*Ḫabirâ*,' and is followed in one place by the geographical suffix *Ki*, 'country' or 'place' (*Ḫabiri-Ki*),[1] which means that the Ḫabiru were a people or tribe emanating from a particular place, or connected more or less vaguely with some district. It is noteworthy, too, that the word *ib-ri-ia*, "my allies," occurs in the Amarna correspondence,[2] but has no *ḫ* in the root as Ḫabiru has. This fact is important and tells against Sayce's theory. The idea also that the Ḫabiru were connected with Hebron as the 'Confederate City' overlooks the fact that in those early times the city was probably known as Kirjath-Arba (Gen. xxiii. 2; Josh. xiv. 15; Judg. i. 10, etc.). No such place as 'Hebron' is mentioned in the Amarna Letters, nor even in the Egyptian geographical lists existing before the XIXth Dynasty, as we would have expected it to be if it were the centre of an important military confederacy. Hebron seems to occur in the Amarna Letters as Rubute (Arba), 'the four-sided' city (see p. 154).

That the Ḫabiru of Abdi-Ḫiba's letters were the Hebrews from the south around Kadesh-Barnea, where the tribes of the Exodus were located, is apparent from a study of the Biblical account. It is generally admitted by Biblical scholars that there was a southern invasion as well as an eastern one from across the Jordan. Whether the two movements were directed by Joshua from a common centre, such as Jericho, after the crossing of the Jordan, and were preceded by a common understanding of how the work of conquest was to be divided and the territories assigned, is a question that is disputed. The consensus of modern scholarship holds that 'Judah' and 'Israel' developed almost entirely independent of each other, and that this dualism which led to two separate kingdoms goes back at least to the invasion of Canaan. Two separate branches, in fact, entered the land from their desert home—the one branch consisting of Judah, Simeon, and others, who moved up from the

[1] Knudtzon, No. 289, l. 24. [2] Knudtzon, No. 126, l. 16.

south through Edom and the Negeb, and the other branch made up of the Joseph tribes, who proceeded round about through Moab, Pisgah, and Jericho.[1] A careful reading of the Old Testament records upholds this view that there was a southern movement quite independent of the other one. We read (Num. xxi. 1–3) that the king of Arad (the modern Tell ʿArâd, about 18 miles south of Hebron) attacked the Israelites in the south, apparently because they were advancing towards his capital, and having routed them carried off a number of prisoners. The Israelites thereupon vowed that, if Yahweh would assist them against the Canaanites, they would place their cities under a ban (*hérem*) and utterly destroy them. On gaining the victory, they fulfilled their vow, and the name of the district was thereafter known as Hormah (a name connected apparently with *hérem*). This was a victory at the very gates of the Promised Land, and it is clear that they must have conquered at this time some portion of the south country, as Arad is about 60 miles from Kadesh-Barnea and only about 18 miles from Hebron. In this case a way must have been opened up for an advance farther north still. If we take this incident along with the one in Judg. i. 16, 17, where we read that Judah and Simeon, together with the Kenites, went up into the Arad district, where they utterly destroyed Zephath [2] and called it Hormah, we see that the two passages refer to the same events, and describe an organized movement from the south. It is evident, as Burney points out, that this movement must have issued in a settlement in the conquered territory by at least the tribes concerned in it,

[1] Cf. Meyer, *Die Israeliten und ihre Nachbarstämme*, pp. 75 ff., 442 f. ; the same view has been expressed by B. Stade, C. Steuernagel, Guthe, G. F. Moore, H. P. Smith, C. F. Burney, and many other Biblical scholars.

[2] The name Zephath has been identified by some with the ruined site *Sebaita*, nearly 30 miles south of Beersheba, but both philology and the circumstances recorded are against this, apart from the fact that there are no remains there older than the third century A.D. Robinson has located the name at *Nakb-es-Safâ* (' Pass of the smooth rock '), a steep pass on the road from Petra to Hebron, east-north-east of *Ǵebel el-Madêrah*, and 25 miles due south of Arad, although there are no traces of any city (*Biblical Researches in Palestine and Adjacent Regions*, 3rd ed., ii. p. 181). But the place was probably farther north than this, nearer Arad.

and in an advance farther north still, for it is difficult to imagine it to have been otherwise, when the victory was so complete.

This matter is of extreme importance in the history of the conquest, and in the elucidation of the Ḫabiru question. According to Judg. i. 16, the conquest was effected by a movement from the 'city of palm-trees.' If we regard this as Jericho, the movement must have proceeded from the north, *i.e.* the tribes of Judah and Simeon, with their supporters, must have made the circuitous journey round by the east of the Dead Sea, and after entering from the other side of Jordan under Joshua's leadership, must have moved south from Jericho, ultimately taking Zephath and settling down in the southern regions. In other words, these tribes must practically have described a circle, which is most unlikely. The statement, however, as to such a movement may have arisen from the redactor confusing the operations of the two branches of invaders, *i.e.* the Joshua tradition of entry has prevailed over the Judahite one; or it may be explained on the ground that the writer quite naturally wished to represent all conquests as part of a great united campaign under the leadership of Joshua. There is some reason, however, for believing that the 'city of palm-trees' here mentioned (as well as in Judg. iii. 13)[1] may have been Tamar ('palm-tree'), which formed the southern boundary of Judah,[2] and which lay somewhere in the vicinity of the ascent of Akrabbim, to the south of the Dead Sea. It is the Asasan Thamar of Eusebius and Jerome, which they identified with Thamara (Thamaro in the Peutinger Tables). At all events, it is apparent from a study of the first chapter of Judges that there was an organized movement into the south country, either from Jericho under the lead of Joshua, or more probably from Kadesh-Barnea in the south, the movement being effected by Judah, Simeon, and probably Levi, in alliance with the Kenites (north Arabian elements) and some groups of Kenizzites (Caleb, Othniel) who

[1] Jericho can hardly be meant in this passage, unless it had been rebuilt and fortified long before the days of Hiel, the Bethelite (1 Kings xvi. 34).

[2] Ezek. xlvii. 19; cf. Josh. xv. 1–4.

were at that time or at least subsequently reckoned as part of Judah.[1] These tribes, the 'Southerners,' were always distinct from the others, the 'Northerners,' who followed Joshua. They were rougher too, more of the bedouin type, and allied somewhat to Edomite and Arabic stock. They had their own views as to the invasion of Canaan. They felt at least that they had a prior claim to the southern districts, and hence they marched direct north into the land, conquered the territory of Arad, settled down in it, and afterwards extended their conquests north and west to Hebron (Judg. i. 10), Kirjath-Sepher (Judg. i. 11 ff.), and numerous other places, till they ultimately took possession of the whole of the southern hill-country known later as Judæa. One exception, at least, to their conquest was Jerusalem and its immediate district, which they were unable to capture or subjugate,[2] but they appear to have attacked and conquered Adoni-Bezek, the chief of the kingdom of Bezek, and to have mutilated him by cutting off his thumbs and great toes.[3]

Joshua's movement, on the other hand, was led by the house of Joseph (Judg. i. 22). The record of it, like that of the southern one, bears all the marks of a genuine tradition, and no doubt contains historical fact. The movement was directed from the east, right across the hill-country, in a line with Jericho (modern *Tell es-Sultân*, 5 miles west of Jordan),

[1] The genealogies reveal a close relationship between Judah, the Kenites, and the Kenizzites.

[2] Josh. xv. 63, Judg. i. 21. The name 'Benjamin' in the latter passage is evidently a misreading for Judah in the former, and has crept into the text because Benjamin's territory afterwards included Jerusalem.

[3] Judg. i. 5–7. The name Adoni-Bezek is regarded by some scholars as a corruption of Adoni-Zedek, the Jerusalem king who appears in the story of the Amorite league against Joshua (Josh. x. 3). But there is no ground for this view, except that the Septuagint substitutes the former name for the latter in the story. Bezek was clearly a place in south Palestine distinct from Jerusalem, and the proper translation seems to be, "They came upon the lord (or owner) of Bezek" (cf. 'the lord of the land,' in Gen. xlii. 30, and 'the lord (or owner) of the hill,' in 1 Kings xvi. 24). The fate of the two men, besides, was entirely different. The only connection of the lord of Bezek with Jerusalem in the narrative is that his followers carried him there after his mutilation, no doubt because it was a well-defended city, secure from Hebrew capture.

Ai (probably modern *Ḫirbet Hayyân*), Bethel (modern *Bêtin*, about 10 miles north of Jerusalem), Gibeon (modern *El-Gîbʿ* 5 miles north-north-west of Jerusalem), and Beth-horon (there were two Beth-horons, Upper and Lower, about 6 miles west-north-west of Gibeon). Joshua appears to have set up the ark at Bethel,[1] and later it was removed to Shiloh, which became the religious centre of the Joseph tribes (Josh. xxiv.). A covenant was made, a simple code of laws was promulgated, and a loosely organized state was established, more or less after the pattern of the Canaanitish states, and to a large extent on friendly terms with the Canaanites and other foreign elements. In this northern confederacy of Joshua we have the commencement of what afterwards became the Israelite nation. His plan of campaign was confined rather to the north and west, and, as shown in Chapter IV., was not nearly so sweeping and successful as the later account in Joshua would lead us to suppose. The statement of Joshua's march into the south, where he is said to have taken Debir, Hebron, and other places (Josh. x.), must have arisen, as we said, from confusion with Judahite traditions, or from a desire to represent everything under his leadership. Probably there was a common understanding with the Judah and Simeon tribes and their allies as to the direction and plan of conquest; and the whole land may have been mapped out in a general way. All the Israelites, of both sections, certainly mingled with each other around Kadesh-Barnea under the leadership of Moses, and had a common bond as Hebrews and worshippers of Yahweh.

From several references in the Biblical account of the Conquest, Joshua seems to have joined hands with those Israelites who had been in Canaan all along (see p. 17), and were probably dwelling among the Canaanites in the Shechem district and perhaps in other places. We know that Jacob had some earlier connection with Shechem, sometimes described as a conquest, sometimes as a purchase, but always put prior to the entry of Joshua. There is a persistent tradition to this effect in the Israelite records, quite separate from the tradition

[1] Judg. ii. 1, where 'Bethel' should be read for 'Bochim.'

regarding the Joshua conquest. Jacob erected an altar at Shechem and sunk a well for his family and cattle. He bequeathed ground here to Joseph's children, and Joseph himself was buried here. Later on, while Jacob lived at Hebron, his sons pastured their flocks at Shechem. Many of Jacob's descendants were probably living in the Shechem district still, at the time when Joshua's forces crossed the Jordan, and they would welcome and support the latter in their occupation of the land. It seems likely, indeed, that the covenant made at Mount Ebal (Deut. xxvii.; Josh. viii.) represents the entry of these Shechem Israelites into the Joshua community and the recognition of their worship by the latter body. At all events, Joshua apparently carried these remnants of Israel along with him in his movements and made them part of the Israelite confederacy which he founded.

A comparison of the Amarna Letters regarding the Ḫabiru-SA-GAZ with this Biblical account of the invasion shows a wonderful similarity. The letters allow us to look behind the scenes in a most interesting way. They visualize the whole southern campaign in particular, and add immensely to our understanding of it. If we assume that Mut-Baal's letter refers to the Ḫabiru aggression, as it apparently does, it accords exactly with the Biblical account of the southern invasion. The towns (so far as identified) which he mentions as being lost to Egypt or captured by the enemy are all in the Arad district,[1] which is the very region stated to have been taken by the Israelites at the time of their initial entry into the land from the south.[2] Of the nine towns mentioned, two (Meshtu, Yabishiba) are unidentified, while seven (Udumu, Aduri, Araru, Magdalim, Ḫinyanabi, Zarki, Ḫawini) have been located in the Arad district, directly between Seir and Hebron. Mut-Baal's letters thus gives us the Canaanite version of the first advances from Kadesh-Barnea directly northward, and forms a most

[1] See the excellent map of the Negeb, printed by the War Office in 1921 for the Palestine Exploration Fund. The map, which is on the scale of 1 inch to 3·95 miles, extends from south of Kadesh-Barnea to Hebron.

[2] Num. xxi. 1–3; Judg. i. 16–18.

interesting commentary on the Biblical narrative. If it were not for the fact that the Biblical record of the southern invasion occupies only a few verses (Num. xxi. 1–3; Judg. i. 1–21), we should, no doubt, have had the mention of some or all of the fallen cities in Mut-Baal's list.

The letters of Abdi-Ḫiba present us with a picture of what happened later, after the southern parts had been captured and when the invaders were coming dangerously near to Jerusalem. "Behold the land of Seir (*Še-e-ri*)," he says, "as far as the city of Gath-Carmel, its princes are wholly lost, and hostility prevails against me."[1] The expression 'the land of Seir' is identical with that in Gen. xxxii. 3 (J), xxxvi. 30 (P), and there can be no doubt that the governor of Jerusalem refers, not to the less known *Mount* Seir (as Sayce suggests), a few miles west of Jerusalem, but to the land of Edom, the territory south and west of the Dead Sea, stretching away to Kadesh-Barnea.[2] His statement goes a long way to show that the invaders must have been none other than the Israelites. It recalls the words of Deborah's song (Judg. v. 4), "Lord, when thou wentest forth out of Seir, when thou marchedst out of the field of Edom." The Carmel mentioned, now the ruined *Kurmul*, lay near the edge of the Judæan hills, about 10 miles north of Arad on the direct road to Hebron. Evidently, therefore, all the country from Seir north to Gath-Carmel (a stretch of about 60 or 70 miles) was by this time in the hands of the Ḫabiru. This accords exactly with Mut-Baal's report, although the latter goes further in giving us the names of the cities captured. The mention of Carmel is also in perfect agreement with the Biblical record, for as the Israelites are stated to have taken Arad and proceeded also to Hebron (Judg. i. 10), they would naturally have to pass through Carmel on their way. The statement of Abdi-Ḫiba in another letter (probably later) that the Ḫabiru

[1] Knudtzon, No. 288, ll. 33–37.

[2] Cf. Dhorme, *Revue Biblique*, 1908, p. 518, "Ces pays de *Še-e-ri* sont la territoire édomite de שֵׂעִיר, limite sud de la Palestine. La voyelle *ê* (*e-e*) accuse la disparition d'un ע." Cf. also Zimmern, *Zeitschrift für Assyriologie*, No. 6, p. 257, n. 13.

had taken Rubute is thought by Sayce, Petrie, Clauss, Dhorme, and others to refer to ‘ Rabbah of Judah ’ (Josh. xv. 60), which is supposed to have been near Kirjath-jearim ; but it is more probable, as Zimmern, Hommel, and others have shown, that Rubute is Hebron, otherwise known as Arba (or Kirjath-Arba, ‘ the city of Arba ’). This is clear from an examination of the two words Rubute and Arba, which are found to be philologically identical.[1] This being so, the correspondence between Abdi-Ḫiba's account and the Biblical one is very close. The progress of the invasion from Seir north to Hebron is identical in both cases. Abdi-Ḫiba's statement that the Ḫabiru had received assistance from Lachish, Ashkelon, and Gezer, and that his caravans had been captured in the fields of Aijalon, refers either to an extended movement to the north-west, as one would expect in any plan of campaign proceeding upward from the south, or to the movements of Joshua westward from Beth-horon. One significant feature common to both the Amarna and Biblical accounts is that the invasion seems to have been directed towards obtaining possession of the walled towns, in contrast to the later operations of Israel against the Philistines and others, when regular campaigns and battles in the open took the place of siege and assault.

That the movements of Joshua across country and up northward are included seems to be apparent. The mention of what is thought to be Shechem in one of Abdi-Ḫiba's letters points to this. “ The same thing will befall us,” he writes, “ now that Labaya and the land of Shechem have given everything to the Ḫabiru.” That is to say, the invaders were already possessed of Shechem, or in special favour with its inhabitants, at the

[1] ‘ *Arba‘* ’ (f) or ‘ *arba‘ath* ’ (m) is the Hebrew word for ‘ four ’ (אַרְבַּע, אַרְבַּעת), but the initial *a* (א) is not in the root, which is simply *rb‘* (*rb‘th*). The *u*-vowel occurs in the participle, meaning ‘ four-sided,’ and probably Hebron was so-called as having been built four-square. Sir John Maundeville (in A.D. 1322) states that at the time of his visit the Jews called the town Arbothe. Cf. Zimmern, *Zeitschrift des Deutschen Palaestina-Vereins*, No. 13, p. 142 ; Hommel, *Ancient Hebrew Tradition*, p. 234 f. ; Weber, in Knudtzon, p. 1342. The old idea that Arba was so called from a man named Arba has been ably controverted by Dr. Moore in his note on Judg. i. 10 (*The International Critical Commentary*).

time Abdi-Ḫiba was disturbed over the southern advance. This cannot refer to the capture of Shechem by Jacob ages before (on our theory of dates). It can only refer to something that had happened just previous to Abdi-Ḫiba's mention of it in his letter; and this is in exact accord with the Biblical record which implies that Shechem was one of the first cities to welcome Joshua's forces (cf. Deut. xxvii. 4 ff.; Josh. viii. 30 ff.), and here an important covenant was entered into, as already referred to. Situated as Shechem was, nearly 40 miles north of Jerusalem, the Ḫabiru to whom it had thus given its support could not have been the southern section, who according to Abdi-Ḫiba's letters had apparently not yet penetrated northward beyond Jerusalem, but probably consisted of the section under Joshua, who are known from the Biblical account to have proceeded northward to Bethel along the main road that led direct to Shechem.

Joshua's movements, too, seem to be implied in the mention of SA-GAZ by rulers immediately north-west of Jerusalem. The mistress of Chephirah informs the Pharaoh that the SA-GAZ had taken Sabuma, and had sent messengers to Aijalon and Zorah. Yapaḫi of Gezer writes in terror of these 'fighting men,' while Dagantakala and Shubanda plead to be delivered from their hand. All these aggressions were going on within 20 or 25 miles of Jerusalem. It is possible, of course, as we have said, that these southern SA-GAZ may have penetrated south from Syria by the coast road and turned inland by the caravan route from Jaffa, but it is not unlikely that some of them at least were part of Joshua's forces from the east, for we know that he struck westward by Gibeon and Beth-horon into the very districts referred to. It may be that the section of Israelites under Joshua, before crossing the river, made an arrangement with these kinsmen for a united attack on the central regions. There seem to be reliable Hebrew traditions (Num. xxi. 20 ff.; Deut. ii., iii.) that Joshua's forces, before crossing the Jordan, proceeded northward far enough to bring them into contact or association with their SA-GAZ kinsmen from the north Syrian desert. They are stated to have proceeded or sent contingents as far north as Bashan, which comprised the districts known as Jaulan and Hauran, lying to some extent beyond the Yarmuk River and almost under the shadow of Mount Hermon. Here they were sure to join hands with their SA-GAZ friends, who are known from the Amarna Letters to have been committing aggressions in this region, for Biridashwa of Yenoam had handed over to them the chariots from the city of Ashtaroth (Egyptian *'Astiratu*).[1] The whole campaign in these northern parts, including the great battle of Edrei (Num. xxi. 33; Deut. iii. 1; Josh. xiii. 12), where king Og was slain, seems likely to have been carried out in association or alliance with the SA-GAZ. For we cannot conceive of two such bodies of men, both of them bent on the invasion of Canaan, and both united by race and lineage, coming into contact with each other without entering into some form of united action. It may be, therefore, that when Joshua crossed the Jordan, he had in his ranks a large body of SA-GAZ allies. In saying this, we do not reject the view that the SA-GAZ in the central regions or some of them may have penetrated southward by the coast road, with the intention of helping their Ḫabiru kinsmen who were entering the land from the south and east. But it seems more likely that large numbers of them entered from the east with Joshua; and this admixture of outside elements helps to explain the different nature of the northern and southern kingdoms, and why the literature of the northern kingdom (the E document) is keener on the use of 'Elohim' than of 'Jahweh.'

The fact that Abdi-Ḫiba was bestirring himself to secure protection for Jerusalem, and that it still remained secure in spite of surrounding peril, accords with the Biblical statement (Josh. xv. 63; Judg. i. 21) that the Israelites were unable to subjugate it. It must not be imagined, of course, that all the events in the campaign took place in a few months. The conquest must have extended over many years, and warfare in the south, west, and north must have been going on for a long time before Abdi-Ḫiba felt in much danger and besought help from the Pharaoh. We know now that he was well pro-

[1] Knudtzon, No. 197, l. 11.

tected from outside attacks. Professor Macalister's excavations at ancient Jerusalem, which were begun at the end of 1923, have revealed Abdi-Ḫiba's city on the eastern hill. They have shown that long before the Amarna age the city had been defended by a great trench, 8 feet deep and 10 feet broad. This trench, older than the Jebusite walls of the city, has been unearthed. It had formed the continuation of a valley and prevented the stronghold from being captured by a rush. Many broken potsherds, including some specimens of Cypriote ware, have been discovered in it, all belonging to the Middle Bronze Age (*c.* 1600 B.C.). About this time, the trench was superseded by the building of a wall, about 3 feet thick, in rude polygonal masonry, of which about four courses still remain. The wall had towers here and there, and although it was not a very substantial one, it must have formed a serious obstacle to hostile attacks. It was superseded, however, just before the Amarna age by a more solid structure, about 20 feet thick, capable of resisting any invasion.[1] If it be possible to draw any conclusions from such excavations, we may see why the Ḫabiru were unable to capture Jerusalem and were forced to leave it in the hands of the 'Jebusites' who occupied it. Surprise has sometimes been expressed that, while there are letters from Jerusalem, there are none from Hebron, Beersheba, Bethel, Gibeon, and other important centres of influence. But the reason is that these cities were already in the hands of the invaders. The silence, of course, may be accidental, but the explanation suggested seems to be the correct one.[2] The letters which we have are from cities which the Israelites, according to the Biblical account, either never conquered or did not conquer till some time after their settlement in the land. This fact and many others are significant, showing a wonderful correspondence between the Amarna and Biblical accounts.

One objection offered to the identification of the Ḫabiru invasion with that of the Israelites is that the names of the

[1] Cf. *Palestine Exploration Fund Quarterly,* 1923 onwards.

[2] Cf. Böhl, *Kanaanäer und Hebräer*, pp. 67 f.

Canaanitish kings in the Amarna Letters do not correspond with those mentioned in Joshua's attack on the land. There happen to be four 'kings,' *viz.* those in Jerusalem, Lachish, Gezer, and Hazor, who are mentioned in both accounts as follows:

	Amarna Letters.	Book of Joshua.
Jerusalem	Abdi-Ḫiba (Knud., Nos. 285 ff.)	Adoni-Zedek (x. 3).
Lachish	Yabni-ilu (Knud., No. 328) Zimrida (Knud., No. 329)	Japhia (x. 3).
Gezer	Yapaḫi (Knud., Nos. 297 ff.)	Horam (x. 33).
Hazor	Abdi-Tirsi (Knud., No. 228).	Jabin (xi. 1).

The objection, however, fails to take in the length of the united campaign and other necessary conditions. An examination of the Biblical account goes to show that the whole combined campaign, both north and south, must have occupied about twenty or twenty-five years (see Chapter XI. on Chronology). It is not to be expected, therefore, that the names of kings mentioned in the Amarna Letters should correspond with those in the Book of Joshua. There are bound to have been changes in the course of years. Take, for instance, the case of Abdi-Tirsi of Hazor.[1] One of the letters from Hazor [2] states that this governor was making all necessary arrangements for the Pharaoh's visit, and as this must refer to the visit of Amenhotep III. to Sidon and the neighbouring places a long time before the latter's death, no doubt, and indeed before the SA-GAZ and Ḫabiru had invaded the land,[3] the date of Abdi-Tirsi's rule must be much earlier than anything in the Book of Joshua; and this is corroborated by Abdi-Ḫiba's letters, which imply

[1] There are only two letters from Hazor (Knudtzon, Nos. 227, 228), both from Abdi-Tirsi, but his name is only mentioned in one of them, and it needs to be said that its reading is rather doubtful, as the tablet is blurred and partly illegible at the particular spot where the name occurs. The middle of the name, especially, is not quite clear (cf. Knudtzon, p. 769, Notes *a* and *b*; Bezold and Budge, *The Tell el-Amarna Tablets,* p. 98).

[2] Knudtzon, No. 227.

[3] This is clear from a letter of Rib-Addi of Byblus (Knudtzon, No. 85) to Amenhotep IV., in which he says, "Since thy father returned from Sidon, since that time, the lands have fallen into the hands of the GAZ-people."

a state of things that could only have developed in the course of many years after a royal visit. Abdi-Tirsi and Jabin, therefore, could not have been contemporary, and they may be eliminated from the above list. Similarly, how many of the other names in the list can be reckoned as contemporary? Twenty-five, even ten or five years is a long time for the same rulers to continue in power in Canaan during such a period of unsettlement, hostility, and intrigue. We read in one of Abdi-Ḫiba's letters [1] that Zimrida of Lachish had been slain, and the same fate may easily have befallen others. Indeed, during the course of the letters, we find no less than three successive governors of Lachish, *viz.* Shipti-Baal,[2] Yabni-ilu, and Zimrida, and there were probably more. Rib-Addi, governor of Byblus, also disappears from the scene, and gives place to Ili-rabiḫ.[3] Many other governors and kings no doubt died, or were driven out of their towns, or were displaced from their position. Add to all this the fact that the records of ancient names are very unreliable,[4] these names being easily forgotten or changed in the course of long tradition, and that persons were frequently known under different names. All this shows that it is unreasonable to expect that throughout the course of so many years the names in the above list should be identical in both cases. Only on the extremely improbable supposition that both lists refer to identically the same period could we expect them to be the same. One has only to imagine the changes that take place in a campaign extending over so many years, in a land seething with internecine conflict, conspiracy, and massacre.

The same reply may be given to other objections of a similar nature. It is asked, for instance, why Abdi-Ḫiba's letters make no mention of Joshua, or why the Biblical account does not refer to Milki-ili, Labaya, Shuwardata, and other leaders. The answer is that Abdi-Ḫiba's letters are concerned mainly with the southern invasion, and the approach of the Ḫabiru

[1] Knudtzon, No. 288, ll. 43 ff. [2] Knudtzon, Nos. 330–332.

[3] Knudtzon, No. 128, l. 21; No. 139, l. 2; No. 140, l. 3.

[4] Horam, for instance, king of Gezer, and Hoham, king of Hebron (Josh. x. 3), both appear in the Septuagint as Ailam.

from Seir, and besides are merely fragmentary. In the same way, the Biblical account of the conquest is only a faint echo of what took place. If the conquest took so many years, multitudes of names and facts must have been omitted from the brief record which we have. The account of the southern invasion is particularly scanty (Num. xxi. 1–3 ; Judg. i. 1–21), occupying only a few verses and mentioning no names at all, whether of kings or native leaders. It is surely unreasonable as well as unscientific to build any argument on the lack of names in such a record.

There is another important aspect of this question of the kings' names. Not all the names in the list may be dissimilar. For one thing, the name Adoni-Zedek (' lord of righteousness ')[1] may be meant for Abdi-Ḫiba. The equivalence is not so far-fetched as it looks. Abdi-Ḫiba's name is Hittite-Mitannian in origin. The first part of it (𒀵) is thought by some scholars to be a Sumerian ideogram standing for ' servant,' and they translate it by the Hebrew or Canaanite ' Abdi ' (עֶבֶד, ' servant '). But as the man appears to have been Hittite or Mitannian, not Semitic, Burney and others[2] prefer to transliterate it ' ARAD,' and take it to represent a Hittite or Mitannian word for ' servant,' which is unknown to us. Gustavs,[3] on the same ground, would render it ' Puti,' the Mitannian root *put* being taken as meaning ' to serve.'[4] But, according to other Assyriologists,[5] whose views seem to have more basis, the expression should be translated ' Arta,' for the first element in Hittite proper names, of which the second element is a divinity (such as Ḫiba), is frequently ' Arta,' as in Arta-tama, Arta-manya, and similar compounds. This ' Arta ' is not from the Baby-

[1] The view that *Zedek* in compound names represents a west Semitic deity is not generally supported by scholars (cf. Burney, *Judges*, p. 42).

[2] Burney, *Judges*, p. lxxxvi.

[3] *Orientalistische Litteratur-Zeitung*, 1911, pp. 341 ff.

[4] Bork (*Mitteilungen der Vorderasiatischen Gesellschaft*, 1909, No. 1, p. 126) regards it as meaning ' to enlist or levy troops ' (*anwerben*). Cf. Weber, in Knudtzon, pp. 1333 f.

[5] Cf. Dhorme, *Revue Biblique*, 1909, pp. 62, 72 ; Hommel, *Sitzungsberichte der K. böhm. Gesellschaft*, 1898 (vi.), p. 10 ; Weber, in Knudtzon, pp. 1333 f. ; Burney, *Judges*, p. lxxxvi. n.

lonian word *ardu*, ' servant,' as Dhorme suggests, but is a form of the later Persian ' Asha,' and corresponds to the old Indian or Sanskrit *Rita* (*Rta*), which means ' moral, social, and ritual order ' in its most general sense, i.e. ' *zedek*,' ' righteousness.' [1] ' Arta ' symbolizes the great law of righteousness presiding over cosmic and human events, a law which, as the Vedas taught, could not fall into unworthy hands without imperilling the existence of the world. Though Indo-Iranian in origin, it represents a higher truth than anything taught in the Babylonian religion or philosophy. It is undoubtedly equivalent to the Semitic ' *zedek*,' for the latter is a word applied to the due observance of duties, rights, and obligations, and to conformity to truth and right. It has to do with proper behaviour among men, and of men towards the gods and even of the gods towards men.[2] It is in accord with this that Abdi-Ḫiba in one of his letters declares himself to be ' righteous ' (*saduk*),[3] thus protesting his loyalty and innocence. This cosmic law of righteousness, in fact, seems to have been connected with the city of Jerusalem from earlier times than those of Abdi-Ḫiba, for in the days of Abraham we find the title ' Melchizedek,' or ' king of righteousness,' applied to its ruler (Gen. xiv. 17–20).[4] In later ages, too, Isaiah predicted that the city, when purged from evil, would become as in olden times the ' city of righteousness ' (Isa. i. 26), and Jeremiah styled it a ' homestead of righteousness ' (Jer. xxxi. 23, l. 7). Thus, from earliest ages onward, Jerusalem seems to have been persistently associated with what is due and right—the idea of what should be. All this leads us to understand the first half of Abdi(Arta)-Ḫiba's name, and to see that it corresponds to the Hebrew ' Zedek.'

We do not know the derivation or meaning of the word ' Ḫiba ' or ' Ḫipa ' (or ' Ghepa,' as Professor Albright would

[1] Cf. Professor Carnoy, *Journal of the American Oriental Society*, 36 (1917), pp. 307 ff. ; Cook, *Cambridge Ancient History*, ii. p. 400.

[2] Cf. Cook, *Cambridge Ancient History*, ii. p. 398.

[3] Knudtzon, No. 287, l. 32 (" *sa-du-uk ana iâši* ").

[4] That is, if ' Salem ' be taken to mean Jerusalem, which appears to be the case, judging from the latter name (*Uru-salim*) in the Amarna Tablets, as well as from references in the Old Testament (cf. Ps. lxxvi. 2).

make it),[1] although it is known from the Boghaz Keui Tablets to have been the name of a Hittite-Mitannian goddess, 'queen of the heavens,'[2] and appears in such names as Gilu-Ḫipa, Tadu-Ḫipa, Pudu-Ḫipa, Ḫiba-malik, etc. The writer or redactor of the Book of Joshua, if he wished to find a Hebrew equivalent for the name of this foreign goddess would search his vocabulary in vain, and indeed it is not likely that he concerned himself with such a matter. It is questionable whether he even knew the name of the king of Jerusalem at the time of the Israelite invasion, or anything about the foreign divinity he worshipped. Taking all the circumstances into consideration, we do not think he did. But he did know that 'righteousness' was the designation applied to the city in those early times, and that every king of it, whatever his name, was a 'lord of righteousness' ('Adoni-Zedek'). Hence, it was natural that he should refer to the king under this description, which he meant to be, not so much a personal name, as a title applicable to any reigning monarch of Jerusalem at that epoch. If in place of the Authorized and Revised Versions, 'Adoni-Zedek, king of Jerusalem' (Josh. x. 1, 3), we substitute 'the lord of righteousness, king of Jerusalem' (cf. 'the lord of Bezek,' and footnote 3, p. 150), we not only have the true meaning of the original, but find no difficulty in reconciling the name Abdi-Ḫiba with the appellative expression 'Adoni-Zedek.'

If the terms Abdi-Ḫiba and Adoni-Zedek may thus represent the same man, as appears to be the case, it follows that this king was one of the five who allied themselves against the Gibeonites, and who escaped to a cave and were put to death by Joshua (Josh. x.). In this case, it is quite evident that Zimrida, governor of Lachish, cannot have been contemporary with Japhia, king of the same city according to the Biblical account, who was one of the five, for the former was killed in Abdi-Ḫiba's lifetime according to one of the Jerusalem letters, while the latter was put to death at the same time as Abdi-Ḫiba

[1] *Journ. of Egypt. Arch.*, x. (1924), p. 6.

[2] Cf. *Boghazköi-Studien*, 8 Heft, pp. 31, 51, 69 ("*bêlat šamê*," "*šarrat šamê*").

(Adoni-Zedek); and as Yabni-ilu is believed by Assyriologists to have predeceased Zimrida, both of these rulers may thus be eliminated from the list as having passed away before the time of Joshua's narrative. Another point worthy of note is that Yapaḫi, the name of the governor of Gezer, is the Babylonian equivalent of Japhia (יָפִיעַ), the Babylonian *ḫ* being a common transliteration of the Hebrew ע. There is nothing more likely, therefore, than that the two names represent the same individual. The fact that in the Amarna Letters he is put down as governor of Gezer and in the Biblical record as king of Lachish is of little consequence, for we know that these two cities were connected in government and closely associated in other ways. Excavation has shown that they were even connected in art and culture.[1] Is it possible that after Zimrida's assassination, Yapaḫi took over the government of Lachish in addition to that of Gezer, and was one of the five 'kings' put to death by Joshua at the cave? At all events, the two names are certainly identical, and this fact alone is very striking. Still another point worth noting is that Joshua does not appear to have attacked Lachish till after the death of the five kings; and it was at the time of this attack that 'Horam, king of Gezer,' is stated to have come to the help of Lachish (Josh. x. 33). The probability, therefore, is that, Yapaḫi being dead, Horam was now his successor. A study of the whole list of names thus reveals a wonderful correspondence with the Biblical record, instead of the divergencies that some have imagined. Considering all the facts, there is no reason for the objection urged on the score of different names, and no cause for Burney's rather severe remarks on Orr's position in this matter.[2]

What we have said of the Ḫabiru invasion in this chapter shows that the date of the victorious entry of the Israelites into Canaan corresponds with that of the Amarna Tablets, *i.e.* it falls sometime between 1400 and 1370 B.C. It is a disputed question how long the initial conquest occupied. Burney, judging from the fact that Joshua was a young man (נַעַר,

[1] Cook, *Cambridge Ancient History*, ii. p. 322.

[2] Burney, *Israel's Settlement in Canaan*, p. 92.

Ex. xxxiii. 11) at the time of the Exodus, and that he is stated to have died at the age of 110, makes the period on the purely Biblical basis fifty years.[1] But the ages mentioned in the Old Testament, especially in the Hexateuch, are a very doubtful basis on which to found any theories. The generality of scholars incline to fix a period of about twenty-five years as being far more probable. Many generations, of course, were to pass before the Israelites obtained full possession, but within a quarter of a century they would be able to make their settlement secure at least, so that they could not be driven out. In this case, supposing them to have made their initial attack on Canaan about 1400 B.C., they would be entering on victorious possession about 1380 or 1375 B.C., just after the weak pacifist Pharaoh Akhenaten (*c.* 1383–1366 B.C.) had ascended the throne, and they would have an excellent opportunity at such a time, when Egyptian foreign government was at its lowest ebb, of settling down and consolidating their position. This agrees with the date of Abdi-Ḫiba's letters, which are spread over a number of years, and are placed by Knudtzon from 1385 B.C. onward.[2]

The Israelites, while located so many years at or near Kadesh-Barnea, would be watching for a suitable opportunity of invading Canaan. They had not been able to enter the land immediately on leaving Egypt, for the Exodus had been followed by the reigns of Thutmose IV. and Amenhotep III., two Pharaohs who turned out to be warriors, ambitious and energetic. Under their government no tribe or tribes could enter the

[1] *Judges*, p. 50.

[2] Knudtzon (p. 53) arrives at this date by the following reasoning: Shuwardata, in one of his letters (No. 280, ll. 30 f.), states that Labaya had died, and Abdi-Ḫiba complains in his letters of the *sons* of Labaya (in one of his letters (No. 289, l. 22), no doubt, he speaks of Labaya himself, but what he says of him can belong to an earlier time than the letter). The sons of Labaya and Abdi-Ḫiba were thus contemporaries. Now, the sons of Labaya lived at the time of Shutatna (Zatatna), who raided a Babylonian caravan that was sent through Canaan during the reign of Amenhotep IV. (Knudtzon, No. 8, l. 19 f.). This places Abdi-Ḫiba partly at least within the reign of this Pharaoh. Cf. also p. 120 of this volume, where we have shown that Abdi-Ḫiba's letters of complaint are somewhat later than the letters mentioning the SA-GAZ in the north.

land of Canaan, for Egypt still held that land securely as her own. In the light of their warlike activity we can understand the policy of the 'forty years'' wandering, during which the Israelites had to remain satisfied with the district of Seir, which scarcely ever, so far as we know, felt the weight of Egyptian arms. But now there were undoubted evidences of a change, and the Israelites, who had been nomads for a generation or more, were getting keen, on the basis of their ancient claim of right, to occupy the 'Promised Land' in which their ancestors had lived centuries before. The time now was specially auspicious. Their SA-GAZ kinsmen and others were already pouring into it from the north-east. Babylonia, Syria, Ḫatti, and Egypt all seemed to be paralysed. They heard repeatedly, in the later years of Amenhotep III., of the growing foreign weakness of this Pharaoh's power and of the withdrawal of Egyptian troops from Canaan. They were closely connected with the trade-routes, and received constant news from caravans as to passing events. Everything told them that Egypt was in a state of indifference as to her foreign possessions, and that the king was not troubled about his subjects or allies in far-distant Canaan. The Israelites felt that they might now at last emerge from their desert wanderings and take possession of the land, unhindered by the forces of the Pharaoh. So, taking advantage of this state of matters, they initiated their attacks, some of them pushing up to Arad, Hebron, and the southern regions, and others entering from the east of Jordan; and later, when Egyptian weakness developed and reached its climax under Akhenaten, they were able to push forward to victorious possession. If we allow the necessary period of about 'forty' years for the nomadic life in the wilderness,[1] it follows

[1] Num. xiv. 33 f., xx. 22 f., xxxii. 13, xxxiii. 38 f.; Deut. ii. 14; Amos ii. 10, v. 25. The expression 'forty years' must be taken as a round number, and though such numbers are often excessive, in this case at least it certainly represents more than forty (cf. Num. xiv. 35, xxvi. 64 f.; Deut. ii. 16). It must be taken as meaning about forty-five years or more, for a whole 'generation,' by which is meant all the adults living when the Exodus took place, could hardly die out in forty years; yet the wilderness existence continued, we are told, till none were left but Caleb and Joshua.

that the Exodus from Egypt must have taken place about 1445 B.C., which is in accord with the Biblical chronology. This would be shortly after Amenhotep II. (*c.* 1447–1420 B.C.) ascended the throne, and he thus becomes the Pharaoh of the Exodus; and it would follow on the long despotic reign (more than half a century) of his immediate predecessor, Thutmose III., who is thus the great Oppressor. This is practically the view advocated by numerous modern Egyptologists of high repute, and it accords with the Biblical account, which indicates that the Exodus followed not long after the death of the Oppressor (Ex. ii. 23, iv. 19 (J)).

Knudtzon agrees that, if the entry of the Israelites into the land, according to the Biblical chronology, could be made to synchronize with the Ḫabiru invasion, there is the possibility of the two invasions being one and the same, which he states is worth considering.[1] This opinion is of importance, and seems to have been overlooked by scholars. He reckons a difference of twenty or thirty years between the two immigrations, but he reaches this result by allowing the bare forty years for the sojourn, and also taking no account of the period over which the conquest spread. If the forty years be reckoned a little longer, as it should be, and the years of the conquest period be taken into consideration, the two immigrations coincide; and Knudtzon may thus be regarded as an upholder of the theory we are advocating.

Most of those who adopt the later date admit that the Ḫabiru-SA-GAZ were Hebrews, though not the particular section of Hebrews who were connected with Egypt. They place the invasion of this latter section about two hundred years later. But what does this imply? It implies that this second body of Hebrews advanced from Kadesh-Barnea and attacked their own kinsmen, who by this time were settling down in possession of the towns and lands. The first body were not like the celebrated Duke, who marched his men up the hill

[1] Knudtzon, p. 49: "Ist die möglichkeit gegeben, dass die genannten zwei Einwanderungen ein und dieselbe gewesen sein können, was wohl zu erwägen ist."

and then marched them down again! The Amarna Letters show that they gained a footing and took possession. The second body thus fought their own kith and kin, who probably spoke the same language and inherited the same customs, and either made them a subject race or put them to the sword. Such a thing is surely improbable, to say the least of it. The inconsistency involved is evidence of the weakness of the theory. The Hebrew records, truly enough no doubt, represent the pre-Israelite inhabitants, not as Hebrews, but as Canaanites, Perizzites, and others, and there is sufficient evidence to show that the first-named group formed the most powerful and probably also the most prominent part of the population. These Canaanites belonged to the same Semitic branch as the settlers in Phœnicia, and it was chiefly these people whom the Israelites upon entering Palestine found in possession, and whom they warred against for many generations. The idea that there was a large and powerful body of Ḫabiru people who invaded the land about 1400 B.C., and another large body two hundred years later who fought against the previous settlers, their own kindred, and seized their cities and lands, is hardly credible. The theory of Dr. Weinheimer,[1] that the Hebrews and Israelites were distinguished both by the writers of the Old Testament and in the Egyptian inscriptions, and that the conquest of Canaan by the Hebrews corresponds with the invasion of the Ḫabiru, while the entrance of the Israelites occurred two centuries later, is improbable for the same reason, for we cannot conceive of the Israelites attacking and slaying Hebrew tribes who must have been closely related to them. Much the same view as Weinheimer's, and equally inconsistent, has been put forth by Theod. J. Meek,[2] who makes Joshua the leader of the Ḫabiru invaders, whom he regards as the northern confederacy of Israel, and makes Moses the leader, two hundred years later, of the Hebrews of the Exodus, who are to be identified, he thinks, with the Judah tribes, who pushed up the country from the south. This latter section

[1] *Zeitschrift d. Morgenländ. Gesellschaft,* lxvi. (1912), pp. 365–388.

[2] *American Journal of Theology,* 1920, pp. 209 ff.

of the Hebrews, he tells us, "seem to have wrested a part of this southern country from the northerners." Such fanciful reconstructions of Israelite history are not only improbable for the reasons we have stated, but out of harmony with reliable history. Even though the previous invaders were not allied by race to the second body, but were simply 'plunderers' of different origin, they certainly conquered the land, or at least the central part of it, and remained on in possession.[1] Therefore, the second body must have found themselves up against newcomers from the desert, instead of against an old and highly civilized population, as the Biblical records represent. Only on the supposition that the first body had quitted the land or had been transformed somehow into Canaanites can the later-date theory be harmonized with history. It is principally on this ground, among others, that Professor Luckenbill supports the Amarna period for the entrance of the Israelites into the land.[2]

[1] The excavations which have been carried out at Jericho indicate the Amarna period as the latest date for the destruction of Jericho. Cf. Sellin and Watzinger, *Jericho*, p. 181.

[2] *American Journal of Theology*, xxii. (1918), p. 39.

CHAPTER IX

THE HYKSOS THEORY [1]

SOMETHING requires to be said regarding the view of Dr. H. R. Hall,[2] who, while identifying the Israelites with the Ḫabiru of Abdi-Ḫiba's letters, holds the theory that they left Egypt with the Hyksos or at least in connection with the same movement. The Biblical Exodus and Expulsion of the Hyksos, he believes, are part of the same historical event. This view is also put forward by Gardiner [3] and others.

The Hyksos (Ὑκ-σῶς) were foreign invaders who poured into Egypt from the north-east, conquered the land, and ruled over it for a considerable period. Little is known of them or their subsequent expulsion by the native kings. The historical remains are scanty, although the researches and discussions of the last few years have thrown some new light on the whole matter. Even yet any views put forward are little more than conjecture: they belong to the probable rather than the certain, and Egyptologists still differ on many important points. The name Hyksos, as Griffith first suggested,[4] is the Egyptian *Hiku-khasut* (pronounced in later times something like '*Hiku-shōs*'), 'Princes of the desert,' [5] which was the usual designation of bedouin chiefs. The Egyptian historian Manetho explains the name as 'Prince of the Shepherds,' by confusion with Shōsu, 'bedouins,' who were generally shepherds, at

[1] See Meyer, *Ägyptische Chronologie*, pp. 80 ff.; *Geschichte des Altertums*[3], 303; Weill, "Les Hyksôs et la Restauration nationale," in *Journal Asiatique*, 1910–13, 1917.

[2] *Ancient History of the Near East*, 5th ed., 1920, pp. 408 ff.

[3] "The Geography of the Exodus," in *Recueil Champollion*, 1922, p. 204.

[4] *Proceedings of the Society of Biblical Archæology*, xix. (1897), p. 296.

[5] Cf. Hall, *Cambridge Ancient History*, i. p. 311.

least those of them who lived on the borders of Egypt. Other derivations are preferred by some scholars, such as Meyer, but the derivation from *Hiku-khasut* seems to be the genuine one, and is accepted by most scholars. Ibsha, the bedouin chief, is so called in Knumhotep's tomb, and Khian, the greatest of the Hyksos rulers, proclaimed himself under this title.

It is generally admitted by scholars that the Hyksos were of Semitic origin, and came somewhere from the region of Amurru, between the Euphrates and the Syrian littoral. This view is supported by the fact that the Hyksos personal names preserved in Egyptian inscriptions and scarabs are mostly west Semitic.[1] Professor King holds another view, that they were desert Arabs, driven northward out of Arabia by the increasing aridity of their country.[2] But the probability lies in favour of their being connected with the region of Amurru. They had, no doubt, been pushed south into Egypt by the pressure of Kassites from Iran and Hittites from Asia Minor. This theory of their origin is borne out by the fact that, when driven out of Egypt, they made a stand at Sharūhen (now *Tell el-Sheria*), a place in southern Palestine (Josh. xix. 6, xv. 36; 1 Chron. iv. 31). They were besieged here by Ahmose I. for three years. We know this from the biography which the naval officer Ahmose inscribed on the walls of his rock-tomb in el-Kab, about 50 miles south of Thebes.[3] "They sat down," he says, "before Sharūhen for three years."[4] Ultimately, they were routed somewhere in northern Syria, on the natural line of retreat to their own land.[5] Josephus, drawing his information from philo-Judaic sources, asserts with Manetho that they were not driven out, but went forth to the number of 240,000 and founded Jerusalem. There is no ground, however, for such an assertion.

[1] Cf. Burchardt, *Zeitschrift für Ägyptische Sprache*, i. (1912), pp. 6 ff.

[2] *History of Babylon*, pp. 119, 132.

[3] Translations have been given by Breasted (*Ancient Records*, ii. 1–16, 38–39, 78–82), and by Sethe (*Urkunden der 18. Dynastie*, pp. 1–6).

[4] Cf. Sethe, *Zeitschrift für Ägyptische Sprache*, xlii. (1905), p. 136.

[5] Cf. Breasted, *Ancient Records*, ii. 1 ff.; Hall, *Ancient History*, p. 212; Luckenbill, *American Journal of Theology*, xviii. (1914), p. 32.

Manetho has given us the account of their invasion of Egypt:[1]

There was a king of ours, whose name was Timaus. Under him it came to pass, I know not how, that God was averse to us, and there came, after a surprising manner, men of ignoble birth out of the eastern parts, and had boldness enough to make an expedition into our country, and with ease subdued it by force, yet without our hazarding a battle with them. So when they had gotten those that governed us under their power, they afterwards burned down our cities, and demolished the temples of the gods, and used all the inhabitants after a most barbarous manner; nay, some they slew and led their children and their wives into slavery. At length they made one of themselves king, whose name was Salatis; he also lived at Memphis, and made both the upper and lower regions pay tribute, and left garrisons in places that were the most proper for them.

Manetho then gives us the names of the immediately succeeding Hyksos kings as follows: Bæon (who reigned 44 years), Apachnon (36 years), Apophis (61 years), Janias (50 years), Assis (49 years). These Asiatic kings made their headquarters at Avaris, which, as Gardiner has shown, probably lay on the fringe of the eastern desert, at or near the later Pelusium. During their occupation of Egypt, they did not rule the upper parts of the land, which still continued under a native Theban dynasty, though tributary no doubt to the northern overlords. As the Hyksos were superior archers and introduced chariots drawn by horses, to which the Egyptian forces were unaccustomed,[2] they were able to harry the Egyptians and maintain their supremacy. How long they continued to rule is a much-disputed point. The longer scheme, laid down by Manetho, and adopted by Petrie and others,[3] allows to their invasion and domination a period of 511 years, from about 2091 B.C. to about 1580 B.C., when they were expelled in the fifth year of the reign of Ahmose I. The shorter scheme of Breasted, Hall, Eric Peet,

[1] As quoted by Josephus, *Contra Apion.*, i. 14.

[2] Cf. Maspéro, *Histoire Ancienne*, ii. p. 51; Petrie, *Hyksos and Israelite Cities*, p. 70; Hall, *Ancient History*, p. 213.

[3] Petrie, *Historical Studies*, ii. pp. 13 ff.

and others gives to it only a period of about 200 years (from *c.* 1780–1580 B.C.), and that of Meyer and others no more than 100 years (from *c.* 1680–1580 B.C.). Though 1580 B.C. is given as the close of Hyksos rule, the country was only gradually freed. There had been a long struggle of a century or more between the Theban king and these Asiatics, and not until Ahmose began to reign was Avaris, the Hyksos stronghold, taken and sacked, and the aliens finally driven out. Even then, they were not disposed of, for their fastness at Sharūhen had to be besieged, and they had to be pursued to northern Syria before complete deliverance was secured.[1]

The view that the Biblical Exodus is the Hebrew version of the expulsion of these Asiatics was first advanced by Josephus. It is in order to confute Apion, who had cast doubts on the antiquity and renown of the Jews, that he quotes from Manetho to prove that they had once ruled over the land of the Pharaohs. According to this view, Abraham becomes the great tribal leader, who in the age of Hammurabi (*c.* 2067–2024 B.C.) led the Hyksos-Hebrews from Haran in Mesopotamia to southern Canaan, from which they afterwards took possession of Egypt. The Israelite nation thus has its origin in the Hyksos movement from Asia, and the Israelite Exodus is identical with the expulsion of these Semitics. Wreszinski [2] has adopted this idea, holding that the tribes of Jacob, Joseph, and Levi entered Egypt with the Hyksos, and were expelled with them under the leadership of Moses.

This theory of Josephus, which has been elaborated by him with patriotic fervour, has been well called by Petrie a " splendidly mistaken one," [3] for the accounts we have of the Hyksos rule and of their defeat by Ahmose do not correspond with the history of the Israelites, even though great deductions be made from the latter. Neither Manetho's account of the expulsion

[1] For an excellent translation and annotation of the Egyptian texts on the expulsion, see Battiscombe Gunn and Alan H. Gardiner, *Journ. of Egypt. Arch.*, v. pp. 36 ff.

[2] " Die Kinder Israel in Ägypten," in the *Deutsche Rundschau*, 1924, pp. 251–268.

[3] *History of Egypt*, i. p. 233.

of the Hyksos nor any other Egyptian account we have of it agrees with the barest tradition of the Exodus. It is clear that the two events were distinct,[1] and even Dr. Hall recognizes this, for, while admitting that the theory of Josephus is a plausible one, he does not insist on identifying the Israelites entirely with the Hyksos, but believes it possible they may have been a small Semitic tribe which entered Goshen during the Hyksos rule, and left the country at the time of the Hyksos expulsion, or shortly afterwards.[2] This point of view is an interesting one, and if correct would open up considerably the early history of the Israelites. But as the Hyksos, or the ruling part of them at least, were expelled about 1580 B.C., Dr. Hall thus extends the period of Israel's nomadic life in the wilderness to about 200 years. He admits that the theory suffers from difficulties, though he believes that this long period of wandering is one of the least of them.[3] Such a long period is too imaginative. It does violence to genuine Hebrew tradition, and leaves no real historical connection between Moses and Joshua. Wreszinski, in order to overcome this difficulty, has been forced to hold that the Exodus condition contains two separate series of historical events mingled together—the one being the expulsion of the Israelites along with the Hyksos, and the other the conquest of Canaan in the Amarna age by a combination of Hebrews, Israelites, and Ephraemites from east of the Jordan, under the leadership of Joshua. Such an idea, however, is artificial and forced. When a theory has to be buttressed by a second one of very doubtful nature, invented to suit the case, it has little credibility. Only on the supposition that the Hyksos were being expelled as late as about 1450 or 1445 B.C. could the theory of Dr. Hall and others be in harmony with reliable traditions of the Exodus. The Hyksos expulsion was no doubt a

[1] Cf. M. V. Schmidt, *Recueil Champollion*, p. 179: "Toute cette hypothèse sur les Hyksôs considérés comme les ancêtres des Juifs est erronée et ne repose sur aucune base solide. La seule source ancienne en est Josèphe. Son témoignage est péremptoire ; il en est tout à fait certain lui-même ; mais il ne fournit aucune preuve de valeur."

[2] *Ancient History*, p. 409 n.

[3] *Palestine Exploration Fund Quarterly*, 1923, p. 126.

gradual affair, and was perhaps going on as late as 1500 B.C.,[1] but it could not have extended as late as the reign of Amenhotep II.

There are other important reasons against it being identical with the Israelite Exodus. For one thing, it is very questionable whether the main body of the Hyksos were expelled from Egypt. There is a good deal to say for the view that most of them became Egyptianized and remained in the land. The king at Avaris was certainly conquered, his capital taken, and his kingdom ended; but as the language of the whole north of Egypt, as well as of the south, was probably Egyptian, and the large majority of the Hyksos were attached in various ways to Egypt, it is not unlikely that these remained as good citizens under the Theban rule, while their leaders and principal people, who were more obdurate and were closely bound to the Hyksos government, preferred to quit the land or were driven out. There is absolutely no proof that the large Hyksos population was expelled from Egypt. On the contrary, it is certain that the inhabitants of Avaris were not thrust out: there is no allusion anywhere to such a thing. Accordingly, there can be little or no comparison between the Hyksos expulsion and the Israelite Exodus, for it is agreed by all critics that the main body of Israelites, probably all who were able, left the land.

Besides, no section of the Hyksos seems to have retreated to the Kadesh-Barnea district, as we would expect them to have done if Dr. Hall's theory be correct. According to Egyptian documents, the whole of them who left Egypt seem to have retreated *via* Sharūhen to the hill country in Syria, where the successors of Ahmose continued to wage war upon them. Even Manetho states that they retired at first to Judæa, and his account does not bear the least resemblance to the Exodus of the Israelites. It is worth quoting: [2]

Thummosis, the son of Alisphragmuthosis, made an attempt to take them by force and by siege, with 480,000 men to lie round about them; but upon his despair of taking the place by that siege, they came to a composition with them, that they

[1] Cf. Naville, *Transactions of the Victoria Institute*, July 5, 1889.

[2] Josephus, *Contra Apion.*, i. 14.

should leave Egypt, and go without any harm to be done them, whithersoever they would; and after this composition was made, they went away with their whole families and effects, not fewer in number than 240,000, and took their journey from Egypt, through the wilderness for Syria; but as they were in fear of the Assyrians, who had then the dominion over Asia, they built a city in that country which is now called Judæa, and that large enough to contain this great number of men, and called it Jerusalem.

Neither this account nor any of the Egyptian ones gives us the idea that the Hyksos settled down around Kadesh-Barnea in the desert between Egypt and Palestine. Indeed, there is fairly good evidence that, after these invaders or their ruling classes were expelled, they became the principal members of the Syrian coalition against Egypt. The danger which they threatened from their northern retreat was only removed by the crushing victories of Thutmose III. and his son Amenhotep II., each of whom took the title 'Smiter of the Hyksos who had attacked him.'[1] All this does not look as if the expulsion of these foreigners had anything to do with the Exodus of a people who are admitted to have escaped to a place in the east, not far away.

Moreover, the narrative in the Book of Exodus implies that the Israelites remained in Egypt for some time after the expulsion of the Hyksos, otherwise the Oppression could not have been of any appreciable duration. There could have been no oppression during the rule of these friendly Semites, but rather the opposite. The lives of the Israelites could only have been rendered bitter after the Hyksos left; and that this period of oppression, referred to in the first chapter of Exodus, was not a short one is clear from the account of the building of the 'store-cities' and the statement (Ex. i. 20) that "the people multiplied and waxed very mighty." This does not agree with Dr. Hall's theory, but accords exactly with the one we are advocating, for it leaves an interval of about 135 years between

[1] Battiscombe Gunn and Alan H. Gardiner, *Journ. of Egypt. Arch.*, v. (1918), p. 39.

the expulsion of the Hyksos and the Exodus. Those who believe the two events to be identical must abandon the period of oppression, which is certainly an integral part of the Exodus story. If there had been no oppression, there would have been no Exodus.

It is clear that only by abandoning a very large part, indeed the main part, of the Israelite tradition, can we harmonize the expulsion of the Hyksos with the Exodus. But there is no call to give up what even advanced criticism regards as genuine tradition. On the same ground, we might have no tradition left at all and no Exodus to discuss. There are certain facts we must accept, and these do not accord with the Hyksos expulsion. The argument that there must be some relation between the two, otherwise there would have been some trace of the Hyksos episode in Israelite history or legend, has little weight when we remember that other great episodes in Semitic history are wanting also from the Israelite records. We know now that great movements took place in the Semitic world, but there is not even the slightest hint of them in the Hebrew records, which make no claim whatever to completeness. If one had to judge, as a mere matter of probability, between Dr. Hall's theory and an Exodus about 1445 B.C., the weight of argument lies in favour of the latter.

CHAPTER X

THE SA-GAZ

THE question of the Ḫabiru is bound up with another one—that of the SA-GAZ. We have stated that the Ḫabiru are mentioned only in the letters of Abdi-Ḫiba, the governor of Jerusalem, who does not refer to any other invaders. In the letters, however, from other rulers, there is no mention of the Ḫabiru, but frequent references are made, especially in the letters from Syria and Phœnicia, to the encroachments of a people, whose name is expressed ideographically as SA-GAZ.[1] These people, like the Ḫabiru of Abdi-Ḫiba's letters, were invaders, for they are described as hostile to the population of the land. Dhorme's theory, that they were nationalists or revolutionaries rising against the controlling power of Syria,[2] is against the picture of them presented to us in the letters. The evidence points to the fact that they were bedouin invaders from the north or north-east, as they are largely associated with the inroads of Abd-Ashirta, the king of Amurru, and his son Aziru. They may have found much sympathy and obtained many fellow-recruits among the settled population of the land, but their origin at least must be traced to the Syrian desert. They are specially mentioned in the letters of Rib-Addi, governor of Byblus (north of Beirût) in Syria, whose references corroborate this view and lead us to conclude that they

[1] Capitals are generally used where the original word in the tablet is an ideogram, *i.e.* a picture or script of some kind representing an idea—not a word written out in syllables. See note 3, p. 46.

[2] *Revue Biblique*, 1909, p. 70: "Ce n'est donc pas du tout de représenter une invasion étrangère, mais bien au contraire de vouloir sauvegarder le pays de l'ingérence de l'Égypte. Aussi leur but est-il faire la guerre à ces *ḫazânu* qui, comme nous l'avons vu plus haut, sont sous la main des Égyptiens."

were aggressive fighters, not unlike freebooters or plunderers, and that their depredations were of a widespread character.

The question has been discussed by scholars, What is the relation of this people to the Ḫabiru? It is generally believed on good grounds by Assyriologists that there is a close connection between the two. SA-GAZ is an old Sumero-Akkadian ideogram, sometimes simply written GAZ, perhaps because the latter could express the same or almost the same idea. It is generally preceded by the determinative denoting 'men,' and followed by the mark of the plural.[1] One theory is that it is an ideogram for Ḫabiru. Every ideogram can be expressed in the ordinary way by means of syllabic writing, and indeed in the Amarna Letters many ideograms are immediately followed by one or more syllables of an ordinary word, so as to obviate any doubt as to the precise meaning.[2] Is the ideogram SA-GAZ, then, to

[1] The ideogram was originally a pictographic script of a knife or cutting instrument, written perpendicularly, thus (see Burney, *Israel's Settlement in Canaan*, p. 70):

But by and by, when Babylonian writing was changed into wedge-shaped signs (cuneiform), written not from top to bottom, but from left to right, the characters were turned sideways. In course of time, GAZ thus became , as in the following line from a letter by Yapaḫi, governor of Gezer:

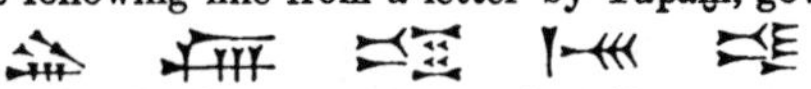

Here the first group is the determinative *amêlu* (*vide* note 1, p. 136), which is always put before a people or tribe, the second is SA, the third is GAZ, the fourth is the ideogram MEŠ, which expresses the plural (being equivalent to the Babylonian word *ma'adu*, 'much,' 'many'), and the fifth is the phonetic complement *-tum* (*vide* note below), denoting *ḫabbatum*, which we refer to later on. The whole line thus reads: *Amêlu* SA-GAZ-MEŠ *tum*, meaning 'The SA-GAZ people' (Knudtzon, No. 299, l. 26). In one case (in a letter from Dagantakala, Knudtzon, No. 318, l. 11), the ideogram is written GA-AZ, but it is possible that the scribe did not know the proper sign, and so expressed it in the way he did.

[2] A peculiar feature of the Amarna Letters is the large number of such glosses (in the form of phonetic complements) that occur. Some of these are explanations of Sumero-Akkadian ideograms by Babylonian or Canaanite words spelt in syllables, the ideogram coming first, and the Babylonian word second, but separated (generally, though not always) from the ideogram by a diagonal wedge ( ). Thus (Knudtzon, No. 155, l. 10):

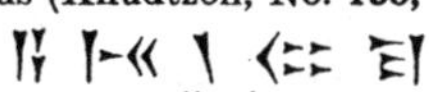

Here is the ideogram A.MEŠ, is the diagonal wedge, and the remainder of the cuneiform is the gloss *miema*, signifying 'water' (Hebrew מַיִם).

be understood as Ḫabiru, 'Hebrews,' so that wherever it occurs we must read that meaning? This is the view of Winckler,[1] as well as of Dhorme in one of his latest articles on the subject,[2] where he says, "La lecture phonétique Ḫabiri remplacerait l'idéogramme SA-GAZ, quel que soit le sens primitif de cet idéogramme." If this be so, then always and everywhere SA-GAZ='Hebrews,' and nothing more. But this view is somewhat incorrect, for the ideogram rather stands for '*hab(b)atum*,' 'fighting man,' 'plunderer,' as we show later, and can only be taken as equivalent to Ḫabiru in the sense that the SA-GAZ belonged generally to the Hebrew race, as did some of the other Aramæan tribes or clans in the Syrian desert, immediately east of Palestine. That they had a close connection with the Hebrew race is proved, not only from the Amarna Letters, in which we find them joining hands with the Ḫabiru, but also from the Boghaz Keui Tablets, in which the expression 'Ḫabiru gods' occurs as a variant for 'SA-GAZ gods.' The fact is that the SA-GAZ invasion was part of a widespread Aramæan movement into Canaan, which history shows took place shortly after 1450 B.C. This is evident from the part played by the SA-GAZ, and is corroborated by the signs of unrest known to exist at the time among Aḫlamû, Sûtû, and other peoples in the eastern desert. It was a movement in which many nomad tribes participated —the next great Semitic movement westward after that represented by Abraham and others over 600 years earlier— and in course of time it gradually swamped or drove out the Amorites and Hittites of the Orontes valley and northern Syria. These Aramæans, of close racial affinity with the Israelites, were pressing into Canaan from the east just before or about the time that the latter began to push into it from the south. Owing to their relationship to the Israelites, it is not unlikely that large numbers of them joined the ranks of the latter when these invaded Canaan.

A glance at some of the references to these fighters or

[1] *Mitteilungen der Orient-Gesellschaft*, xxxv. p. 25.

[2] *Revue Biblique*, 1924, pp. 12, 14.

plunderers will give an idea of their widespread aggressions. We have already referred to the complaints of Rib-Addi, governor of Byblus, regarding them, and given quotations from two of his letters (see Chapter III.). His authority seems to have extended over the greater part of Phœnicia, and included the strong fortress of Simyra, about 50 miles farther north than Byblus. One by one, however, his cities were taken from him by Abd-Ashirta and his active son Aziru, with the help of the SA-GAZ. In one letter he writes, "Powerful is the hostility of the SA-GAZ against me"; in another, "All countries desire to join the SA-GAZ." He mentions many towns which have either been captured and plundered by them, or had thrown in their lot with them, including Shigata, Ambi, Batruna (? Simyra), Ammia, Inamta, and others in Syria, and Phœnicia. Beirût had also fallen, he states, and the enemy were closing in on Byblus. In over fifty letters to the Pharaoh, as well as in numerous letters to Egyptian officials, he makes appeal after appeal for help, but without any result. Even some members of his own household had joined the enemy, but he still protests his unswerving loyalty, and only in despair does he threaten to abandon Byblus and renounce his fealty to the Egyptian king. His letters show that the SA-GAZ ultimately took possession of all the coast land between the Orontes and Beirût, undoubtedly with the connivance of the Amorites under Abd-Ashirta, who were in alliance probably with the Hittites against Egypt. Majarzana of Ḫazi, a town believed to have been near Tyre, makes similar complaints of the SA-GAZ. His letters state that they had conquered, pillaged, and burned Tushulti;[1] they had also taken the towns of Maḫzibti, Giluni, Magdali (? Migdal-el, Josh. xix. 38), and Ushte,[2] and would have captured Ḫazi itself, if he had not victoriously repulsed them. Zimrida of Sidon writes that all the towns which the Pharaoh had handed over to him had joined the SA-GAZ, and he asks for troops to retake them.

[1] A town which lay just to the north of the modern *Bekâ'* valley of the Orontes (the Amki valley of the Amarna Letters).

[2] All these towns lay just to the south of the *Bekâ'* valley.

Abimilki [1] of Tyre, the author of ten letters, reports that the king of Ḫazura (Hazor) [2] had abandoned his fortress and gone over to the SA-GAZ, and that "the whole land of the Pharaoh was lost." Itakama of Kinza states that Namiawaza, governor of Ube (the Damascus region), had handed over all the towns in Taḫshi [3] and Ube to them, but that these had been regained and the enemy driven off. Namiawaza, writing in defence of himself, offers to place his own SA-GAZ and Sûtû at the disposal of the Pharaoh, and states in another letter that Biridashwa (governor of Yenoam) had taken the chariots belonging to the town of Ashtaroth and given them to the SA-GAZ. Baiawa, a governor in Syria, complains that, owing to the absence of Yanḫamu, the High Commissioner, all the lands round about had fallen to the SA-GAZ. Biridiya of Megiddo writes that their hostility was powerful in his district, and that the two sons of Labaya had given (?) their money to them. Yapaḫi, governor of Gezer, makes frequent complaint about them. He announces that his younger brother had surrendered to them, and that they and the Sûtû were so powerful that Gezer would be annihilated, unless the Pharaoh could save it. A chieftainess, who is the only one mentioned in the letters, and who calls herself *Bêlit*-UR-MAḪ-MEŠ,[4] writes to the Pharaoh that the SA-GAZ had taken Sabuma and had sent word to Aijalon and Zorah, and that they had nearly slain the two sons of Milki-ili. Dagantakala, who is believed to have been governor of some town in south Palestine,

[1] Hebrew Abimelech (אֲבִימֶלֶךְ), a name given to several kings of Philistia, Gath, Gerar, etc.

[2] Identified with *el-Ḫurebeh*, to the west of Lake Hûleh. The name survives in *Merdj-Ḫadireh*, which is applied to the region round about.

[3] Probably the Aramæan Taḫash (Gen. xxii. 24), sometimes written Tiḫshi.

[4] Knudtzon, No. 273, ll. 18 f. *Bêlit* is the Hebrew בַּעֲלָה, 'mistress,' while UR-MAḪ-MEŠ is an ideogram, meaning 'lions,' the syllabic equivalent of which is *nêsê*. The whole name seems to be 'Mistress of Chephirah" (כְּפִירָה, a 'young lion'), which was a city (modern *Kefîrah*), 5 miles south-west of Gibeon. Chephirah seems preferable to Leba'oth (לְבָאוֹת, 'lionesses'), which was situated in the far south, about 3 miles north of Arad. The language implies that the city was not far from Aijalon and Zorah.

begs the Pharaoh to deliver him out of their hand and the hand of the Sûtû, while an unknown ruler reports that the SA-GAZ had been making raiding expeditions, and thirteen people connected with Egypt had been wounded by them.

These references from a few of the letters clearly represent the SA-GAZ as invaders of the plundering or bedouin type. Sayce takes the name as equivalent to the Assyrian *saquisi*, 'slayers' or 'murderers,'[1] and it seems to correspond to that of the Shōsu, given by the Egyptians to the bedouins east of the Red Sea. The references to them imply that they were in opposition to the *ḫazanutu* or *amêlûtu*, who were the governors or prefects charged with administering the country under the authority of the *rabisu* or commissioner installed by the Pharaoh. They seem to have been largely at the disposal of Abd-Ashirta, the king of Amurru, who was apparently in league with the Hittites and was seeking to extend his Amorite kingdom to the shores of the Mediterranean. What was the relation of these people to the Ḫabiru of Abdi-Ḫiba's letters? Were they identical with them to such an extent that the one name, wherever it occurs, may always be taken for the other? In this case, as we have said, the Ḫabiru could not have come from Kadesh-Barnea in the far south. In other words, they could not have been the Israelites of the Exodus, but must in all likelihood have been SA-GAZ from the north who permeated into the central and southern regions. This is the view adopted generally by those scholars who uphold the later-date theory of the Exodus, and most of them (except Burney and others, whose views we have referred to in a previous chapter) regard not only the SA-GAZ but the Ḫabiru of Abdi-Ḫiba's letters as mercenary soldiers, professional fighting men, in the pay of the Hittite or Amorite armies. This view, however, of the complete identification of the two peoples has little or no basis on which to rest. That they were not identical, except racially as belonging to the Hebrew stock, is apparent for several good reasons:

First, the SA-GAZ appear almost entirely in the letters

[1] *Expository Times*, xxxiii. p. 43.

from the north, mostly the far north. This is recognized by the later-date scholars, who connect them with the Hittites and Amorites. Everything goes to show that they were nomad fighters or plunderers from the north Syrian desert, who invaded the land principally under the lead of Abd-Ashirta of Amurru. Rib-Addi, in a letter to Amanappa, a high Egyptian official, states that the SA-GAZ were with Abd-Ashirta, and that through their support this ruler's influence and authority had become strong.[1] Abd-Ashirta seems to have had sufficient command over them to gather them all together against any one place.[2] It was under him that they marched against Shigata, Ambi, Byblus, Simyra, and numerous other towns.[3] Through his exhortation they turned their faces to Rib-Addi after the arrival of Amanappa.[4] Letter after letter, indeed, shows that they were mercenary fighters under this Amorite king, and Dhorme is correct when he speaks of him as "le chef de SA-GAZ."[5] It must be remembered, too, as Weber has pointed out,[6] that in many places in Rib-Addi's letters, where only Abd-Ashirta and his sons are mentioned, the SA-GAZ are also meant. Such facts seem to show that these fighting hordes entered the land from the north-east. There are complaints of them as far north as Kadesh on the Orontes, 70 miles beyond Damascus, and at Simyra, and Arvad on the coast, farther north still (about 200 miles north of Jericho). Even Itakama, prince of Kinza, away in the Belikh basin of the Euphrates,[7] refers to them in terms which show them to have been well known in his district. It is true, we read of SA-GAZ as far south as near Jerusalem, but this group may have penetrated southward by the coast-road, or come direct from the eastern desert. According to the whole correspondence, the SA-GAZ attacks were not so much in Palestine proper as

[1] Knudtzon, No. 82, ll. 6–9, 21 ; No. 71, l. 21.

[2] Knudtzon, No. 85, l. 78.

[3] Knudtzon, *Šigata*, No. 71, l. 29; *Ambi*, No. 76, l. 18, No. 73, l. 29, No. 81, l. 13, No. 74, l. 29 ; *Byblus*, No. 91, l. 24, No. 132, l. 21 ; *Simyra*, No. 68, l. 18. No. 76, l. 37, etc.

[4] Knudtzon, No. 79, l. 10.

[5] *Revue Biblique*, 1909, p. 55

[6] Knudtzon, p. 1148.

[7] See note 2, p. 45.

away in Phœnicia and Syria, and appear also to have commenced somewhat earlier than those of the Ḫabiru.[1] On the other hand, the Ḫabiru are not once mentioned in any of the letters from the north, but only in the letters from Jerusalem. They are described as coming from 'the land of Seir,' and their operations seem to have covered a much more limited area than those of the SA-GAZ. This is significant as showing that the particular people whom Abdi-Ḫiba terms the Ḫabiru appeared only in the southern regions, and must have had their seat in the south. If the terms SA-GAZ and Ḫabiru be so identical that they are interchangeable, and if both came as one and the same people from the north or north-east, why is their name only written ideographically in the northern letters and only syllabically in the letters from Jerusalem? One would expect that some of the governors or scribes in the northern parts would have used occasionally at least the syllabic form, or that the governor of a large city like Jerusalem, who must have known either himself or through his scribes the ideogram SA-GAZ, would at least have employed it once or twice as a variant for Ḫabiru. But nothing of the kind has happened. Abdi-Ḫiba seems expressly to avoid the word; and Knudtzon states that, if the two expressions be identical in the sense referred to, this fact remains a great enigma to him.[2]

Second, there is evidence that the syllabic equivalent of the ideogram SA-GAZ was generally *ḫab(b)atum* (or *ḫab(b)atu*), 'warrior,' 'fighting man,' 'plunderer,' and not Ḫabiru, 'Hebrew.'[3] In other words, SA-GAZ was in all likelihood understood and pronounced *ḫab(b)atum*. There are several proofs of this. Thus we have a case[4] where it is followed by the syllable *ḫa*- ('*amêlu* GAZ-MEŠ 𒑱 *ḫa*- '), and another case[5] where it has the syllable *-tum* after it ('*amêlu* SA-GAZ-MEŠ *tum* '), both these

[1] See p. 120, and note 2, p. 164.

[2] Knudtzon, p. 51: "Aber wie wäre es dann zu erklären, dass diese richtige Benennung [Ḫabiru] nicht bloss so äusserst selten, sondern nur in den Briefen des Abdiḫiba von Jerusalem vorkäme? Das bliebe mir ein grosses Rätsel."

[3] Cf. Burney, *Judges*, pp. 75 ff.

[4] Knudtzon, No. 207, l. 21.

[5] Knudtzon, No. 299, l. 26.

syllables being phonetic complements added as glosses to explain the ideogram.[1] That is to say, the ideogram was equivalent to a Babylonian word beginning with *ḫa-* and ending in *-tum*. Unfortunately, in the former case the tablet is broken and illegible after the syllable *ḫa-*, so that it is almost impossible to discover what immediately followed. But there is no other Babylonian word than *ḫabbatum*, beginning in *ḫa-* and ending in *-tum*, and having a likely meaning. Some light, too, is believed to be thrown on the matter in Dagantakala's letter, where he begs the Pharaoh to deliver him from the hand of the "*amêlûtu* SA-GA-AZ-MEŠ, *amêlûti ḫabati*, *u* [and] *amêlûtu Sûti-i*."[2] Dhorme makes three groups out of this sentence,[3] on the ground that the determinative *amêlûtu*, 'men,' precedes each one; but it is generally believed by Assyriologists that we have here only two (the SA-GAZ and Sûtû), the second expression being merely an explanatory gloss on the first. It is true, the usual diagonal wedge denoting a gloss does not occur before the second expression, but the wedge is sometimes omitted.[4] So far as can be gathered from the Amarna Letters, there were only two distinct classes of enemies in the northern parts, the SA-GAZ and the Sûtû,[5] and there seems no reason for regarding the *ḫabati* as a distinct group by itself. We thus conclude that the full equivalent for SA-GAZ was the term *ḫab(b)atu*. Knudtzon is inclined to exclude this word on the ground that the indistinct strokes after *ḫa-* in the case quoted do not seem to be *ba* or *bat*, whatever they may be.[6] But what we have said is corroborated by the Babylonian inscriptions. In a tablet

[1] A phonetic complement was a syllable or syllables of a Babylonian or Canaanite word added to an ideogram to show the precise meaning of the latter. In this way an ideogram could be used without the trouble of writing it out in syllables. See note 2, p. 178, and Burney, *Israel's Settlement in Canaan*, p. 72, where examples are given.

[2] Knudtzon, No. 318, l. 11.

[3] *Revue Biblique*, 1924, p. 14.

[4] See Knudtzon, No. 148, l. 31; No. 288, l. 34; Louvre, AO 7093, l. 69.

[5] Cf. Namiawaza's letter (Knudtzon, No. 195, l. 27), where he offers his SA-GAZ and Sûtû for the help of the Pharaoh.

[6] Knudtzon, p. 50, where he gives a facsimile of the cuneiform script in question.

quoted by R. C. Thomson,[1] the ideogram SA-GAZ has the gloss *ḫabbâte* after it; and in a Babylonian syllabary (*i.e.* a vocabulary of difficult words or signs) given by Rawlinson,[2] SA-GAZ is represented as equivalent to *ḫab-b(atum)*. The evidence is thus fairly conclusive that, wherever the ideogram SA-GAZ occurs in the Amarna Letters, it was probably meant to be read and understood as *ḫabbatu*, 'warrior,' 'smiter,' 'plunderer,' a word which seems to be connected with the Hebrew and Arabic root *hbt* (חָבַט) 'to strike or beat.'[3] It is unlikely that the ideogram should represent two words, *ḫabbatu* and Ḫabiru, or that it should represent the former outside the Amarna Letters, and the latter within them, as Dhorme seems to hold.[4] Such a view is lacking in consistency, for the ideogram means either the one thing or the other. Knudtzon takes up a sound position when he says that, although the two peoples were in one sense identical, he "cannot accept under any circumstances the idea that 'Ḫabiru' is the syllabic equivalent ('denomination') of the SA-GAZ people."[5]

SA-GAZ was not a proper name, such as the name of a clan or tribe or nation, but rather a descriptive title. It is true, in two occurrences of '*amêlûtu* SA-GAZ' we find *KI* added,[6] which is a geographical suffix denoting some country or locality, no doubt the north Syrian desert; but this does not prevent the ideogram being also a class term, having reference to certain characteristics. It is found outside the Amarna Letters, and in every case has the same meaning. An ancient Sumerian incantation, for example, describes the *gallû* demon as the "SA-GAZ *šunugi*," 'the smiter who is not turned back.'[7] Tette, king of the north Syrian State of Jaruwata (Arvad) is

[1] *The Reports of Magicians and Astrologers of Nineveh and Babylon*, i. No. 103, obv. 7.

[2] *Cuneiform Inscriptions of Western Asia*, ii. 26, 13 *g–h*.

[3] The word *ḫabbatu* occurs frequently in the Amarna Letters. See No. 7, ll. 74, 75, 77; No. 9, l. 28; No. 113, l. 14; No. 131, l. 37; No. 286, l. 56.

[4] *Revue Biblique*, 1924, p. 14.

[5] Knudtzon, p. 51.

[6] Knudtzon, No. 215, l. 15; No. 298, l. 27.

[7] Lutz, *Selected Sumerian and Babylonian Texts*, No. 127, obv. l. 7.

referred to as an " *amêlu* SA-GAZ," [1] *i.e.* a 'warrior or fighting man.' There can be little doubt that the enemies of whom the Syrian and Phœnician governors complain as attacking their towns under the lead of Abd-Ashirta were Aramæan (Ḥebrew) nomadic tribes living in the Syrian desert, particularly in the north part of it, bordering on Amurru and Mitanni, and that their depredations and fighting powers warranted the application of SA-GAZ to them. Namiawaza, the governor of Ube, had managed to enlist some of them among his own troops, and could speak of " my SA-GAZ," as he could also of " my Sûtû." [2]

Third, the SA-GAZ were closely connected with the Sûtû, who are known to have belonged to the north Syrian desert, adjoining Amurru.[3] In certain passages they are named along with these desert nomads. Rib-Addi of Byblus not only complains of the aggressions of the SA-GAZ, but of the Sûtû having killed his Sherdan mercenaries. According to Namiawaza's letter, both peoples were in his service as paid soldiers; from Dagantakala's references, we find they both committed depredations on his district; and if Knudtzon's transliteration be correct, Yapaḫi of Gezer complains of both.[4] The SA-GAZ must therefore have come, like the Sûtû, from the north-eastern or eastern regions, which are known from both Babylonian and Biblical records to have been the home of the Aramæans or Hebrews. We know that the Sûtû had been troublesome to the kings of Assyria and Babylon. Ashuruballit, king of Assyria (*c.* 1386–1369 B.C.), complains in one of the Amarna letters [5] that they had detained the envoys of Amenhotep IV., and we can understand this reference when we reflect that these messengers would have to cross the north Syrian desert. One of the kings of Babylon, Kadashman-Harbe I. (*c.* 1370 B.C.),

[1] *Keilschrifttexte aus Boghazköi*, iii. 3, Vs. i. 7; Hrozný, *Hethitische Keilschrifttexte aus Boghazköi*, i. pp. 136 f.

[2] Knudtzon, No. 195, l. 27.

[3] Cf. Knudtzon, No. 16, ll. 38, 40; No. 169, ll. 25, 29.

[4] Knudtzon, No. 297, l. 16. The first syllable of the name of the people here is not quite clear, but seems to be *su* or *zu*, and Knudtzon takes the word to be 'Sute' (the same as in Rib-Addi's letter).

[5] Knudtzon, No. 16.

found it necessary to drive the Sûtû farther westward. From a Babylonian record given by Winckler,[1] we learn that this king marched against these predatory nomads, destroying their power from east to west, and establishing a chain of blockhouses as a barrier against their inroads. According to another record, one of the kings of Assyria, Arik-dên-ilu (*c.* 1345–1305 B.C.), carried on warfare against the Sûtû, as also against the Aramæan nomadic tribes, the Aḫlamû and Kûtû.[2] From these and similar historical references we conclude that the Sûtû were a nomadic tribe inhabiting the country south and east of Amurru, and that the SA-GAZ, who are so closely linked with them in the letters, must have been Aramæans from the same region. This is corroborated by their presence with Abd-Ashirta, whose kingdom of Amurru extended at this time from the Lebanon to the Euphrates, precisely the regions inhabited by Aramæan and Hebrew nomads. There is absolutely no ground for identifying the Ḫabiru in the southern part of Palestine with the SA-GAZ to the extent of their being one and the same people, all entering the land together from the north-east. Such an identity, indeed, would have to be extended to the Sûtû also. The SA-GAZ invasion was clearly from the Amurru direction, whereas Abdi-Ḫiba's letters imply a southern invasion and a concentration south and west of Jerusalem.

Efforts have been made by some critics to prove, by comparison of the terms SA-GAZ and Ḫabiru in the letters, that both peoples were identical in all respects, but the arguments advanced are not of any weight. The statement of Abdi-Ḫiba, for instance, is quoted, " Behold, this deed is the deed of Milkiili, and the deed of the sons of Labaya, who have given up the land of the king to the Ḫabiru." [3] This is compared with the statement of Labaya himself to the Pharaoh, " I do not know whether Dumuia [4] has gone with the SA-GAZ," [5] and the words of Biridiya of Megiddo, " Behold, two sons of Labaya

[1] *Altorientalische Forschungen*, 1893, p. 115.

[2] Burney, *Israel's Settlement in Canaan*, p. 75, n. 3.

[3] Knudtzon, No. 287, ll. 29 ff.

[4] Supposed to be Labaya's son.

[5] Kundtzon, No. 254, ll. 32 ff.

have given (?) their money to the SA-GAZ and to the Kashi people."[1] From this comparison it is concluded that the two peoples must be identical. But all that is implied is that the sons of Labaya (who appears to have been governor of Shechem) had found it advantageous to secure the help of the SA-GAZ for some purpose or other. If they were Hebrew by race, as some think, it is not surprising that they should make some compact with their Aramæan or Hebrew kinsmen; and apart from this motive, they were only doing what was done by other Canaanitish rulers, such as Namiawaza, who enlisted both SA-GAZ and Sûtû in their service. There is not a shred of evidence in the comparison to prove the identity of the SA-GAZ and Ḫabiru. On the same ground, indeed, the Ḫabiru must also be identical with the Kashi people, for the sons of Labaya are said in the same clause to have given their money to them also. As another sample of how weak the argument for identity is on the ground of comparison, the statement of Abdi-Ḫiba regarding the Ḫabiru, "Should there be no troops this year, all the lands of the king, my lord, will be lost,"[2] is placed alongside a similar statement by Baiawa as to the SA-GAZ, "Unless Yanḫamu comes this year, all the lands will be lost to the SA-GAZ,"[3] and it can hardly be doubted, we are told, that the "reference in each case is to the same peril."[4] Such an argument would imply that similarity of thought and language in describing invasions carries with it identity of invaders. As we have said, the language of these ancient scribes was very limited, and the danger from an invasion of bedouins, whether in the north or south, could only be expressed in words almost similar.[5]

Winckler's discovery at Boghaz Keui of Hittite tablets, on several of which the expression 'gods of the Ḫabiru' occurs as a variant for 'gods of the SA-GAZ,' has been supposed by some scholars to prove that the two terms are equivalent in every

[1] Knudtzon, No. 246, ll. 5 f.
[2] Knudtzon, No. 288, ll. 51 ff.
[3] Knudtzon, No. 215, ll. 9 ff.
[4] Burney, *Israel's Settlement in Canaan*, p. 73; so also Dhorme, *Revue Biblique*, 1924, p. 13.
[5] See p. 54.

sense. But all that the reading proves is that the SA-GAZ were of Hebrew stock, their gods being the gods of the Hebrew race. Being of Hebrew stock, what other gods would they have than *ilâni* Ḫabiri ('gods of the Hebrews')? It is thus apparent that *ilâni* SA-GAZ = *ilâni* Ḫabiri, and this equivalence could have been stated before the discovery of the tablets, though probably with less certainty. Boghaz Keui is a modern village of Asia Minor, in the district known in early Christian ages as Cappadocia. It occupies the site of an ancient city called Ḫattushash, the once flourishing capital of the Hittite empire. Here Shuppiluliu, to whom we have already referred as encroaching on Palestine at the time of the Amarna Letters, reigned for about forty years (*c.* 1400–1365 B.C.), and from here he directed his powerful empire. Among the buried ruins of this city, the national archives were unearthed (in 1906–7, and 1911–12) by Professor Winckler and Makridy Bey, consisting of an immense number of cuneiform tablets, some of them inscribed in the Babylonian language and others in the Hittite.[1] Among these

[1] The work of deciphering the tablets proceeds so rapidly and the bibliography is increasing to such an extent that only the barest references can be given here. We are only concerned here with the tablets so far as they refer to the Ḫabiru-SA-GAZ question. Figulla, Weidner, Walther, Hrozný, and other scholars have issued texts, and articles are constantly appearing in the Oriental journals. For the more important literature, cf. Winckler, *Mitteilungen der deutschen Orient-Gesellschaft*, No. 35 (1907), pp. 32 ff.; Weidner, 58 (1917), pp. 55 ff.; Forrer, 63; *Zeit. der Deut. Morgenländ. Gesell.*, 1922, pp. 174–269; Winckler, *Orientalische Literatur-Zeitung*, 1910, pp. 292 ff.; Schachermeyr, 1921, pp. 66–70; Böhl, *Theologisch Tijdschrift*, 1916, pp. 162 ff.; Figulla and Weidner, *Keilschrifttexte aus Boghazköi*, 1916 ff.; Meissner, *Zur Geschichte des Chattireiches*, 1917, iv. pp. 5 ff.; Hrozný, *Hethitische aus Boghazköi*, 1919; Luckenbill, *American Journal of Semitic Languages and Literatures*, xxxvii. (1921), pp. 161 ff.; and Weidner, *Politische Documente aus Kleinasien*, Leipzig, 1923. See especially *Boghazköi-Studien*, edited by Otto Weber, Leipzig, 1917 ff., which includes some of the publications just mentioned, as well as other important ones. There are also numerous stray publications in German journals which deal with Assyriology. A bibliography up to 1922 is given by Weidner, *Die Assyriologie*, pp. 188 ff. (J. C. Hinrichs'sche Buchhandlung, Leipzig). A grammar of the Hittite language with vocabulary was published by Hrozný, *Die Sprache der Hethiter*, Leipzig, 1917. Hrozný and Forrer agree in regarding the various dialects of this language (at least six in number) as largely Indo-European, akin to Latin indeed, though their views have been criticized by Bork, Weidner, Bloomfield, and others.

documents are some remarkable treaties made by the Hittite kings with the peoples of Mitanni, Nuḫashshi, Kizzuwadna, and other states. The treaties include oaths taken for their due performance, and in these oaths a large number of deities are invoked. In one treaty, for instance, between Shuppiluliu and Mattiuâza, which contains a long list of gods, occur the words, "The god Kunijawannish of the city Landa, the Lulaḫi-gods, the SA-GAZ-gods [*ilâni* SA-GAZ], the male gods, the female gods of the Hittite land."[1] On the other hand, in a treaty between Shuppiluliu and Tette, king of Nuḫashshi, a north Syrian district, there is a list of over fifty gods invoked, and near the end the following passage occurs, "Ninpisan-pisan-na of Kinza, the Lebanon Mountains, the Sharijana Mountains,[2] the Bîshaisha Mountains, the gods of the Lulaḫḫi, the gods of the Ḫabiru, [the goddess] Ereshkigal, the male gods, the female gods of the Hittite land."[3] There are other places in the texts where Ḫabiru seems to take the place of SA-GAZ when the gods are referred to.[4] On the ground of these equivalent readings, the view that SA-GAZ and Ḫabiru are interchangeable terms, identical in every respect, is supposed by some to be placed beyond question. Such a deduction, however, does not follow. All that the variant reading proves, as we have said, is that the SA-GAZ were connected generally with the Hebrew

[1] Weidner, *Politische Documente aus Kleinasien* (1923), 8 Heft, p. 31, ll. 50, 51. A variant copy has "gods of the Nulaḫḫi, gods of the SA-GAZ-people [*ilâni ša amêlu* SA-GAZ]." For the interchange of *l* and *n*, cf. Weidner, *Boghaz-Stud.*, 6 Heft, p. 77. Hrozný regards the Lulaḫi people as related to or the same as the Lulubi, but as they are nearly always mentioned in the Boghaz Keui Tablets along with the SA-GAZ, they were probably more closely related to the latter.

[2] The Hermon Range. Cf. שִׂרְיֹן, Deut. iii. 9; Ps. xxix. 6.

[3] Weidner, *Politische Documente aus Kleinasien* (1923), 8 Heft, p. 69, ll. 35–38.

[4] So far as known at present, there are five places in the Tablets where the expression '*ilâni* Ḫabiri' occurs, and two where the form '*ilâni* SA-GAZ' is found. See Appendix, p. 272, where translations from all these texts will be found in parallel columns. The first four texts are in Babylonian, and the other three in Hittite. Weidner has been good enough to give the writer translations of the latter. It will be noticed that in the Hittite texts the names have Hittite endings. Thus Ḫabiru appears as Ḫabirijâš, or Ḫabiriêš.

stock, their gods being those of the Hebrew race. There were numerous tribes or clans which were descended from Eber, the great Hebrew ancestor. We have already seen that there were Hebrews as far away as Babylonia, for the term Ḫabiru occurs in inscriptions at Larsa and other places. The Israelites were only a small branch from the great stock, which included not only many tribes along the Euphrates valley, but the SA-GAZ people and other Aramæan nomads of the Syrian desert. Hence it is quite natural that the expression *ilâni Ḫabiri* should take the place of *ilâni* SA-GAZ. The one is quite a natural equivalent in this sense for the other. Nor is there anything out of the way in the use of the plural word 'gods' as applied to the Ḫabiru.[1] "The Hittite treaty," says Professor Langdon, "speaks of their gods, and that need not surprise us. Only the branch of their people led by Abraham, and descended through the line of Jacob, received the revelation of monotheism." [2]

It is noteworthy, and in accordance with all we have stated, that there were SA-GAZ also in Babylonia and other parts. Being nomadic 'fighters' or 'plunderers' of Hebrew extraction, they were found not only in the districts adjoining Amurru and Mitanni, but along the valley of the Euphrates, the ancient home of the Hebrews. They are mentioned as *amêlu* SA-GAZ in several Larsa records in Yale University, going as far back as the reign of Warad-Sin, over 2000 B.C.,[3] and the reference implies that they were Hebrew. In six at least of these records, quoted by Miss Grice, we read of sheep being bought for the SA-GAZ or 'fighting men.' From a letter published by Professor L. W. King[4] we find that the *amêlu* SA-GAZ also served in the armies

[1] As Forrer has pointed out (*Zeitschrift der Deutschen Morgenländ. Gesellschaft*, 1922, p. 251), the expression AN(-MEŠ) in these cases in the Boghaz Keui texts never stands as a plural of majesty (like the Hebrew *Elohim*, etc.) for a single god, but only before an actual plural (a god-group). AN is the ideogram for 'god' (*ilu*).

[2] *Expository Times*, xxxi. pp. 324 ff.

[3] Miss Grice, *Records from Ur and Larsa*, Nos. 33, 47, 50, 46, 51, 52, 53.

[4] *Letters and Inscriptions of Hammurabi*, No. 35. See also Ungnad, *Babylonische Briefe*, No. 26.

of Hammurabi, king of Babylonia (*c.* 2067–2024 B.C.), in the days of Abraham, and their captain bore a Semitic Babylonian name, Anum-pî-Sin. As already shown, these 'fighting men' are mentioned in the Hittite treaties in Asia Minor. In King's Hittite Texts (37. 4, 5) we also read on one tablet of 600 SA-GAZ. The tablet is an Akkadian fragment, which has unfortunately been much injured, but the reference, according to Weidner,[1] seems to be connected with military service. All this agrees with the fact referred to in a previous chapter that the Hebrew race was a wide one. By the name Hebrew we have to understand not Israel alone, but all the Hebraic peoples whom the traditions of Israel claimed as kindred. They formed various communities, some of them mere unorganized hordes, speaking closely related dialects, and found here and there in the vast extent of territory between the Euphrates and the Mediterranean.

Most of the upholders of the late-date theory of the Exodus find it necessary, as we have said, to adopt the view that the SA-GAZ and the Ḫabiru were not only related racially, but were one and the same people, identical in all respects. For if they were to admit any distinction between the two, they would make it possible for the Ḫabiru of Abdi-Ḫiba's letters to be the Hebrews of the Exodus who were dwelling round Kadesh-Barnea. Thus, Professor Langdon regards them both as one people—as professional mercenary soldiers in the Hittite army, having probably an official or legal status.[2] Sayce adopts a similar view and believes them to have been mercenaries who formed the bodyguard of the chief rulers of western Asia.[3] So far as the SA-GAZ were concerned there may be some truth in this, although we think these 'fighting men' were rather connected with the Amorite than the Hittite armies. But as for the Ḫabiru of Abdi-Ḫiba's letters, it takes some imagination to picture these invaders of southern Palestine forming royal Hittite bodyguards. Pharaoh certainly would not so understand the word Ḫabiru—he would give it the meaning to which he had long been accustomed. When we

[1] In a communication to the writer.

[2] *Expository Times*, xxxi. pp. 334 ff.

[3] *Op. cit.*, xxxiii. p. 43.

read, too, in one of Abdi-Ḫiba's letters that the Egyptian High Commissioner 'loved' the Ḫabiru, it seems impossible that these people could have been official Hittite soldiers, who were the sworn enemies of Egypt. Would he favour the very armies whose encroachments it was his duty to watch against? Would he allow them to advance as far south as Jerusalem and settle down there? And would Abdi-Ḫiba oppose them so strongly when he was Hittite-Mitannian himself?

We have already referred to the view of Burney,[1] who, while not holding the complete identity of the two peoples, makes the Ḫabiru to be a part or subsection of the SA-GAZ, and regards them as entering the land at the same time and from the same direction. He endeavours to show that the Ḫabiru were the Jacob tribes re-entering Canaan after returning from Aram. They were now coming back in increased force, along with the SA-GAZ, on the wave of Aramæan immigration. They were thus *included* among the SA-GAZ or *ḫabbatu*, though separate from them. This, too, was the view expressed at one time by Dhorme, who regarded them as a special clan within the great population of the SA-GAZ.[2] In proof, Burney endeavours to show from a sentence in one of Abdi-Ḫiba's letters that the Ḫabiru mentioned by the latter were connected with the north of Palestine as much as the south. The sentence is quoted by him as follows:[3] "When there was a ship (*or* a fleet) at sea, the king's strong arm held the land of Naḫrima and the land of Kapasi (?); but now the Ḫabiru hold all the king's cities."[4] It is concluded from this that the Ḫabiru of Abdi-Ḫiba's letters were holding "either the cities of Naḫrima in the north, or (more probably) the Phœnician cities which it was necessary for Egypt to hold in order to maintain her footing in the ports," and hence the SA-GAZ, to whom the governor of Byblus refers so often, were included in Abdi-

[1] See p. 144. Cf. *Israel's Settlement in Canaan*, pp. 72 ff.

[2] *Revue Biblique*, 1909, p. 69.

[3] *Israel's Settlement in Canaan*, p. 74.

[4] This is Winckler's translation (No. 181, ll. 32 ff.). Knudtzon (No. 288, ll. 32 ff.) makes it, "I once had a ship on the sea when the mighty arm of the king . . ."

Ḫiba's use of the word Ḫabiru. It needs to be said, however, that the interpretation of this sentence is recognized as very difficult by Assyriologists, and that little word "all" ("*all* the king's cities"), which gives some force to Burney's argument, has accidentally crept into the text, for it does not occur in the original, the words being simply *alâni šarri-ri*, 'the cities of the king.' Naḫrima (Naḫarin) is another name for Naḫaraim (*i.e.* Mitanni), or at least that part of it to the west of Carchemish, while Kapasi, if this word be another reading for Kashi, as Weber thinks,[1] was a district farther north still, never completely subjugated even by the Hittites. There is no doubt that when the Egyptian fleet held a base on the coast of Phœnicia, as it had done in the victorious campaigns of Thutmose III. and his immediate successors, the Egyptian army could at least reach Naharin without serious difficulty and keep down revolt there and in the adjoining regions. But Abdi-Ḫiba could not have meant that the Ḫabiru were now in possession of these far northern lands. We know, indeed, they were not, for the Amarna and Boghaz Keui Tablets show that these lands were still independent and strong, and in the very zenith of their power. Even Burney cannot reconcile himself to such a conclusion, for he substitutes for these far-away lands "the Phœnician cities" as the only way to uphold his argument, although he thereby shows its weakness. The fact is that both Winckler's and Knudtzon's translation of the text are incorrect. Professor W. F. Albright gives what is now regarded as the correct translation as follows:[2] "As sure as there is a ship in the midst of the sea, the mighty arm of the king will seize Naharîm and Kapasi, but now (meanwhile) the Hebrews are seizing the towns of the king." This rendering puts a different construction on the matter and removes all support from Burney's argument, for it does not imply that

[1] Knudtzon, pp. 1340 f.

[2] *Journ. of Egypt. Arch.*, x. (1924), p. 6. Albright shows that in the text *šaknati* (at end of l. 32) = *šaknat*, and belongs to the previous sentence, and not to the one we are discussing. The latter begins with the word *enûma*, which introduces an oath or asseveration.

the Ḫabiru of Abdi-Ḫiba's letters were holding or seizing any of the towns in the far north. That the southern towns are intended is evident from the fact that Abdi-Ḫiba, in proceeding to give proof of his assertion, does not mention any in the north (as we would expect him to do, if Burney's interpretation were correct), but cites what has happened at Lachish and Zilu, two cities not more than 30 miles from Jerusalem.[1] Indeed, the expression 'cities of the king,' used only this once by Abdi-Ḫiba, must be interpreted according to the other expression "lands (or land) of the king," which is so common in his letters and which undoubtedly signifies the lands around Jerusalem or in south Palestine, with which Abdi-Ḫiba was more immediately concerned. "Let the king send troops," he says, "that I may restore the king's land to the king." [2] "The lands of the king, my lord, have all fallen away." [3] "Let the king send fifty garrison men to protect his land! The whole land of the king is in revolt." [4] It cannot be imagined that Abdi-Ḫiba intended to restore the whole of Palestine himself and with a few garrison troops too, to say nothing of the distant countries of Naharin and Kapasi. As the governor of Jerusalem, he was mainly concerned with the lands and cities in his own district, and it was obviously these that were in his mind when he appealed to the Pharaoh for help.

Any comparison of Abdi-Ḫiba's letters with those from the north of Palestine shows that the Ḫabiru were a separate invading force. They could not have come into the land from the north-east along with the SA-GAZ, although being nomads themselves from the desert around Kadesh-Barnea

[1] Zilu has been variously identified, but the context implies that it was not far from Lachish, and an important place with gates and walls. Such identifications as Zelah, an insignificant village of Benjamin, just north of Jerusalem, and Selah in Edom (Clauss, *Zeitschrift der Deutschen Palästina-Vereins*, 1907, p. 73), not to mention Shiloh, as suggested by Conder (Tell el-Amarna Tablets, p. 146, n. 2), are unsatisfactory. The idea of Professor Albright that Zilu was Sile (or Sellê), a frontier fort of Egypt proper, seems equally far-fetched, for it would surely be outside Abdi-Ḫiba's province to offer information of events occurring at the gate of Egypt.

[2] Knudtzon, No. 290, ll. 19 ff.

[3] Knudtzon, No. 289, ll. 42 ff.

[4] Knudtzon, No. 286, ll. 35 f., l. 56.

and being so closely related to the latter, they may have been regarded as the same by many Canaanites, and were no doubt classed as such by many southern rulers. To many natives of Palestine every Hebrew nomad from the desert was put down as a SA-GAZ or ' plunderer.' Thus, many of the Israelites may have been looked upon as such, and in spite of the restraints of the Mosaic law many of them were real plunderers, not a whit better than others from outside. But in reality the SA-GAZ dwelt in the country between the Euphrates and Syria, probably under the suzerainty of the king of Amurru. They were an unorganized people, of semi-nomadic habits, generally peaceful under a strong governing hand, but ever ready to give their services as mercenary fighters to those who wanted them, willing to engage themselves for plunder and aggressive warfare, and capable of becoming dangerous enemies. They were now invading north Palestine, along with the Sûtû who were allied to them ; and Abd-Ashirta was clever enough to secure their assistance in his endeavour to extend his kingdom to the Mediterranean shores. Historians can place the movement as a widespread Aramæan one, the third of the main eruptions of the Semites. It was a movement similar to that which brought Abraham and his clans to Palestine, and was thus a repetition of much earlier events. The Ḫabiru who left Egypt and settled at Kadesh-Barnea were related to these northern invaders, being of the same Hebrew stock, *i.e.* of the line of Arpachshad, Eber, and Peleg, and their ancestors had all lived together at one time in the Syro-Babylonian region. They and the SA-GAZ people were not only fellow-nomads, but kinsmen, speaking the same language or dialects of it. Knudtzon suggests that the two peoples may have received different names from the city governors of Palestine because they penetrated into the land from different directions, or at different times, or for both reasons.[1] This may be so,

[1] Knudtzon, p. 52 : " Die Ḫabiru und die (SA.)GAZ-Leute können nun auch sehr gut Stammesgenossen gewesen sein, welche von der Landesbevölkerung verschiedene Namen erhalten haben, etwa weil sie zu verschiedenen Zeiten oder in verschiedene Gegenden eingedrungen sind, oder aus beiden Gründen."

but more probably it was because the term Ḫabiru was particularly connected in Abdi-Ḫiba's mind with that section of the Hebrew race which had been in Egypt. They were the section within easiest reach of him, and of whom he must have heard the oftenest; and they were also the nearest and best known to the Pharaoh. Both to Abdi-Ḫiba and the Pharaoh they were *the* Ḫabiru, in contradistinction to others.

We have seen that there was probably an alliance between Joshua and the SA-GAZ to invade the central regions. This opens up a still larger conception, *viz.* Was there some previous arrangement between the whole Ḫabiru forces and their SA-GAZ kinsmen in the Syrian desert to attack Canaan together and about the same time, the one section from the north and the other from the south? There was, as we have said, a great Semitic movement at this time from all sides to press into Canaan, and the Israelite invasion thus becomes simply a part of this widespread movement. Looked at in this light the conquest, as depicted in the Biblical records, appears more reasonable and understandable than if it had been an isolated event from Kadesh-Barnea. Thus, Professor Peet says: "Is it not possible that the Hebrews under Joshua, after reaching the east of the Jordan, combined with other elements of allied race in a united attack on the whole of Syria-Palestine, the Joshua-group forming the southern wing of this huge immigration?"[1] There is a second view, however, which may be more probable, *viz.* that the Ḫabiru at Kadesh-Barnea, hearing that their SA-GAZ kinsmen in the Syrian desert were invading Canaan and capturing its strongholds, resolved to seize the opportunity for which they had so long waited and to enter the land also. This view seems the correct one. It still makes the Israelite conquest part of the great Semitic movement from all sides, and accords with the fact that the letters regarding the SA-GAZ are somewhat earlier in date than those of Abdi-Ḫiba.

[1] *Egypt and the Old Testament*, p. 119.

CHAPTER XI

BIBLICAL CHRONOLOGY

THE evidence adduced has shown that the entry of the Israelites into Canaan is identical with that of the Ḫabiru in the Amarna Letters, and that the Exodus must have taken place about 1445 B.C. How does the date thus arrived at from external sources agree with Biblical chronology on the subject? In reply, it may be said that it accords remarkably well with it, a fact which furnishes an additional argument in favour of the theory. In saying this, we are not to be understood as laying any special emphasis on Biblical chronology, especially of the pre-monarchic period, which we admit to be largely artificial, belonging, as it undoubtedly does, to the post-exilic or latest stratum of the Old Testament. But the generality of Biblical critics, without assigning to it more importance than it possesses, acknowledge at any rate that it gives some reasonable indication, though only in round numbers, of the time at which certain great events happened. We cannot reject the Biblical chronological system in its entirety. It contains at least trustworthy material, not unlike what we find in all ancient historical works, such as those of Herodotus or Berosus. With the mass of authentic external evidence that we possess at the present day, it is possible to disentangle the probable from the improbable, and the reliable from the doubtful or inaccurate.

The old attempts to form some comprehensive scheme of Biblical chronology, founded mainly on the Hebrew records, are gone for ever. Such was the scheme of Julius Africanus, who reckoned 5500 years from the Creation to the Birth of Christ, that of Eusebius, who made all his dates dependent on an era of Abraham, and that of Ussher (published in 1650–54), which found its way into the margin of the Old Testament, and which allowed 4000 years between the Creation and the Birth of Christ, on the fanciful idea that the world would last 6000 years, *viz.* 2000 before the Law, 2000 under it, and 2000 under the Messiah. Such schemes were artificial, ambiguous, and untrustworthy. Within recent years, however, real progress has been made in fixing accurate dates for certain Biblical events, and thus solving some difficult problems. This is due to the large accumulation of ancient historical and archæological material at our disposal now. Sometimes, no doubt, these sources of information conflict with one another, and it is difficult to decide between them, but on the whole finality is being attained on certain points.

An examination of the Biblical chronology before the days of Solomon shows that, while it is not lacking in precision, it is chiefly an artificial system, often inconsistent with the narratives in which it is found, and the result of complicated editorial processes extending to post-exilic times. Its peculiar character is due to the old Jewish practice of dating periods and historical events by the number of 'generations,' in much the same way as the Greeks made use of their early pedigrees. This is obviously a very inaccurate method; for a 'generation,' whatever signification we put upon it, may vary, and genealogical lists may have names interpolated or withdrawn in the course of the ages. It is a very rudimentary though elaborate system, originating in the simple life of the early Hebrew families. But it is not to be despised on that account as utterly wanting in truth. It is not unlikely that there was some kind of synchronism between Palestinian and Egyptian records,[1] as seems evident from the statement (Num. xiii. 32) that Hebron was built seven years before Zoan (Tanis) in Egypt; and there are other evidences that the Biblical chronology has trustworthy elements.

In connection with our subject, let us examine Biblical chronology from the Exodus to the monarchy. In 1 Kings vi. 1 we are told that 480 years elapsed between the Exodus

[1] Cf. S. A. Cook, *Cambridge Ancient History*, i. pp. 156 ff.

and the foundation of Solomon's temple in his fourth year. We shall discuss this statement directly—meantime let us discover the date of the latter event. We are not dependent on Biblical chronology for it: we can fix it astronomically from Assyrian inscriptions. These inscriptions are dated by the Assyrian Canon or calendar (the *limmu* lists), every year of which bears the name of an Assyrian officer, a sort of 'eponym.' This calendar exists in several copies, all consistent with each other, and so far as yet found covers the period from 893 B.C. (during the reign of Adad-nirari II.) to about 650 B.C. (during the reign of Ashurbanipal). The date of all the years is determined from the mention of a solar total eclipse which is stated to have occurred in the ninth year of Ashur-dan, in the eponymate of Bur-sagale of the city of Gozan, in the month of Sivan. Astronomers have discovered that this eclipse, visible at Nineveh, occurred on June 15, 763 B.C. By means of this authentic guide it is easy to determine all the dates in the Assyrian Canon. In this way the date of the battle of Karkar, at which 'Ahabbu Sir'lai' (presumably Ahab, king of Israel) was present in his twenty-first year, in alliance with Hadad-idri of Damascus (the Ben-hadad II. of 1 Kings xx. 33), and at which this confederation of kings was defeated by Shalmaneser III., has been accurately fixed at 854 B.C.; and if we reckon backward from this date by lengths of reigns, the documentary evidence for which is partly contemporary and therefore sufficiently trustworthy, we arrive at 970 B.C. for the accession of Solomon and 966 B.C. for the foundation of the temple in his fourth year.

By the other method, the purely Biblical one, we reach almost the same figure, if we adopt the synchronistic system of calculation, which is the best Biblical one for this period. In 1 and 2 Kings we have a complete list of the monarchs of Judah and Israel, and the length of their reigns from Solomon's time onward. As the length, however, of each reign is dated by the year of the contemporaneous king in the other kingdom, and there are thus many cross-reckonings and overlappings to be taken into account in adding the reigns together, a careful system of synchronisms is necessary before accuracy can be obtained. By this method it is found that 243 years elapsed between the foundation of Solomon's temple and the fall of Samaria, which latter event is known from the Assyrian calendar to have occurred in 722 B.C. This makes the date of the former event 965 B.C., being a difference of only one year from the result obtained by the first method. If we remember that under either method we have to assume the correctness of the round number of forty years for Solomon's reign, and that round numbers have usually been found to be excessive in such cases, we can see that even if the date were brought down a year or two it might not be incorrect.

Taking 965 B.C., however, as the date of the foundation of the temple, and adding the 480 years which are stated to have intervened from the Exodus, we obtain the date 1445 B.C. as the Biblical one for the Exodus. This date accords with the theory we are advocating, making the Israelites identical with the Ḫabiru of the Amarna Letters and strengthening our argument considerably. It is clear that both Egyptian and Biblical records point to the same date.

The statement, of course, in 1 Kings vi. 1 as to 480 years intervening has been the subject of keen controversy. Grave doubts have been urged against the genuineness of the text, especially by the advocates of the late-date theory, who naturally find it to conflict with their views. For one thing, attention is drawn to the fact that the Septuagint reads 440 instead of 480, a discrepancy which seems suspicious and argues some amount of incertitude. But this is a point that need occasion no difficulty when we reflect that in volume iii. of the valuable works of Constantine Oikonomos no less than 130 pages are devoted to the differences of chronology between the Septuagint and the Hebrew text of the Old Testament. Any one who knows the history of the Septuagint will understand this. The Septuagint version of 1 Kings, for example, is expressly cited in still existing documents as having its source in the Hexapla, the first Greek Polyglot Bible, put together by Origen with the object of recovering the original text of the Septuagint. But Origen could not possibly have produced an authentic Septuagint version by the unsatisfactory method he adopted. He used the Hebrew Manuscripts that were at his disposal (where he got them we do not know), along with the Greek versions of Aquila, Symmachus, and Theodotion, but he started with the false conception that the original text of the Septuagint must be that which coincided most nearly with the current Hebrew text. Indeed, the result of his labours has been to hinder rather than promote the recovery of the genuine Septuagint. The situation was rendered worse after his time. His followers, Pamphilus and Eusebius, made careful copies of the Septuagint column, placing on the margins the most notable various renderings from the other versions; but later copyists in their thoughtlessness completely neglected the whole of Origen's critical marks, thus producing *krypto*-Hexaplaric copies and spoiling the value of the Septuagint. The copy for 1 and 2 Kings in the Codex Alexandrinus is unfortunately of this nature.

It is obvious from this that the Septuagint of 1 Kings vi. 1 cannot be regarded as an original Septuagintal text, seeing that the principles on which Origen chose his version were so unsatisfactory. Where our Authorized Version has 480 and the Septuagint 440, the former has every chance of being the correct figure. It is found, moreover, in Aquila, Symmachus, and the other Greek versions, as well as in the Syriac Peshitta, believed by many scholars to be one of the oldest versions of the Bible.[1]

Most scholars are agreed on this point, but some, especially those who uphold the later date of the Exodus, lay weight on the view that the "480 years" is a very late addition or interpolation, probably inserted in post-exilic times by some redactor.[2] There may be some truth in this. We know that the Book of Kings, though edited for the first time prior to the destruction of Jerusalem in 586 B.C., was not finally completed until some time after Jehoiachin's death (which must have taken place after 561 B.C., the year of his release from captivity); and the book no doubt underwent still later revision in post-

[1] Cf. Köhler, *Bib. Gesch.*, i. p. 242; ii. pp. 36, 39.

[2] So Burney, *Judges*, pp. l–liv; *Notes on the Hebrew Text of the Book of Kings*, pp. 58 f.

exilic times. Another point that seems to weigh against the figure is that it coincides with the 480 years from the foundation of Solomon's temple to the foundation of Zerubbabel's (536 B.C.) at the close of the Exile. This, of course, is not the case *actually*, for the second period, correctly estimated, amounts to only 429 years ; but the total lengths of the reigns mentioned in 'Kings' from Solomon's fourth year onward, together with fifty years of Captivity added (although the true length of the Captivity is quite uncertain),[1] make 480 years. The coincidence between the two periods, it must be admitted, cannot be accidental, and marks the Biblical chronology as artificial and the statement in 1 Kings vi. 1 as probably a post-exilic insertion. Of course, we must not overlook the possibility that the post-exilic redactor, finding perhaps that the lengths of some of the reigns had not been preserved, may have supplied them by conjecture (this seems borne out by the artificial and symmetrical nature of the figures), so as to make this second period in Israel's history exactly equal to the first. This would not only form a kind of chronological analogy similar to others in the history of Israel and of the world, but would be helpful to the memory. This view, however, which would leave the first period untouched and would imply that the statement of its length was in existence before the redactor's day, is considerably weakened by the fact that, according to the Jewish custom of reckoning, the figure 480 simply represents twelve generations of forty years each which were supposed to cover each of the two periods. By 'generation' here is not meant single successions in natural descent from father to son. The word *dôr* in the Old Testament (Hebrew דּוֹר, Arab. *dârum*), usually translated 'generation,' does not have this signification, though Greek γενεά frequently does, as well as our English word 'generation.' There is no likely instance of such usage, and such texts as Gen. xv. 16

[1] The usual reckoning of seventy years (Jer. xxv. 11 ff.; Zech. i. 12; etc.) is too long. According to Josephus (*Contra Apion.*, i. 21), the temple was desolate for fifty years, and this agrees with the accession of Cyrus which has been definitely fixed at 538–537 B.C., and the foundation of the new temple in 536 B.C. (Ezra iii.).

and Job xlii. 16 are incorrectly cited in favour of it. The word, as used by the Hebrew writers, has various meanings, but generally speaking signifies a *period of time* (περίοδος), either past or future,[1] and as such was commonly reckoned at about forty years. The Hebrew writers, in their zeal to conform to the number of the tribes and the frequent use of twelve in the Scriptures, came to regard twelve such generations or periods as intervening between the Exodus and Solomon's temple, and between Solomon's temple and Zerubbabel's.

Such a method of noting time was valueless, but its origin and development are easily accounted for. Reliable data for the earlier genealogical lists, especially those before Solomon, were not available, for during the pre-monarchic period lines of individual descent could not be carefully preserved. In the wilderness the nomadic conditions of Israel made family archives impossible, while in Canaan for several centuries the laws of inheritance were not sufficiently complicated to require their preservation. The only method of retaining them was by memory, but all the branches of a family tree could not be preserved in this way. Consequently, in the absence of sufficiently authentic records, the writers naturally fell back upon their own judgment, and chose the number of names, especially in the priestly genealogical lists, so as to fit in with the supposed chronological scheme of twelve generations. In doing so, they must naturally have omitted many links, and only recorded those names which, for some reason or other, they were best acquainted with, or which were traditionally renowned or the most deserving of remembrance, just as the genealogies of Christ recorded in the Gospels appear to have a form of great completeness and yet undoubtedly have certain links omitted. An examination of Eleazar's list (1 Chron. vi. 3–10) bears out what we have said. It contains 22 names,

[1] Cf. Isa. li. 8; Ps. x. 6 (margin); Ps. cii. 24; etc. Another Hebrew word *tôledhôth* (תּוֹלְדוֹת), also translated 'generation' in the Old Testament, generally means 'begetting,' from *yāladh* (יָלַד), 'to beget,' 'to bear children.' The Septuagint translates it by γένεσις. Cf. Gen. x. 32, xxv. 13; Ex. vi. 16, 19; 1 Chron. v. 7, vii. 2, 4, 9, viii. 28; etc. This word is only found in P, Ruth iv. 18, and Chronicles.

beginning with Eleazar, a son of Aaron, and ending with Jehozadak, who was carried away at the Babylonian Captivity (1 Chron. vi. 15); and it was manifestly intended, according to the compiler's view, to furnish a list of high priests from the settlement in Canaan up to the time of the Captivity.[1] Including Aaron's name, the number from the date of the Exodus is 23, and if we allow forty years or a supposed 'generation' (*dôr*) for each one, this gives $(40 \times 12) + (40 \times 11)$, which accords with the two periods of 480 years each, for the Captivity occurred in the eleventh generation of the second period. Hence, these 22 names seem chosen to accord exactly with the supposed chronological data; and this is still further evident from the statement expressly made (in verse 10) that Azariah, the thirteenth priest (including Aaron), ministered in Solomon's temple.[2] The list, it is easily seen, cannot be historically correct, but must on the whole be artificial.[3] It is not even in harmony with the statements made elsewhere in the historical books. The order of the priests appears incorrect, and there is no mention of the priestly line through Eli (1 Sam. xiv. 3, xxii. 10), nor of other priests such as Jehoiada, Zechariah, and Urijah, who are known to have existed. Other two instances of the same type of genealogy occur, where ten or eleven names are given between the Exodus and the earlier years of David, *viz.* the genealogy from Shimei to Asaph (1 Chron. vi. 39–43), containing eleven names, and that from Mahli to Ethan (1 Chron. vi. 44–47), containing ten. It is clear that all these lists were inserted as representing the well-developed notion of twelve generations of forty years each. Most Biblical scholars now accept this view as to the origin of the 480 years, though some of them think that originally the twelve generations from the Exodus to Solomon were really reckoned by assigning forty years each to the twelve great leaders, *viz.* Moses, Joshua, Othniel, Ehud,

[1] Cf. Professor E. L. Curtis, *Hastings' Dictionary*, ii. p. 123.

[2] Verse 10*b* must be transferred to 9*b*, according to Bertheau in *Kgf. Handb.*, 1873, Öttli in *Kgf. Komm.*, 1889, and Zöckler in *Lange's Commentary*, 1876.

[3] Cf. Kittel, *Sacred Books of the Old Testament*; Wellhausen, *Prolegomena to the History of Israel*, 1885; Curtis, *Hastings' Dictionary*, ii. p. 123.

Barak, Gideon, Jephthah, Samson, Eli, Samuel, Saul, and David.[1]

Looked at in this light, the figure 480 (40 × 12) in 1 Kings vi. 1 appears to be fictitious, or at least too artificial to be of much value. But, as Professor Luckenbill says in regard to such Biblical figures,[2] " Have we really disposed of them, when they are bracketed and declared late insertions in the text ? Where did the later writers get hold of them ? Out of their thumbs ? " Before we can quite discredit the statement as to 480 years, we must show reason why it may not have been regarded as a rough estimate at least, and we must show cause for doubting the preservation of such an estimate in Hebrew traditions or writings. Why did the redactors choose twelve priests, representing a period of forty years each ? Because they had already an estimate amounting to about 480 years. They filled it in with 12 × 40 years, but they had it to begin with. It is worth noting that the building of Solomon's temple marked a specially important epoch in Israel's history, and justified an exceptional reference to the birth or emancipation of the nation ; and it is unreasonable to think that the historians and prophets in preexilic times did not investigate the length of the period from the Exodus, and come to some conclusion regarding it. It is argued that there was no settled calendar or official registration of events during the early period, and that the condition of affairs was disorganized without any central authority. This is no doubt true, but state annalists, who certainly existed as early as the reign of David (cf. 2 Sam. viii. 16, xx. 25) and probably before his time, must surely have set themselves to compute the figure, approximately at least, from such chronological data as were available, and their conclusions would be contained in the sources open to later writers and redactors. There are, of course, chronological figures in the Book of Judges. According to the data in that book, the enumeration of the years of the judgeships, oppressions, and other events

[1] Burney, *Israel's Settlement in Canaan*, pp. 4 f. ; so also Driver in *Ency. Brit.* (article, " Bible "), although he prefers Deborah to Barak.

[2] *American Journal of Theology*, xxii. (1918), p. 39.

from the Exodus to Solomon amounts to over six hundred years; but as many of the figures are mere round numbers (usually excessive) and several of the events overlap each other, their summation could not have been intended to represent the actual length of the period. The author of 1 Kings vi. 1, whether he was the first writer of 'Kings' or a late redactor, must have had all the chronological details of the Book of Judges before him precisely as we have now, and yet he puts the figure at 480, showing that he must have had some other independent sources. It is admitted that he based his work on state and other records, and it would surely be remarkable if there was no calculation, though only of a rough and approximate nature, in any of them as to the important period from the Exodus to the founding of the temple.

Those who reject the statement of 1 Kings vi. 1 admit that, by taking the date 965 B.C. (Solomon's temple) + 480 + 430 (Israel's period in Egypt) + 215 (Patriarchal period), we reach an authentic date for Abraham's departure from Haran, *viz.* 2090 B.C., a date which would place his later years well within the reign of Hammurabi, in accordance with the tradition of Gen. xiv.[1] Yet these same scholars, while admitting that the exterior dates in this calculation, *viz.* 965 B.C. and 2090 B.C., are approximately correct, and that this period of 1125 years accurately represents the time between a date in Solomon's reign and one quite close to Hammurabi's, do not accept the correctness of the 480 years or of the other sectional periods within the external limits.[2] Some Jewish chronologist, they tell us, who lived in Babylon during the Captivity and probably had access to Babylonian sources, would have no difficulty in going back to Hammurabi's reign, owing to the accuracy with which the Babylonian officials preserved their chronological data, but he would be unable to secure any information about the intervening periods. This view of the matter, however,

[1] The date of Hammurabi's reign, according to latest discoveries, is discussed on p. 221. For Israel's period in Egypt, cf. Ex. xii. 40; and for the Patriarchal period, Gen. xii. 4, xxi. 5, xxv. 26, xlvii. 9.

[2] So Burney, *Israel's Settlement in Canaan*, p. 90; and others.

overlooks the fact that in Israel's own state records or annals there must have been sufficient information, traditional at least, for fixing approximately the intervening periods, especially the more recent ones, and any capable redactor, even though post-exilic, who set himself to the task would be able to produce a sufficiently trustworthy figure. There are many Egyptologists, strange to say, such as Petrie,[1] who accept the statement of the priestly redactor (P) as to the 430 years for the 'sojourn' in Egypt, but reject the statement as to the 480 years which followed, though this later period was several centuries nearer the age of the redactor. They reject it evidently because it conflicts with their theory of an Exodus in the reign of Merenptah. To such inconsistencies does this theory lead!

The fact that 965 + 480 years take us back to the Ḫabiru invasion (after deducting the wilderness period) is surely a very significant thing, and points to the figure 480 being at least roughly or approximately correct. We are not upholding the perfect accuracy of the figure. The correct number may have been only 475 or thereabouts, and the fondness of the Hebrew historians for the figure twelve may have led them to put it roughly at 480. But that there is an element of correctness in it is not to be doubted. Otherwise, it would certainly be a most remarkable coincidence that the Old Testament records should point to about 1400 B.C. as the date of the Israelite entry into the land, and that we should read in the Amarna Tablets of a powerful Hebrew invasion at this very time. Hommel, who had been an upholder of the late-date theory, abandoned it, principally on this chronological ground, and adopted the theory we are advocating.[2]

One other point requires to be stated here. What we have said as to the origin of the three priestly genealogical lists shows that these cannot be taken as containing twelve generations in natural descent from father to son. Several links are

[1] *Egypt and Israel*, p. 37.

[2] Orr, *Problem of the Old Testament*, p. 422, n. 2, p. 424, n. 2. Hommel gives the reasons for his change of view in the *Expository Times*, February 1899. He had advocated the later-date view in his *Ancient Hebrew Tradition*.

omitted. Indeed, we know that there were far more than twelve such generations from the Exodus to Solomon.[1] In 1 Chron. vi. 33–37 there are no less than eighteen given between Korah, who was the head of a family at the Exodus (Ex. vi. 21), and Heman, who was the head of a family in the earlier years of David (1 Chron. xv. 17). This would imply about twenty up to the founding of Solomon's temple. It follows that Petrie and others, who base one of their main arguments for the late-date theory on the existence of twelve generations in natural descent from the Exodus to Solomon, or ten up to the earlier years of David,[2] and Weigall and others who do the same for their Akhenaten theory,[3] are building upon false premises. Petrie, for instance, on this erroneous basis, has no difficulty in reducing the period in question from 480 years to 210, and in this way placing the Exodus as late as 1220 B.C., during the reign of Merenptah (according to his dating of that reign). He also falls into the error of taking the low figure of 21 for a 'generation,' whereas the *average* length of the period representing the age of a father at the birth of his first-born son (*i.e.* the length of a generation in natural descent) is more than this. Some, indeed, would reckon the average from about 30 to 33 years, which was the usual significance of the word 'generation' in Greek (γενεά), as it is in English. "Three generations of men make a hundred years," says Herodotus.[4] Besides, the priestly lists, on which Petrie bases his argument, are not necessarily those of eldest sons. Eleazar, for instance, who follows Aaron, was his third son. The preference which existed in early times for making first-born sons priests can hardly at any time have been strictly carried out in practice. Other Egyptologists fall into the same error as Petrie, and found most important theories upon this idea of twelve generations. For any one to do this because twelve names happen to be mentioned

[1] Cf. Kessler, *Chronologia judicum et primorum regnum*, 1882, p. 12.

[2] *Egypt and Israel*, pp. 55 f.

[3] *Tutankhamen and Other Essays*, pp. 90 ff.

[4] ii. 142, *et al.*; cf. also Heraclit., in *Plut. def. orac.*, c. 11; Thayer-Grimm, *New Testament Lexicon*, *sub* γενεά.

or implied in two or three cases in the Book of Chronicles is to misunderstand entirely the nature of these genealogies.

Something requires to be said about the chronology of the Book of Judges, which seems to conflict with the statement in 'Kings.' If the lengths of the judgeships, oppressions, and peaceful periods mentioned in 'Judges' be regarded as consecutive, and if we add to them the 'forty years' of sojourn, and the other events which fall into the period between the Exodus and the founding of Solomon's temple, we reach a total, as already mentioned, of over 600 years. The entire period may be seen in detail as follows:

The sojourn in the wilderness	40	years.
The conquest under Joshua.	x	"
Oppression under Cushan-Rishathaim (Judg. iii. 8)	8	"
Deliverance by Othniel (Judg. iii. 11), peace for .	40	"
Oppression under Eglon (Judg. iii. 14)	18	"
Deliverance by Ehud (Judg. iii. 30), peace for .	80	"
Oppression under Jabin (Judg. iv. 3)	20	"
Deliverance by Deborah (Judg. v. 31), peace for .	40	"
Oppression under Midian (Judg. vi. 1)	7	"
Deliverance by Gideon (Judg. viii. 28), peace for .	40	"
Abimelech's reign (Judg. ix. 22)	3	"
Tola's judgeship (Judg. x. 2)	23	"
Jair's judgeship (Judg. x. 3)	22	"
Oppression under Ammon (Judg. x. 8)	18	"
Jephthah's judgeship (Judg. xii. 7)	6	"
Ibzan's judgeship (Judg. xii. 9)	7	"
Elon's judgeship (Judg. xii. 11)	10	"
Abdon's judgeship (Judg. xii. 14).	8	"
Oppression under the Philistines (Judg. xiii. 1) .	40	"
Samson's judgeship (Judg. xv. 20, xvi. 31) . .	20	"
Eli's judgeship (1 Sam. iv. 18)	40	"
Samuel's judgeship (1 Sam. vii. 2)	y	"
Saul's reign	z	"
David's reign (1 Kings ii. 11)	40	"
Part of Solomon's reign (1 Kings vi. 1) . . .	4	"
Total	$534+x+y+z$	

Various figures have been suggested for the unknown periods, x, y, z. For x (the Conquest), we must include not only the time of the Conquest proper, but also some additional years, for we are informed (Josh. xxiv. 31) that Israel remained faithful all the days of the elders that outlived Joshua,[1] and that the oppression under Cushan-Rishathaim only began when apostasy took place (Josh. iii. 7 f.). Burney, as already stated, puts the Conquest alone at 50 years, but 35 is a much more likely figure for the Conquest and eldership combined. For *y* (Samuel's judgeship), a period of 20 years is generally assigned (1 Sam. vii. 2), on the ground that his administration continued so long as the people remained faithful to Yahweh, and ceased on their choosing a king. For *z* (Saul's reign), some scholars assign 40 years, but Professor Welch has pointed out [2] that this would make Saul about 80 years of age when he fought at Mount Gilboa, an idea which it is impossible to accept. The length given by Josephus,[3] *viz.* 20 years, seems far more probable. All this adds 75 years to the above list, making a total of 609 years [4] instead of 480.

Nöldeke, Moore, Budde, and others attempt to explain this excessive number by deducting the years of oppression and usurpation, amounting to 114, and making two or three changes on the doubtful figures.[5] In this way they reduce the total to 480. They hold the view that it was customary in Oriental chronologies not to count years of oppression or usurpation, these being included in the years of rest under lawful rule. This custom, however, was by no means general, and it is doubtful whether the writer or editor of 'Judges' had such an idea in his mind. The form of his narrative is clearly against such an exegesis. It forbids us, for example, reckoning the 8 years of Cushan-Rishathaim's foreign domination into the 40 years of peace under Othniel, for the latter period could only begin

[1] According to the Hebrew (literally), 'lengthened out their days after Joshua' (הֶאֱרִיכוּ יָמִים אַחֲרֵי יְהוֹשֻׁעַ).

[2] *Hastings' Dictionary*, iv. p. 415*a*.

[3] *Ant.* x. viii. 4; vi. xiv. 9.

[4] This figure comes very close to that of Josephus (*Contra Apion.*, ii. 2), who makes it 612.

[5] Nöldeke, *Untersuchungen zur Kritik des A.T.*, 1869, pp. 173 ff.; Moore, *Judges*, p. xli f.; Budde, *Kürzer Hdcomm.*, 1897, p. xviii.

when the foreign yoke was shaken off. In the same way, the 7 years of invasion by the Midianites cannot be reckoned into the 40 years under the watchful rule of Gideon, during which the Midianites could not lift up their heads. The correct explanation of the excessive number is not to be found in this way, but rather in the twofold fact that the list contains many round numbers, which being conjectural are generally over the mark, and that several of the oppressions and judgeships are synchronistic or overlap.

The fact of the round numbers, especially the frequent recurring 40, at once raises suspicion, and requires the deduction of many years from the total. Thus, we have 40 years representing the intervals of peace after the victories of Othniel, Barak, and Gideon, as well as the intervals of the oppression by the Philistines, and the judgeship of Eli.[1] Twice 40 is given for the peace which supervened after the Moabite oppression, and half 40 for the oppression by Jabin and for the judgeship of Samson. Nowhere in the Old Testament do round numbers like these occur with such frequency as in the chronology of 'Judges' and 'Samuel.' It is reminiscent of the ancient Babylonian method of reckoning, in which there was the tendency to use the figure 60, which was a unit in the Sumerian system. Such round numbers, indeed, were common in early records among all nations; and after all due allowance has been made for exceptions, it is evident that they can only be taken in an approximate sense. Even at the present day in Persia, 'forty years' means nothing more than 'many years,' and there what we call the *centipede* (Ger. *tausendfuss*) is known as the 'forty-foot.'[2] Among the Arabs the number forty is very frequently employed in the same indefinite sense; and among modern

[1] The 40 years given for the reign of David is probably not a round number, for a number can hardly be regarded as round, when portions of time are enumerated which make it up exactly. This is the case with David's reign, which occupied 7+33 years (2 Sam. v. 5). Cf. the τεσσαράκοντα ἔτεα of the reign of Battos of Cyrene (Herod. iv. pp. 157 ff.), which were composed of 2+6+32 years, and which have been wrongly regarded by some people (Hirzel included) as a round number.

[2] Cf. König, *Hastings' Dictionary*, iii. p. 563*b*.

Turks, too, the number 40 in proper names is often used, according to Sir W. Ramsay, with little or no reference to its numerical value.[1] The psychological origin of the employment of all such round numbers leads to exaggeration, and hence they are usually excessive. The inscription on the Moabite Stone (*c.* 850 B.C.) supplies an interesting example of this, for there the occupation of Mehēdeba during Omri's reign and half of his son Ahab's reign is represented as 40 years,[2] whereas we know (1 Kings xvi. 23, 29) that Omri only reigned 12 years and Ahab 22, so that the whole period of occupation could only have been 23 years at the most. All this goes to show that the round numbers in the above list tend to the excessive side, and that on this account alone a reasonable deduction falls to be made from the total.

Further, it is clear from the narratives in 'Judges' that in some cases the judgeships and oppressions overlap, and in others they run parallel to one another, being events that were going on in different parts of Canaan at one and the same time. It is here that Nöldeke, Moore, and similar chronologists principally fail in their schemes: they make the various events consecutive, overlooking the fact that they are largely synchronistic. For a century or two after the Israelites entered Canaan, the leaders could not possibly exercise jurisdiction over the people as a whole, for Israel did not form a corporate unity of twelve tribes till long afterwards. There was bound to be a large amount of disorganization and even disunion among the tribes, and the judges mentioned can only be regarded as local and not successive rulers over all Israel. This is borne out by some of the statements made. We read, for instance (Judg. x. 7), that "He (Yahweh) sold them into the hand of the Philistines, and into the hand of the children of Ammon," which implies that the oppression of the Ammonites (x. 8 ff., xi. 4 ff.),

[1] *Thousand and One Churches*, p. 6.

[2] "So Omri obtained possession of the land of Mehēdeba, and (one) dwelt therein during his days and half the days of his son, forty years." For the original, see Smend and Socin's copy, and Driver's *Notes on the Hebrew Text of the Books of Samuel*, Appendix to Introduction, pp. lxxxvi ff.

which occupied 18 years, and that of the Philistines (xiii. 1 ff.), which covered 40 years, occurred at the same time. Again, it is clear (from Judg. xv. 20) that the judgeship of Samson (20 years) was contemporaneous with the oppression of the Philistines. Evidence thus goes to show that the oppressions and judgeships were in most cases, if not in all, merely local and not general. The eastern tribes, for example, may have been suffering from the oppression of Eglon, king of Moab, about the same time that the western tribes were under the heel of the Philistines; and some judge in the far north, such as Elon, who belonged to the tribe of Zebulun there (Judg. xii. 11), may have been exercising authority over the tribes in that region at the time that some other judge in the far south, such as Ibzan, who belonged to the tribe of Judah (Judg. xii. 8), was ruling over the people in the southern district.[1] M. Vernes truly says that the editor of the Book of Judges has placed "bout à bout des évènements qui ne s'enchaînent en aucune façon."[2] Petrie has endeavoured to frame a scheme whereby the events are divided up among three districts, *viz.* north, east, and west, allowing a period of 118 years to the north, 122 to the east, and 121 to the west;[3] and other scholars have similar schemes, but dividing the events into more groups than three. The fault of all such schemes, however, is that they are forced and artificial, giving an idea of far greater chronological exactitude than can be possible. The round numbers, too, are taken at their exact arithmetical value, and there are other defects. It is obvious to any casual reader of 'Judges' that the events, as we have them, cannot be forced into an artificial scheme. The book is a mere collection of episodes, some of them no doubt consecutive, but others parallel with each other or overlapping each other, and with the meagre facts at our disposal a strict scheme of chronology cannot be drawn from the book. All that can be done is to allow for the synchronisms and overlappings by making, as in the case of round numbers,

[1] Cf. Burney, *Judges*, p. liii.

[2] *Précis d'histoire juive*, 1889, p. 199.

[3] *Egypt and Israel*, p. 55.

a general deduction from the total. It is easy to see that in this way the figure 609 may be reduced without any hesitation to 480, and that the apparent discrepancy is of no importance.

It will be seen that the upholders of the late-date theory of the Exodus, most of whom fix it about 1220 B.C. or later, involve themselves in serious and quite insuperable chronological difficulties. According to their theory, the period between the Exodus and the foundation of the temple in 965 B.C. is reduced to about 250 years, or little more than half of the 480. Is it likely that the Hebrew writer or redactor, whatever plan he went on, would have made such a large error? "It is worthy of note," says Professor Peet, "that if the Exodus took place under Merenptah, who came to the throne in 1225 B.C., then Hebrew tradition has made an error of about 230 years, or nearly half the whole figure, an error which, though not inconceivable in dealing with very remote events, is a little unlikely in dealing with comparatively recent times."[1] It means that the period of the wanderings, the Conquest, the oppressions and judgeships, and the reigns of Saul and David are condensed into a most inadequate number of years. The theory of Eerdmans, who places the Exodus later still, at about 1130 B.C., is even worse, for all the events have to be crowded into a period of 165 years. Looking at matters in this way, the late-date theory will not bear investigation from the chronological point of view, any more than from others.

In regard to the period of Israel's residence in Egypt, there seems to be no reason why we should not accept the figure of 430 years (Ex. xii. 40 (P)) as genuine. It is not a multiple of twelve or forty at least, or a round number, and though it may belong, as some critics think, to the latest stratum of the narrative, this does not discredit it. The idea that it is based on a supposed absurdity—the assumption of four generations of one hundred years each—is partly traceable to the genealogical lists, where only four 'generations' from father to son are given

[1] *Egypt and the Old Testament*, p. 112.

as existing from Joseph to Moses, or five to Joshua. Thus, we have :

(Ex. vi. 16–20; Num. xxvi. 59).	(Ex. vi. 16–21; Num. xiv. 1).	(Ex. vi. 16–21; Lev. x. 4).	(Josh. vii. 1).	(Ex. vi. 14; Num. xxvi. 7–9).
Levi	Levi	Levi	Judah	Reuben
Kohath	Kohath	Kohath	Zerah	Pallu
Amram	Izhar	Uzziel	Zabdi	Eliab
Moses	Korah	Mishael	Carmi	Dathan
			Achan	

But why should these 'generations' not have extended to about one hundred years each ? They were not generations in single succession, any more than the twelve were from the Exodus to Solomon. There were far more descents in the English sense during this period, as we know from the genealogies of the daughters of Zelophehad (Num. xxvii. 1) and of Joshua (1 Chron. vii. 23–27). Any one who is acquainted with Oriental expressions knows that 'son of' generally signifies 'descendant of' or 'of the house of,' just as 'father' frequently means 'forefather.' [1] The members of any guild or clan are frequently referred to as 'sons' (cf., for example, the 'sons' of Jeduthun). We also read that Gilead begat Jephthah (Judg. xi. 1), by which is simply meant that the latter belonged to the Gilead tribe (as is evident from vers. 1*a*, 7). The terms 'son' and 'father' are often used in the Old Testament in a very wide sense, with the result that an indefinite number of links (unimportant ones) in the genealogies are omitted—a fact for which we have positive evidence in the most important of all genealogies, that of Christ, as well as in that of Ezra and others. Only four connecting links are given in the case under consideration, and these are simply meant to represent four well-known traditional stages or periods of time in the long descent.

The idea of four generations is also traceable to Gen. xv. 16 (J), where Abraham is informed that his seed would be oppressed in a foreign land for 400 years, but would return to Canaan in

[1] Ashur-uballit in a letter (Knudtzon, No. 16) calls Ashur-nadin-aḫi his 'father,' but we know his father was Erba-Adad, and Ashur-nadin-aḫi was his forefather. Cf. Hall, *Ancient History*, p. 16 n.

"the fourth generation." The meaning of this statement, however, which has been the subject of much discussion, is apparent. The 400 years, being a round number, may be taken without any objection as equivalent to the 430, and the four 'generations' are not to be taken here, any more than in the genealogical lists, as referring to single successions, but simply as epochs or periods of time (the word used is *dôr*),[1] varying in length, and each one no doubt connected with some particular descendant or great leader. The passage may be paraphrased, "They shall be afflicted for about 400 years, and in the fourth *dôr* or great epoch [that of Moses] they shall return." While, therefore, the statement of 430 years in Exodus stands by itself on its own merits, independent of any artificial system of 'generations,' it is evident that even though we connect it in the writer's mind with such a system, there is good reason to accept the figure as approximately correct.[2]

The Septuagint and Samaritan versions of Ex. xii. 40 add the words "and in the land of Canaan," thus making the 430 years include the whole patriarchal period as well as the sojourn in Egypt; and as the former lasted 215 years according to Biblical chronology, the latter is therefore reduced to the remaining 215. But this reading is rejected by the majority of scholars of all schools. Not only do the most ancient Greek codices agree with our Hebrew text, but the Septuagint and Samaritan versions both place the inserted clause differently, thus revealing it as a gloss. The clause was apparently added in an effort to lessen the difficulty of the 'four generations.' There can be no doubt that at an early time some of the Jews who did not know better felt the difficulty of reconciling the 430 years with the genealogies, for if Levi were the grandfather of Moses on the mother's side through Jochebed, and separated

[1] Cf. γενεά in Col. i. 26, "hid from all ages and generations."

[2] It is wonderful what shifts some writers put themselves to, quite unnecessarily, in order to overcome the supposed difficulty of 'four generations.' Thus Eerdmans (*Expositor*, 1908, pp. 193 ff.), in finding it necessary to distinguish the 'Hebrews' from the 'Israelites,' dates the entrance of the former into Egypt about 1500 B.C. (so as to agree with the 400 years), and that of the latter about 1205 B.C. (to agree with the 'four generations')!

only by two descents on the father's (through Kohath and Amram), it was clear that a period of 430 years could not be accounted for, and hence their effort to remove the difficulty by the additional words. The reading was followed by Paul (Gal. iii. 17) and by many ancient Jewish and Christian authorities. It was not adopted, however, by Stephen (Acts vii. 6), nor consistently by Josephus. In one passage (*Ant.* ii. 15. 2) Josephus appears to follow it, but in others he distinctly asserts that the period of hardship in Egypt after the death of Joseph lasted 400 years (*Ant.* ii. 9. 1; *Wars of the Jews*, v. 9. 4). As Driver says, the Septuagint reading "cannot be the original text; not only has Israel's sojourn in Egypt alone to do with the present context, but until the birth of Jacob's sons there were no children of Israel to dwell in Canaan at all."[1]

Assuming the correctness then of the figure 430, and adding this number to 1445, we obtain a date about 1875 B.C. for the Israelites' entry into Egypt.[2] This would date the entry during the Hyksos period, according to the longer scheme of Egyptian chronology, or about a hundred years before it, according to the shorter scheme. The entry of Israelite tribes could have occurred most easily under the Hyksos, for these rulers were probably Semites themselves. Under these friendly 'shepherd-

[1] Driver, *Exodus*, p. 102.

[2] The well-known scene picturing the arrival of Hebrews in Egypt, which is taken from the tomb of Khnumhotep at Beni Hasan, is generally thought by some to represent the arrival of Abraham in Egypt. According to Dr. Hall's scheme of dating, it certainly comes near to that time (Abraham must have visited Egypt about 2070 B.C.). But the scene gives us a good idea of what the arrival of the Israelites would look like. It describes the coming of thirty-seven Syrians or Aamu, bearing green eye-paint, in the sixth year of Senusret II. of the XIIth Dynasty. The leader's name is Ibsha, the men are armed with spears, bows, and throwsticks, and are accompanied by baggage animals. Some of them have 'coats of many colours,' one is carrying a water-skin slung on his shoulder, and another is playing on a lyre. They are evidently men, women, and children of Hebrew race. The facial characteristics are totally un-Egyptian, and correspond to those of the Israelites. They seem to be coming to Egypt with presents or tribute; and when we read in the inscription that Ibsha brought some valuable eye-unguent to the chief of the land, we are reminded of Jacob's speech to his sons, "Carry down a present to the man" (Gen. xliii. 11).

kings,' the Israelites would be well received in Egypt, and placed in "the best of the land" (Goshen), as the Hebrew records testify (Gen. xlv. 17–20, xlvii. 6). According to George the Sincellus (ninth century A.D.) and other chronographers of his day, it was during the lengthy reign (61 years) of the Hyksos king, Aphophis (*i.e.* Apopi I.), in his seventeenth year, that the Israelites entered the land.[1] This date was probably arrived at, as Maspéro suggests,[2] by combining the Biblical 430 years with what was regarded as Egyptian data. Unfortunately, we have no means of determining the date of this king's reign. Petrie places him in the XVth Dynasty, from about 1898 to about 1837 B.C., being precisely the period within which, on our reckoning, the descent into Egypt took place; but other well-known Egyptologists, such as Hall and Breasted, who accept the shorter scheme of Hyksos rule, place him over a century later.[3] According to the shorter scheme of chronology, the Israelites would enter Egypt about one hundred years before the Hyksos invasion, and in such a case it is clear that they would give a ready welcome to these Semitic princes and would be encouraged to remain on during their friendly rule.

Biblical chronology assigns a period of 215 years from the "call of Abraham" (*i.e.* his departure from Haran) to the entry of the Israelites into Egypt.[4] This agrees with Babylonian data, for it places the former event about 2090 B.C., within or at least immediately before the reign of Hammurabi, who belonged to the first dynasty of Babylonian kings, and who has been identified with Amraphel of Gen. xiv., a contemporary of Abraham. That the two names are identical

[1] Edition Goar, p. 62: *ἐπὶ πᾶσι γὰρ συμπεφώνηται ὅτι ἐπὶ Ἀφώφεως ἦρξεν Ἰωσὴφ τῆς Αἰγύπτου.* Cf. also pp. 69, 107. On p. 107 the seventeenth year of Aphophis is mentioned.

[2] *Struggle of Nations*, p. 71.

[3] For an account of him, see Hall, *Ancient History*, pp. 215 ff.

[4] The 215 years are made up as follows: 25 till the birth of Isaac, 60 till that of Jacob, and 130 till Jacob's entry into Egypt (Gen. xii. 4, xxi. 5, xxv. 26, xlvii. 9). These are all statements by the priestly redactor, but without accepting the implication as to the ages of the patriarchs, there is nothing to hinder us accepting the total of 215 years as approximately correct for the whole period.

has been disputed by some critics, but the general consensus of scholarship is now in favour of the identity, which Schrader first pointed out in 1887.[1] King has shown that the name was also pronounced Ammurapi (without the initial ḫ) in Babylonia,[2] and several reasonable explanations have been given of the final *-el* in the Hebrew.[3] " On the whole," says Professor Peet, " it may be said that the identification is distinctly probable." [4] " There can be little doubt," says Dr. Hall, " that Amraphel is the historical Hammurabi, that Chedorlaʿomer is an Elamite Kudur-Lagamar whom we do not yet know from contemporary records, and that Tidʿal " king of the Goyyim " was a Hittite Dudḫaliya . . . whatever we may think of ' Arioch of Ellasar.' " [5]

There used to be much dubiety as to the date and length of Hammurabi's reign, but within recent years the Dutch astronomer Kugler, as well as Hommel, Langdon, and others have all made most careful investigations of the matter. Some time ago, the astronomer Kugler, by working out certain observations of the heliacal rising and setting of the planet Venus taken in the reign of king Ammi-zaduga, the tenth king of the First Babylonian Dynasty, and recorded on a cuneiform tablet, fixed the accession of this monarch at 1977 B.C. As the Baby-

[1] *Sitzungsberichte der Berliner Akademie*, 1887, p. 600.

[2] This arises from the fact that the ḫ represents the softer sound of the aspirate, corresponding to the softer sound of the Hebrew ע (Arab. ع, *'Ain*). This softer sound is represented in the Septuagint by only a light breathing and is sometimes omitted in the earliest manuscripts. Numerous instances of this ḫ being dropped in Hebrew are found in the Amarna Letters.

[3] Dr. Lindl, for instance, has called attention to the fact that the name is found written Hammurabi-ilu on a Babylonian contract tablet belonging to the period of the First Dynasty (Tablet, No. 657, *Das Priester und Beamtentum der altbabylonische Kontrakte*, 1913), though the name here is not that of the monarch. Cf. also Dhorme, *Revue Biblique*, 1908, p. 208, where an explanation of Hommel's is adopted, *viz. -bi*= *-pil* in the cuneiform : " Une lecture *-pil* au lieu de *-bi* a pu très bien donner naissance à la terminaison d'Amraphel. Le processus serait ; *Am-mu-ra-bi*, *Am-mu-ra-pil*, אַמְרָפֶל . . . L'auteur du chapitre xiv. de la Genèse a pu utiliser un original cunéiforme."

[4] *Egypt and the Old Testament*, p. 50.

[5] *Journ. of Egypt. Arch.*, ix. (1923), p. 253.

lonian lists place Hammurabi's accession 146 years earlier than that of Ammi-zaduga, he thus obtained for the former the date 2123 B.C. As Hammurabi is known to have reigned for 43 years, this would place him from 2123 to 2080 B.C. Professor Langdon, who has studied the matter carefully for many years, also reached a date according with Kugler's, but he has since lowered the dates of the whole dynasty by 56 years as a result of the Oxford prism [1] and evidence supplied by Dr. Fotheringham, the Oxford astronomer, who states that the year of Ammi-zaduga's accession could only have been 1921 B.C. Langdon's modification would thus place Hammurabi from 2067 to 2024 B.C. Some Assyriologists, especially the German ones, would prefer a lower date still. Thus, Weidner would lower Kugler's date by 168 years,[2] while Kugler himself would now reduce it by 176 years. But Langdon, on good grounds astronomical and historical, definitely rejects these much lower dates, as do also Professor Albright,[3] Waterman,[4] and others. Whichever view we adopt for Hammurabi's accession, whether 2123 or 2067 B.C., it will be seen that the date at which we have arrived for Abraham's leaving 'Ur of the Chaldees' (2090 B.C.) accords well with the fact that Hammurabi was a contemporary (Gen. xiv. 1). If we accept Langdon's calculation, Abraham's departure for Haran and Canaan would fall only twenty-three years before Hammurabi ascended the throne. This quite accords with Gen. xiv. 1, for the Biblical narrative implies that the Battle of the Nine Kings did not take place till many years after Abraham entered Canaan. He went down into Egypt and probably spent several years there before the battle took place. All this affords a strong confirmation of our theory of

[1] *Oxford Editions of Cuneiform Texts*, in the Weld-Blundell Collection of the Ashmolean Museum, vol. ii., *Historical Inscriptions, containing principally the chronological prism* (Oxford, 1923). This is a large prism, with eight columns of closely written chronological material which gives the entire Sumerian lists of dynasties before and after the Flood to the end of the Isin Dynasty in 2076 B.C. It is the most important document of its kind ever recovered in cuneiform literature.

[2] *Könige von Assyrien.*

[3] *Revue d'Assyriologie*, xviii.

[4] *American Journal of Semitic Languages and Literatures*, xxxix.

the date of the Exodus. It is certainly a very striking coincidence that, if we come forward 215 + 430 years from a point in or near Hammurabi's reign, and come back 480 years from the foundation of Solomon's temple, we reach practically the same point, 1445 B.C.

It is worth noting that the date of Hammurabi's reign involves the late-date theory of the Exodus in additional chronological difficulties. For if the Exodus did not take place till about 1220 B.C., and if we go back 430 + 215 years from that date, we find ourselves about 1865 B.C., over 150 years at least after the death of Hammurabi. In order to avoid this difficulty, Petrie and others, who admit the identity of Amraphel and Hammurabi, have had to extend the patriarchal period from the Biblical 215 years to 460.[1] No stretch of imagination, however, can harmonize Biblical data with such a long interval between Abraham and the descent into Egypt. It is clear that the later-date theory breaks down chronologically both in its forward direction (towards the founding of the temple) and in its backward direction (towards Hammurabi).

[1] *Egypt and Israel*, p. 38.

CHAPTER XII

MERENPTAH'S VICTORY STELE

THE conclusions at which we have arrived in the preceding chapters as to the probable date of the Exodus, and which are based on the Ḫabiru-SA-GAZ question and a consideration of Biblical chronology, find excellent confirmation in the great triumphal slab of Merenptah. This Pharaoh, who began to reign over Egypt about 1233 B.C., not only fought the Libyans and the pirates of the coast-lands, who tried to establish themselves in the Delta, but seems to have carried out or at least organized a campaign in Palestine. He refers to his numerous victories in an inscription on the back of a fine large black syenite stele, over 10 feet high and over 5 feet wide, which had originally been set up by Amenhotep III. of the previous dynasty to commemorate his buildings. Merenptah placed the fine block of syenite in his funerary temple wall at Thebes, turning its face inward; and on its polished back he inscribed the story of his victories. The date of the inscription is not later than the fifth year of Merenptah's reign (*i.e.* about 1228 B.C.). The stele, which was discovered by Flinders Petrie in 1896, contains a carved figure of the god Amūn at the top in the middle, with one of the king on each side of him, the goddess Mut being behind the king on the left, and the god Khonsu behind him on the right.[1] Below the carved figures is the lengthy Hymn of Victory, containing twenty-eight closely

[1] Cf. Petrie, *Contemporary Review*, May 1896, where an account of the discovery is given; *Six Temples at Thebes*, 1897; *History of Egypt*, iii. p. 114; Breasted, *Ancient Records of Egypt*, iii. 602 ff.; W. M. Müller, *Ammerkungen*; Naville, "Les dernières lignes de la Stèle mentionnant les Israëlites," *Recueil de Travaux*, xx. (1898); etc.

packed lines of inscription. The name 'Israel' is mentioned, though for the first and only time in Egyptian history, so far as existing discoveries have gone. It occurs in the latter part of the text, where other triumphs are enumerated besides that over the Libyans. The following are the sentences, in the order here given :

> "The kings are overthrown, saying 'Salām!'
> Not one holds up his head among the Nine Nations of the Bow.
> Wasted is Tehenu [Libya],
> Kheta [Hittite Land] is pacified,
> Pekanan [the Canaan] is captured with every evil circumstance,
> Ashkelon is carried captive,
> Gezer is taken,
> Yenoam is brought to naught,
> Israel is destroyed, its seed is not,
> Kharu [Palestine] has become as a widow [*khare*] for Egypt,
> All the lands together are at peace,
> Every one that is turbulent is bound by king Merenptah."

Ashkelon and Gezer are the two well-known Biblical cities in south Palestine, the former on the coast of Philistia, and the latter in the Shephelah. Yenoam is believed to have been east of Tyre. The determinative sign for 'land' accompanies the names Tehenu, Kheta, Ashkelon, Gezer, and Yenoam, but the determinative for 'people' is used with the name Israel (*Ysir'al*, cf. the Assyrian *Sir'il*), indicating that it denotes a people (the 'Israelites'), not a city or country.[1] The expression, "its seed is not," has been understood by Chapman, Griffith, Petrie, and many others to mean that Israel's *crops* were destroyed, but it does not necessarily have such a signification. It may refer to *posterity*, which is identical with 'seed' in nearly all languages. Breasted has pointed out that the expression is found five times elsewhere of conquered foes, and in some of these places at least the reference to 'crops' is out of the question. Ramesses III., for example, referring to

[1] For this reason alone, it cannot be meant for 'Jezreel,' as Sir Peter Renouf and others suggested at the time of the discovery. An Egyptian *s*, moreover, could not take the place of a Hebrew *z*.

the defeat of the 'sea-peoples' who endeavoured to invade Egypt during his reign, says, "Those who reached my border are desolated, their seed is not." Presumably in such a case the word cannot mean 'crops,' unless the invaders had been long enough in the land to plough and sow, and hence the expression in Merenptah's case may merely be a conventional one signifying the defeat and plundering of an enemy.[1]

The importance of the inscription, so far as we are here concerned, lies in the fact that Israel, or a large part of Israel, is here mentioned for the first time as being outside Egypt, and evidently in Palestine as a settled community. This has been a serious difficulty to the upholders of the late-date theory of the Exodus, for it is clear that if the Israelites left Egypt in Merenptah's own reign, and wandered in the desert for forty years or more, they could not have been settled in Palestine as early as the fifth year of his reign. The inscription, indeed, makes the late-date theory practically impossible. We have no real corroborative evidence for a Palestinian campaign by this Pharaoh. He may only be following the fashion of his age by assuming to himself the victories of his predecessors. If this be so, it only strengthens our argument by proving that the Israelites had been away from Goshen for a very long period. But in spite of Naville's view that there was no such campaign,[2] we think there cannot be any satisfactory reason to doubt the testimony of the stele that Egyptian forces in the reign of Merenptah had been in conflict with the Israelites somewhere in Palestine. The inscription does not imply that Merenptah

[1] Cf. Breasted, *Ancient Records*, iii. 604. As the line mentioning Israel is important, we give here a few of the various translations:

Breasted . "Israel is desolated, his seed is not."
Petrie . . "The people of Israel is spoiled, it has no corn."
Griffith . . "The people of Israel is laid waste, their crops are not."
Peet . . . "Israel is destroyed, its seed is not."
Naville . . "The Israelites are swept off, his seed is no more."
Maspéro. . "Le peuple d'Israël est rasé, et il n'y a plus de sa graine."
Spiegelberg . "Israel ist verwüstet und seine Saaten vernichtet."

[2] *Journ. of Egypt. Arch.*, 1915, pp. 195 ff.

himself was present in the campaign,[1] or that he was the conqueror himself, or indeed that he personally did anything to bring about the result. If he did, it is probable that according to the usual boastful method of commemorating the great deeds of the Pharaoh, there would have been some reference to the fact. Nor does the text state that the victory was achieved by the Egyptian home army, or by troops sent specially from Egypt. So far as we know, Israel's 'defeat' may have been inflicted by the Egyptian garrisons in Syria, or by native vassals of the Pharaoh, or even—which is not at all unlikely—by outside allies or other people incited by Egypt to the attack.[2] The essential fact for our present argument is that the Israelites, or the main body of them at least, are recognized in the inscription as being settled in Palestine by the time of Merenptah, a fact which conflicts directly with the late-date theory and confirms the one we are advocating.

The expression "Israel is destroyed, his seed is not," cannot be taken as representing Merenptah's own version of the Exodus. Strange to say, when the discovery of the stele was

[1] Breasted and others incline to believe that the Pharaoh was present. Breasted bases his view partly on the evidence of a campaign afforded by the day-book of a frontier official which is found on the blank backs of a papyrus (Anast. iii., plates vi. and v., *verso*), and which he regards as of importance "as showing that Merenptah in his third year was in Syria" (*Ancient Records*, iii. 271). The document is a record of letters which the official sent to various places by different messengers.

[2] The date would appear to coincide with the oppression of Israel by Midian, and if 'seed' be taken to mean 'crops,' the Biblical circumstances correspond (Judg. vi. 3–6, 11), "So it was, when Israel had sown, that the Midianites came up, and the Amalekites, and the children of the east . . . and destroyed the increase of the earth till thou come unto Gaza, and left no sustenance in Israel. . . . They came into the land to destroy it, and Israel was brought very low because of Midian." The same account tells us how Gideon tried to hide his wheat from the invaders. All this accords exactly with Merenptah's statement, "Israel is destroyed, his seed is not," and also with the determinative 'people,' which includes women and children as being involved. On the theory that the Exodus took place near the beginning of the reign of Amenhotep II., the invasion of Midian would appear to fall during the reign of Merenptah. This is significant, and it is not at all improbable that Merenptah's statement refers to this invasion, when Israel's seed is known to have been destroyed.

made, there were a few who regarded it in this light, considering the flight of the Israelites into the waterless desert to be equivalent, in Merenptah's mind, to their destruction. Deeper reflection, however, led them to see the improbability of this view. The mere fact that the name of Israel is mentioned in the midst of Palestinian cities and localities, thus forming an element in the same group with them, is proof that the expression has nothing to do with the departure of Israel from Egypt.[1] Nor can it be taken as referring retrospectively to the repressive measures of Pharaoh in Egypt prior to the Exodus (as mentioned in Ex. i.), though several scholars took this view at the time of the discovery.[2] Thus, Sayce refers it to the destruction of the Israelitish males by Ramesses II., so that "no seed was left" to the people. "The expression used in regard to them [the Israelites]," he says, "is a most remarkable parallel to what we read in Ex. i. 10–22."[3] Such an interpretation, in addition to being what Professor Orr has called "a harmonistic makeshift,"[4] overlooks the fact that the edicts ordering the slaying of the male children (Ex. i. 16, 22) must have been nearly a century old at the time of Israel's departure from Egypt. They must also have been for a long time practically inoperative, otherwise there could not have been a younger generation existing at the time of the Exodus, as there certainly was, nor any large body of people at all to form the Israelite nation. Whichever way we look at the phrase, "Israel is destroyed, his seed is not," it cannot be regarded as upholding the assumption that the Exodus took place as late as Merenptah's reign, but goes to prove that it happened much

[1] The view that the inscription refers to the Exodus is still held by some. Sir Hanbury Brown, K.C.M.G., upholds the suggestion in the *Journ. of Egypt. Arch.*, 1917, pp. 6 ff., but the arguments advanced are far from convincing. He adopts the mistaken idea (see next page) that the name Israel, being accompanied by the determinative signifying a 'people,' implies that they had no "fixed and recognized habitation of their own," and overlooks the fact that the name occurs in a group of Palestinian references.

[2] *Expository Times*, July–September 1896; Dr. Sellin, *Neue Kirchzeitschrift*, No. 6.

[3] *Expository Times*, September 1896.

[4] *Expositor*, 1897, p. 161.

earlier. The obvious implication is that Israel was already living in Palestine at the beginning of this Pharaoh's reign, and along with other tribes there had come into hostile contact with Egyptian forces of some kind.

It is said by some that the name 'Israel,' being accompanied by the determinative denoting a people, not a country, must be taken as indicating a non-territorial or *roaming* Israel, *i.e.* it must refer to the time when the Israelites were still 'wandering' in the wilderness. This is the view adopted by those who place the Exodus a few years prior to the date of the stele.[1] To such desperate shifts are some of the late-date theorists driven! The determinative undoubtedly represents a people, but why 'roaming'? This is adding an idea not contained in the text. All that the determinative implies is that the Israelites could not yet be described by any territorial name, as the Libyans could be who were known to dwell in Tehenu, or the Canaanites who inhabited Canaan, or the Hittites who were in Kheta; and consequently the determinative for 'people' was the only one that could be rightly used of them. This fact, moreover, accords with the history of the Israelites for some time after their entry into Palestine. Their conquest of the land was a very gradual process. For the first one or two centuries they were compelled in many parts to settle down on sufferance alongside the Canaanites, without actually possessing much territory or giving a name to it. It was not until they had strengthened their hold by racial vigour and increase of families that they eventually gained superiority. For many ages they had no king or national organization, and there was no 'Israel-land' or other territorial name connected with them, to which the determinative signifying 'land' could be applied, and thus the only correct determinative that could be employed was the one denoting 'people.' The form of the expression, "The Israel-people is destroyed" shows the grammatical accuracy of the scribe.

[1] So Gressmann, who puts the Exodus and Conquest somewhere between 1260 and 1225 B.C.; cf. also J. S. Griffiths, *The Exodus in the Light of Archæology*, pp. 50, 73.

Most of the late-date upholders apply the text to Israelite tribes in Canaan who had never descended into Egypt with Jacob, or to a portion who had left Egypt when the great famine was over or at the time of the Hyksos departure, or at all events before the Biblical Exodus. According to Burney, for instance, only the Joseph tribes (Ephraim, Manasseh, Benjamin) were settled in Egypt and were led by Joshua across Jordan, while other Israelite tribes continued in Palestine without a break. The Zilpah tribes (Gad, Asher) and Bilhah tribes (Dan, Naphtali), with Reuben, Zebulun, Issachar, and a nucleus of Judah, were in Palestine all along, while Simeon and Levi were in the desert to the west of Edom.[1] Petrie and others do not take such an extreme view, though they hold it probable that some parties of Israelites at least remained in Palestine during most, if not all, of the time that the others 'sojourned' in Egypt.[2] No doubt there is some truth in these views, as we have already stated in Chapter I. Some of the proofs, however, usually advanced for them should be abandoned. One supposed proof is the fact that in the lists of Syrian places captured by Seti I. and Ramesses II., the immediate predecessors of Merenptah, we find a district called *'Asaru* (*'-s-r* in Egyptian), corresponding, it is said, to the hinterland of southern Phœnicia,[3] which is exactly the position assigned in the Old Testament to the Israelite tribe of Asher after the Exodus. Hence the later-date scholars assure us that the tribe of Asher must have been in Canaan all along, since it was there before their date for the Exodus! The identity of *'Asaru*, however, with Asher of the Biblical records must be regarded as most uncertain. The word *'Asaru* is believed to be a transliteration, not from the Hebrew, but from some non-Semitic language;[4] and the geographical location is also a matter of dispute owing to the town-lists of the Pharaohs not being in strict geographical order.

[1] *Israel's Settlement in Canaan*, pp. 36, 84, and map v.

[2] Petrie, *Egypt and Israel*, p. 35; P. S. P. Handcock, *Latest Light on Bible Lands*, 1913.

[3] Cf. W. M. Müller, *Asien und Europa*, 1893, pp. 236 ff.

[4] Cf. Eerdmans, *Vorgeschichte*, 1908, pp. 65 ff.

But even though the identity of the two names were placed beyond doubt, it would afford little encouragement to the later-date theorists. While it might be regarded from their point of view as proving the existence of the Asher tribe in Canaan prior to the Exodus—though it should be remembered that after all the existence of the Asher tribe in Canaan does not explain the word 'Israel' on the stele—it would supply a far stronger confirmation of the early-date theory we are advocating. For if the Israelites entered Canaan about 1400 B.C. or a little later, as the Amarna Letters go to prove, there was nothing to hinder the tribe of Asher being found in its assigned district by the time of Seti I., nearly 100 years later. It is exactly what the Biblical account would lead us to expect.

A second proof brought forward is the occurrence of two town-names which are supposed to read Jacob-el (*Y-ʿ-k-b-'â-ra*) and Joseph-el (*Y-š-p-'â-ra*) respectively, in the long list of south Syrian places inscribed on the pylons of the temple at Karnak during the reign of Thutmose III., about 1479 B.C.[1] It is inferred from this that Israelite tribes existed in Canaan at that time. But here again the equivalence of the names, especially of the latter one in which the sibilants do not correspond, is recognized as rather doubtful. Besides, they are the names of places, not tribes; and if the reading be correct, it would only prove that some Semites, probably descendants of Abraham, had left their names on places in Palestine in early times, perhaps even before the Israelites went down into Egypt. The name Jacob, especially, must have been well known in the Semitic world in those early ages. Among the names of autonomous Hyksos chieftains inscribed on Egyptian scarabs, there are two which appear to read Jacob-el and Jacob-baal.[2] It is possible that these chieftains may have been called after the patriarch, whose name may have been in high favour at the Egyptian court, but—what is just as likely—he may have

[1] See note 2, p. 36.

[2] Petrie, *Hyksos and Israelite Cities*, pp. 68 f.; Hall, *Ancient History*, p. 217; Spiegelberg, *Orientalistische Literaturzeitung*, vii. (1904), col. 131; Sayce, *Patriarchal Palestine*, p. 167.

had no connection with them. Indeed, there is now evidence that the names Jacob, Joseph, Abraham, and others are much older than the date of the patriarchs. Dr. Pinches has discovered the personal name *Ya'kub-ilu* [1] on contract tablets of the time of the Babylonian king Sin-muballit, the predecessor of Hammurabi, as early as about 2090 B.C., and the contracted or hypocoristic form *Ya'kubu* (exactly like 'Jacob') also occurs.[2] We have thus monumental evidence that the name Jacob was well known, perhaps common, in the Semitic world before this patriarch was born.[3] It is exceedingly doubtful, therefore, if the place-names Jacob-el and Joseph-el in southern Syria, assuming the reading of them to be correct, prove the existence of what may be called Israelite tribes in that district in the reign of Thutmose III. It is admitted by all scholars, Burney included, that the Joseph tribes can hardly have been in Canaan at this date; [4] and as for Jacob-el, all that may be safely concluded from it is that some Semitic chieftain, perhaps the Biblical patriarch, had implanted his name on a place in Palestine, or that some of his descendants had done so. But whether the place was inhabited by tribes who could be described as Israelites, we have no means of determining.

At the same time, apart from these considerations, we think there is sufficient evidence that there were numerous Israelites in Canaan all along, who never migrated to Egypt. Whether Burney's theory be correct that only the Joseph tribes sojourned

[1] Similarly we find *Yašup-ilu*, *Yarbi-ilu*, *Yamlik-ilu*, *Yakbar-ilu*, etc. (where *ilu*=*el* or God) on tablets of the same age.

[2] Hommel, *Ancient Hebrew Tradition*, pp. 61, 96, 112, 203.

[3] The name *Išre-il* or *Išre-el* has also been found on a Babylonian cylinder-seal of the era of Narâm-Sin (*c.* 2680 B.C.), several hundred years before the patriarch Jacob (cf. Père Scheil, *Revue d'Assyriologie*, 1916, p. 6; *Recueil de Travaux*, xxii. (1900), p. 55). On this account it has been thought by some scholars that the Israelites mentioned by Merenptah may not have been the Biblical tribes of this name, but some sheik and his people not related to them at all. All the circumstances, however, are against such a view. Merenptah's stele was meant to be read by the inhabitants of Egypt, and these were acquainted with only one body of Israelites—those who had dwelt in Goshen. At all events, they must have known these tribes better than they did any common Canaanite sheik.

[4] *Israel's Settlement in Canaan*, p. 89.

there, is a matter on which little or no direct evidence is available. But judging from what usually happens in such cases, some Israelite families must undoubtedly have remained in Palestine (especially in parts where the famine was not so severe) during the residence of the others in Egypt. A number of them would certainly continue to dwell among the Canaanites in the Shechem district, where Jacob bought ground and erected an altar. It is quite likely, too, that small detachments may have left Egypt from time to time and settled and multiplied at Hebron, round the tombs of the patriarchs or elsewhere. We know at least that parties of Israelites made raids from Goshen into Palestine during the sojourn (1 Chron. vii. 21, 22), and if the road were open for such raiders, it must have been used frequently by peaceful Israelites who wished to return to their ancestral domains. Intercourse certainly went on between the Israelites in Goshen and Palestine (cf. Gen. l. 4–14), and there was nothing to hinder any returning after the famine was over. The fact that all the family heritages were well known at the time of the Conquest seems to confirm these views, for if no Israelite families had remained in Canaan, and there had been no coming and going for over four centuries, the location of these sites would have faded from memory. It seems probable, therefore, that there were Israelites in Canaan, in stray detachments at least, during the time the others were in Egypt.

But while this is no doubt true, it affords no ground for the view that the term 'Israel' on Merenptah's stele refers to these people. Even though we assume the extreme position of Burney, and hold that many of the tribes remained in Canaan, this gives no satisfactory explanation of the statement on the stele. For the tribes of Asher, Gad, Dan, and Naphtali, who were among those that remained in Canaan according to his theory, were not regarded as of true Israelite stock. They were descended from sons of handmaids, not full wives, and as they were not purely Israelite by race, they were considered, even long after the Exodus, as holding an inferior position, without full tribal rights or claim to a full position in Israel. This is admitted by

Burney himself.[1] Their full entrance into the Israelite community was not won till the final settlement of all the tribes in Canaan. This explains the terms in which Dan is mentioned in the blessing of Jacob (Gen. xlix. 16). It accounts also for the failure of Asher, Gad, and Dan to respond to Deborah's call to arms (Judg. v. 17), and their evident separation from the common interests of Israel at that time. No doubt the Naphtali tribe also would have withheld their support from Deborah, if their geographical position had not made their adherence necessary. The names, too, of Asher, Gad, and Dan imply that these tribes were not at first pure Yahweh worshippers, but adhered to pagan forms of cultus. 'Asher' is known to have been a form of the moon-god. 'Gad' was the god of Fortune (Isa. lxv. 11, R.V.),[2] and 'Dan' was a title of the sun-god. The worship of these tribes must therefore have been marked by pagan and naturalistic characteristics, which differentiated them from Israel proper. Both in their descent from handmaids and in their form of worship, these Zilpah and Bilhah tribes were regarded for many ages as hardly entitled to a position in Israel. They were mere clans, whereas Israel was an organized community comprising several clans, with a strong religious bond represented by its Yahwism and having its origin in an Exodus from Egypt. Thus, one can easily see that Merenptah's statement, "Israel is destroyed," cannot refer to these tribes, who could not have been known under the name of 'Israel.' Would the Pharaoh or his scribe apply the name Israel to some concubine tribes who were known not to be purely Israelite by race and to whom the Israelites proper denied full tribal privileges? It is apparent that Merenptah's forces were up against the real Israel.

It is difficult to see how the stele can refer to any of the other tribes who are thought to have remained behind. In the inscription, Israel is distinguished from Ashkelon and Gezer (coast-land), Yenoam (in the north), and Kharu (really south

[1] *Judges*, pp. cvi f.

[2] Cf. Baal-Gad, Migdal-Gad (Josh. xi. 17, xii. 7, xiii. 15, xv. 37). The name also occurs frequently in Phœnician and Aramaic inscriptions.

Palestine), and thus represents a central Palestine people,[1] exactly in accordance with what we have already said as to the Israelite settlement for the first two or three centuries (see Chap. IV.). This seems to exclude the main part of Judah, which Burney has placed to the south of Edom during the sojourn in Egypt, as well as Simeon and Levi which he has located around Kadesh-Barnea. Hardly any of the tribes appear to have been left in the central regions, unless it be Reuben and a nucleus of Judah, and there is no certainty that the former tribe was west of Jordan at the time, for it is believed to have finally crossed eastward and found a home in southern Gilead, adjoining Moab.[2] There must have been, of course, as already indicated, numerous scattered families of Israelites even in central Palestine who had not migrated to Egypt, but these were not sufficiently large or important to warrant our application of the inscription to them. The fact is that the statement on the stele cannot possibly refer to any mere section of Israel or to stray detachments. From the wording of it, it is clear that it refers only to the main body, the 'Israel-people' as a whole. In the fact that Merenptah singles out 'Israel' so distinctly lies the suggestion, if not the proof, that it was the dominant race in the country. One cannot imagine Pharaoh applying to a mere portion or to some scattered fragments in Canaan the particular name which represented the entire confederacy. The statement can only be explained on the supposition that Israel as a settled and organized whole was located in Palestine at the time.

There is another way of looking at the matter. If the Exodus had not yet taken place, as the upholders of the late-date theory assert, the main body of Israelites must still have been in Goshen. These people were known to the Egyptians as 'Israel.' As a part of the wide Hebrew race, descended from Eber, they were spoken of as '*'Ibhri*' or Hebrews, and foreigners generally referred to them as such, but in other connections and among themselves, the name 'Israel' was

[1] Cf. S. A. Cook, *Cambridge Ancient History*, ii. p. 381.

[2] Cf. Burney, *Israel's Settlement in Canaan*, p. 50, and map v.

used. "Who is Yahweh," said Pharaoh, "that I should obey his voice to let Israel go (Ex. v. 2)?" "Let us flee from Israel," the Egyptians said, "for Yahweh fighteth for them (Ex. xiv. 25)." "There was not one of the cattle of the Israelites dead (Ex. ix. 7)." These and similar references may be to some extent a reading back of the name into the period of the sojourn, but it is admitted that the tribes which dwelt in Egypt were well known in the land under the name 'Israel.' Is it not very strange, then, that the Pharaoh should set up a stele in Egypt with the statement "Israel is destroyed," meaning a people in Canaan, while at this very time the only people known throughout Egypt as 'Israel' was still dwelling secure and untouched in Goshen? Who would the Egyptian readers of the stele understand by the term? Acquainted as they were with only one 'Israel,' the people who had dwelt for several centuries in their own midst, they must have regarded Merenptah's statement as inexplicable and even absurd, while the numerous Israelites who looked at it must have been amazed at its evident misrepresentation or falsity. The statement can only be satisfactorily explained on the assumption that the Exodus had already taken place, and that the people known to the Egyptians as Israel was now settled in Canaan and coming into prominence as a powerful confederacy.

CHAPTER XIII

THE ʿAPERU

SOME of the Egyptologists who prefer a later date still than the reign of Merenptah lay weight on the reference in Egyptian documents of the XIXth and XXth Dynasties to a people called *ʿAperu* or *ʿAperiu*, a name which is preceded by the determinative denoting foreigners or foreign land. As these people have been identified by several scholars with the Hebrews, the fact that they are alluded to four or five times as dwelling in Egypt during these dynasties, much later than Merenptah's time, is regarded as conclusive that the Exodus cannot have taken place till long after that monarch's reign.

We find the ʿAperu first mentioned in a folk-story about the siege of Joppa under Thutmose III. (*c.* 1501–1447 B.C.). The story is contained in the Papyrus Harris 500, which was written during the XXth Dynasty. It relates how, when Joppa was taken by a stratagem, one of Thutmose's generals, Thutiy, sent a message to the Egyptian troops outside by one of the ʿAperu. As the context is damaged, it is difficult to determine whether the ʿAperu were in the Egyptian army or belonged to the inhabitants of Joppa, though the former supposition is regarded as the more probable. The ʿAperu are mentioned on a stele of Seti I., discovered by the members of the Pennsylvania Museum in the foundations of a Byzantine church at Beisân (Beth-shean).[1] In two papyri preserved in the museum of Leyden, and dating from the reign of Ramesses II. (*c.* 1301–1234 B.C.), the ʿAperu are represented as hauling stones for temples built by this Pharaoh. In the Harris Papyrus of the reign of Ramesses III. (*c.* 1204–1172 B.C.), we read of a large

[1] See p. 59, and *The Museum Journal*, Philadelphia, xiv. (1923), 4–7.

number of ʿAperu connected with the endowments of the temple of Tūm at Heliopolis, together with "sons of foreign chiefs" and "Maryn" (Syrian warriors of some kind).[1] Even as late as the time of Ramesses IV. (*c.* 1172–1166 B.C.), we find an inscription on a rock in the Hammâmât Quarries (a little north of Thebes) stating that 800 ʿAperu, drawn from the "Anu-troops," or, as some translators put it, from "the foreign residents in the east of Goshen," were employed by Pharaoh on some kind of expedition there.

These people were evidently Egyptian mercenary troops or forced labourers, like the Hebrews under the Oppression (Ex. i. 11 ff.), in connection with the building operations of the Pharaohs, especially the quarrying and transportation of stone, and it is an interesting question as to whether they were Hebrews. Long ago the identity of the two peoples was asserted by some scholars, such as Chabas, Ebers, and others, and is upheld still by arguments of much force.[2] Maspéro, Breasted, Böhl, and some others reject it,[3] while Heyes, Driver, Skinner, and others are inclined to favour it.[4] Max Müller explains the name as that of a coast-dwelling people named Afri, who were Carthaginian Phœnicians and gave their name to Africa;[5] and there are even some scholars who connect it with that of Ephraim. We think, however, there can be no doubt that the name ʿAperu is the Egyptian form of 'Hebrew,' corresponding to the Babylonian Ḫabiru and the Hebrew *ʿIbhri*. In Egyptian it is merely written *ʿprw* or *ʿpryw*, the ʿ repre-

[1] Cf. Peet, *Egypt and the Old Testament*, p. 124; Breasted, *Ancient Records*, iv. 150.

[2] Chabas, *Mélanges Égyptologiques*, i. (1862), pp. 42 ff.; ii. (1864), pp. 108 ff.; Ebers, *Ägypten und die Bücher Mose's*, 1868, p. 316; *Durch Gosen zum Sinai*, ed. 2, 1881, pp. 505 ff.; Eerdmans, *Die Vorgeschichte Israels*, 1908, pp. 52 ff.

[3] Maspéro, *The Struggle of the Nations*, ed. 2, 1910, p. 443 n.; *Contes Populaires*, p. 119; Breasted, *Ancient Records*, iv. 281; Böhl, *Geschichte des Volkes Israel*, ed. 2, i. (1912), pp. 453 ff.

[4] Heyes, *Bibel und Ägypten*, 1904, pp. 146 ff.; Burchardt, *Die Altkanaanäischen Fremdworte und Eigennamen in Ägyptischen*, 50; Driver, *Exodus*, pp. 41 f.; Skinner, *Genesis*, pp. 218 ff.

[5] *Mitteilungen der vorderasiatischen Gesellschaft*, 1913, p. 255.

senting the Semitic guttural ע (as in עִבְרִי, 'Hebrew'), the *w* being simply the plural ending, and the vowels being unwritten (as is usual in Egyptian script) and consequently unknown to us. Several well-known Egyptologists regard this *'prw* as equivalent to 'Hebrew.' It is known that the Hebrew *b* sometimes becomes *p* in Egyptian (though not very often), as it does in the Canaanitish word *hereb* (חֶרֶב), 'sword,' which becomes *hurpu* in Egyptian. The word *habši* in the Amarna Letters,[1] supposed to mean 'arm,' 'thigh,' 'strength' (cf. Hebrew חָבַשׁ 'to gird,' 'to restrain'), is the Egyptian *hpš*. In Babylonian, too, the Hebrew *b* is frequently written as *p*. It is thus apparent that 'Aperu was the Egyptian form of Ḫabiru, *'Ibhri*, Hebrew.

Assuming, therefore, that these people were Hebrews, their presence in Palestine in the time of Seti I., nearly a century before Merenptah ascended the throne, is an argument against the late-date theory of the Exodus, unless we choose to regard them as distinct from the Israelites, that is to say, as Hebrews in the wider sense of the word. The later references to them would quite well agree with the earlier period for the Exodus, for the later 'Aperu may have been re-immigrants or prisoners of war from Palestine. The mention of them as slaves or forced labourers in the time of Ramesses II. would point to their having been captured in the Palestinian wars of Seti I. and Ramesses after their entry into Canaan, while the mention of them later still might refer to the descendants of these prisoners or to voluntary Hebrew soldiers serving in Egypt.[2] At all events, if we regard the word *'Aperu* as equivalent to 'Hebrews,' we have a fairly good argument in Seti's stele in favour of the earlier date of the Exodus.

The Hebrew race, of course, was a very wide one, the Israelites being only a small section of it, as we have shown in the chapter on the Ḫabiru. Hebrew tribes, descended from their common ancestor Eber, were scattered over all lands from the Euphrates to Asia Minor. We readily admit, therefore, that if the 'Aperu were not Israelites, they may have belonged

[1] Knudtzon, No. 147, l. 12.

[2] Cf. Hall, *Palestine Exploration Fund Quarterly*, 1923, p. 131.

to the great Hebrew stock. The Egyptian records show that thousands of Semitic people, many of whom must certainly have been Hebrews, were brought into Egypt as captives by the Pharaohs, or migrated there themselves, and were employed in the heavy manual work of quarrying, brickmaking, and building. In eleven campaigns under Thutmose III. alone, there are no less than 7548 captives, male and female, mentioned as being brought from the Asiatic provinces. The country simply swarmed with Semites, including Hebrews. Hence it is, that by the time of the XIXth Dynasty numerous Hebrew words and idioms are found in Egyptian literature, long before they appear in the writings of the Old Testament. An instance of the extent of the Hebrew penetration is found in the tomb of a general of cavalry and archers, Pa-hem-neter, in the reign of Ramesses II., where the scribe-engraver's name appears to be a Hebrew one, Yehu-nama, 'Yahweh speaks.' There were no doubt many such skilled workers of Hebrew race, who had probably become heathenized (this one calls himself 'Osirian'), and were engaged in carving figures or pursuing some craft connected with the gods of Egypt.[1]

Still, in spite of this view of the matter, it is apparent that if we equate '*Aperu* with 'Hebrews,' as there seems to be good philological and other reasons for doing, the probability at least is that these people who are mentioned as being in possession of the citadel of Beth-shean in the time of Seti I. belonged to the Israelitish tribes who had entered Canaan in the time of Abdi-Ḫiba, and that the later ones in Egypt were prisoners of war taken in the later campaigns, or their descendants. We see nothing against this view, and indeed much in its favour. It should not be forgotten that to the Egyptians the name 'Hebrew' referred particularly to that section of the race which had lived in Goshen. To the Pharaoh and his rulers they were *the* Hebrews.

Those who place the Exodus later than the reign of Merenptah, *e.g.* in the reign of Seti II. or Ramesses III., involve themselves in many difficulties. Several of these have already

[1] Petrie, *Expository Times*, xxxvi. (1925), p. 156.

been referred to in the preceding chapters. One more may be mentioned here. That the Israelites were away from Egypt by the early years at least of Merenptah's reign is evident from the Egyptian papyrus known as Anastasi VI., written in the eighth year of this Pharaoh's reign. This papyrus contains a letter from an Egyptian frontier official who had charge of the eastern entrance into the Wady Tumîlât, within the land of Goshen, in which he says: "We have finished causing the bedouin tribes of Edom to pass the fortress of Merenptah, belonging to Theku, towards the pools of Pithom (of) Merenptah, belonging to Theku, in order to feed themselves and feed their flocks." [1] From this letter it is apparent that the rulers of the XIXth Dynasty were in the habit of admitting the bedouin tribes and their flocks into Goshen as early as the reign of Merenptah, and it is difficult to see how such a custom could be possible if the Israelites were still inhabiting the district, which was a region of only limited extent, covering not more than 100 square miles. "The population of this district," says Petrie, "is stated to have been 4000 Bedawyn a century ago; it is now improved by agriculture to support a farming population of 12,000 persons. As the Israelites were essentially pastoral, probably the Bedawy population shows most nearly what numbers Goshen formerly supported." [2] That is to say, the district of Goshen could not carry a pastoral population of more than 6000 or thereabouts, living as they must have done in tents or huts scattered over the country, with their flocks and herds. The fact that there was room in Goshen in Merenptah's time for bedouin tribes from the eastern desert is only explicable on the supposition that the Israelites were no longer there. There is little doubt that the custom of admitting these tribes had been in existence since the days of Amenhotep II., when the district was vacated.

[1] See p. 29, and n. 1 there; cf. also Peet, *Egypt and the Old Testament*, p. 65; Breasted, *Ancient Records*, iii. 636–638.

[2] *Egypt and Israel*, p. 30.

CHAPTER XIV

THE OPPRESSION

ACCORDING to the Biblical account, the bondage of the Israelites during the latter part of their sojourn in Egypt, and especially just previous to the Exodus, took the form of forced labour. Instead of being allowed to continue at their pastoral avocations, they were driven under the task-master's lash to brickmaking, building, and other hard work. This is exactly in accord with the conditions at the period to which we have traced the Exodus. We know too much weight cannot be placed on such arguments, as large building enterprises were carried on by various Pharaohs both of the XVIIIth and XIXth Dynasties, but in connection with the view we are advocating, it is necessary to show that conditions were pre-eminently suitable to Thutmose III. (*c.* 1501–1447 B.C.) being the great Oppressor, and his successor Amenhotep II. (*c.* 1447–1420 B.C.) being the Pharaoh of the Exodus. The upholders of the late-date theory lay much emphasis on the large amount of building carried on by Ramesses II. at Memphis, Abydos, and other places, and his use of bondmen and foreign slaves for this purpose, but the circumstances under Thutmose III. are in every way just as applicable, indeed far more so.

Ever since the king arose " who knew not Joseph " (Ex. i. 8), and who was no doubt Ahmose, the first king of the XVIIIth Dynasty (*c.* 1580–1558 B.C.), who expelled the Hyksos or ' Shepherd-Kings ' under whom Joseph lived, the Israelites had been oppressed and their lives embittered by slavery in brick-fields and quarries. The years during which they had enjoyed the friendship and favouritism of the ruling caste were gone, and instead of being treated with respect and goodwill, they were now regarded, along with their friends the Hyksos, as "vile Asiatics," and threatened with various coercive measures. During the Hyksos rule, architecture and art had sunk into oblivion. Instead of works of art or important edifices being built, the first few of the rulers are believed to have destroyed the beautiful monuments erected during the first empire; but with the expulsion of the Hyksos, building recommenced, and by the time of Thutmose III. it had developed enormously. This powerful ruler and conqueror spent many years in quarrying, brickmaking, and building. In this respect, his character, length of reign (54 years), and oppressive measures correspond accurately with the description in Exodus. Remains of his works are to be found everywhere on Egyptian soil—in Nubia, in the Saite lands, in the Delta, and in the mines and quarries of Sinai. To his reign belongs the well-known picture of captives employed at brickmaking, so often used to illustrate the bondage of the Israelites. The overseers with their rods or lashes are seen standing over the slaves and commanding them not to be "idle" (cf. Ex. v. 17). The picture, which is given completely by Wilkinson,[1] is from the tomb of Rekhmara, vizier of Thutmose III., at Abd-el-Kurnah, opposite Luxor. Men are seen drawing water from a tank to moisten the mud; others carry the mud in baskets, place it in moulds, expose the bricks to dry, pile them in rows, and build walls with them. The gangs of slaves thus engaged were under masters chosen out of the Egyptian army, although the workers had also officers of their own.[2] This picture tallies exactly with the Biblical account, where we find the Pharaoh of the Oppression setting the Israelites hard and difficult labour at brickmaking, and appointing overseers to look after them and see that they produced a certain quantity of bricks daily. Probably, while engaged in this labour, they were housed together closely in brick huts and were often beaten unmercifully. Relying on their long-suffering and captivity, he increased their burdens to such an extent that we are told "their cry came up unto God by reason of the bondage"

[1] *The Manners and Customs of the Ancient Egyptians* (1878), i. p. 344.

[2] Cf. Erman, *Life in Ancient Egypt*, pp. 417 f., 128.

(Ex. ii. 23). It is thought by some that the mention of straw and stubble in the story may simply be a piece of local colour on the part of the writer, as the want of these things would not add to the labour of brickmaking.[1] Straw or stubble was not by any means universally employed; generally plain mud and sand, or mud and pebbles were used, and it was far more important to produce the requisite number of bricks than to be too particular about the straw. But even allowing for this, and without taking the grievances of the Israelites too seriously, there can be little doubt that for years their lives were embittered with oppression, and this state of matters accords exactly with the conditions existing under the reign of Thutmose III., who combined huge building undertakings with a liberal use of forced labour by Semitic bondmen and slaves. We have evidence that large numbers of such people were compelled to work under taskmasters in the construction of his great monuments and buildings,[2] especially the latter, just as Saladin built the citadel at Cairo with the forced labour of captive Crusaders.

This great conqueror, in fact, was not less active as a builder than as a warrior. No previous Pharaoh had shown such extraordinary activity in the erection of temples to the gods. Everywhere in Egypt these buildings of his arose—in Thebes, in Memphis, in Heliopolis, indeed in every town of importance throughout the land from the Delta to the third cataract. At Thebes he made an immense addition to the central shrine of Amūn. A great hall was built, over 130 feet long, supported on two rows of pillars. Numerous chambers opened around it, forming a complex mass of nearly fifty halls and rooms; and on a pylon, which he added to the numerous gateways of the temple, he inscribed lists of the various towns and districts abroad which he had captured. The brick wall around the whole of the buildings was also his work. At Dêr-el-Baharî he erected two enormous obelisks in celebration of his having

[1] Cf. Peet, *Egypt and the Old Testament*, p. 99; Petrie, *Hastings' Dictionary*, i. 326*b*.

[2] Breasted, *Ancient Records*, ii. 756–759.

crossed the Euphrates. These are believed to have weighed about 800 tons each, and to have stood 185 feet high. They no longer adorn the site, but a fragment of one stands at Constantinople and bears the record of that great achievement. At Heliopolis, where he also carried out great building operations, he reared two other huge obelisks in commemoration of his fourth jubilee. In the eighteenth year of the Emperor Augustus (*i.e.* 12 B.C.) they were removed to Alexandria, where they remained till 1877, when one of them, 68 feet in height, which had fallen, was removed to London, where it stands on the Thames Embankment and is known as Cleopatra's Needle ; two years later, the other one, a foot higher, was shipped across the Atlantic to a site in the Central Park, New York. Probably few of the thousands who gaze at these obelisks are aware that they are the monuments of one of the greatest building monarchs of ancient times. Although all his monuments in Egypt have either perished or been removed, the modern world thus possesses a line of them reaching from Egypt through Constantinople and London to the United States. In Sinai, amid the rocks of Serabît-el-Khâdem, he carried on building operations begun by Queen Hatshepsut and the earlier kings, and added a pylon to the temple there. At Dêr-el-Baharî he continued the work of Hatshepsut's terraced temple, though he endeavoured to efface almost every vestige of her connection with it. At Koptos he entirely rebuilt the temple of Min, the god of the gold country. At Elephantine, Kom Ombo, Edfu, and many other places his architects and labourers, native as well as foreign captives and bondmen, were employed for many years. Even in Nubia his building operations have been traced at Kalabsheh, Amâda, Wady Halfa, Kummeh, Soleb, and Semneh, where he restored the temple of his great ancestor Senusret III. Throughout all these extraordinary building activities, thousands of forced labourers must have been driven under the threatening lash to the work of making bricks, or quarrying huge blocks of granite.

In Thutmose III. we see the 'Alexander the Great' of

Egyptian history. He was a man of enormous energy unknown in any Pharaoh before or after. The portrait statue of him when a young man, discovered at Karnak by M. Legrain, reveals a handsome intelligent face. But a study of his mummy shows that in stature he was short, as his great ancestor Ahmose, the conqueror of the Hyksos, was, and as many other great soldiers have been. His chin was strong and heavy, and his nose a Roman one with a prominent bridge, as befitted a conqueror. Few who have read his history and studied his character will doubt that the conditions of the Oppression were fulfilled in him to a remarkable extent. As great conqueror, mighty builder, lynx-eyed administrator, his character stands forth with more individuality and clearness than that of any other king of early Egypt, except perhaps Akhenaten. He could launch his armies upon Palestine, Syria, and even distant Mesopotamia with one hand, and with the other drive his thousands of slaves and captives to the brick-fields and quarries. The Hymn of Victory to him, written by some unknown poet and inscribed on a stele discovered in the temple of Karnak, does not exaggerate. Amūn is represented as saying, among other things :

> I have given thee might and victory over all lands ;
> I have set thy will and the fear of thee in all countries,
> Thy terror as far as the four pillars of Heaven ;
> I have magnified the dread of thee in all creatures,
> I have caused the roaring of thy majesty to go among the Nine Bows.
> The chiefs of all lands are gathered in thy grasp ;
> I myself have stretched forth my two hands and bound them for thee.
> I have bound together the Antiu of Satet by myriads,
> And the northerners by hundreds of thousands as captives.
> I have struck down thine enemies beneath thy sandals ;
> Thou hast smitten the host of rebels according to my command.
> The earth in its length and breadth, Westerners and Easterners, are subject to thee.[1]

His reign marks an epoch in the ancient history of the world. Never before had a single ruler wielded the resources of so great

[1] Hall, *Ancient History*, p. 250 ; Budge, *History of Egypt*, iv. p. 49.

an empire with such remarkable efficiency, so as to make his name feared both abroad and at home. His genius, which led him from the obscurity of the priestly office at Thebes to become one of the first world conquerors and the embodiment of stern discipline and cruel oppression, eclipses that of Alexander or Napoleon. "The inevitable chastisement of his strong arm," says Breasted, "was held in awed remembrance by the men of Naharin for three generations. His name was one to conjure with, and centuries after his empire had crumbled to pieces it was placed on amulets as a word of power."[1] His long reign of over half a century, his powerful figure, his stern rule, his enormous building operations, and his well-known employment of Semitic slaves and captives under the lash of Egyptian officers, are all in exact accord with the description given in Exodus of the Pharaoh who ruled immediately prior to the escape of the Israelites, and he thus stands out as the great Oppressor. In all these respects he appears a much more likely figure than Ramesses II.

In 1448 B.C., he made his son Amenhotep II. co-regent, and about a year later, when within six weeks of the end of his fifty-fourth year on the throne, he died, and was buried in the Valley of the Kings. His body still survives, his mummy being in the Cairo Museum. There was no break in the succession, and Amenhotep, who appears to have been young, perhaps not more than twenty or twenty-five years of age at the most, thus succeeded at once to the throne of his mighty father. He has been described by Dr. Hall as a "tall man, of imposing presence, and with an intelligent stern face."[2] He fell heir to a kingdom embracing many lands and tongues, and stretching from the Upper Nile to the distant Euphrates. The wealth of Asiatic trade, which once flowed eastward to Babylon, now poured into the Nile Delta, and all the world traded in the markets of Egypt. But as often happens in the history of nations, when Thutmose died the tributary princes revolted. In Syria and the northern provinces, including Naharin, the vassal rulers made every effort to throw off the Egyptian yoke, with its

[1] *History of Egypt*, p. 321. [2] *Ancient History*, p. 252.

annual tribute and other heavy burdens. The young king marched into Syria in April, 1447 B.C., a few weeks after the death of Thutmose, and succeeded in quelling the turbulent enemy. He returned with 740 captives, who were driven before him, together with 210 horses and 300 chariots. He had the bodies of seven chiefs fron Taḫshi, whom he had slain with his own club, hung up head downward on the bows of his boat, as he sailed up the Nile to Thebes. Six of them were afterwards displayed in front of the walls of Thebes, while the seventh was sent to Napata, on the Upper Nile, to be hung on the walls there, so that the natives in the south might see it and tremble. This reminder of his treatment of rebels was apparently sufficient, as no further attempt seems to have been made against his suzerainty in Asia or elsewhere. He now (*c.* 1447 B.C.) devoted himself to works of construction, probably using Semitic slaves and captives, as his father had done. In Thebes he built his mortuary temple, long since vanished, while he also set up the columns which Queen Hatshepsut had removed, and restored the long dismantled hall. He also built largely at Heliopolis and Memphis, and restored the famous quarries of Troja opposite Gizeh, from which the blocks for the Gizeh pyramid had been taken. We can easily see that the Israelites, toiling hard under a burning sun in brick-fields and quarries, and chafing daily under the officers' rods, would make efforts immediately after the death of Thutmose III. to throw off their serfdom. The death of an old and powerful king such as Thutmose, and the accession of his young and inexperienced son, together with other favouring circumstances, gave them the long looked-for opportunity. Their day, indeed, had now arrived, and with the help of Moses, who had come to their help from the land of Midian, they managed at length to escape from the land (*c.* 1445 B.C.). The whole circumstances agree with the picture painted in Exodus, and the date accords with the one at which we have arrived from a study of the Amarna Tablets, the Biblical account of the entry of the Israelites into Canaan, the Merenptah stele, and chronological data. It is singular, too, that Manetho and Chœremon, though their accounts of the Exodus are largely legendary lore, both state that the Pharaoh of the Exodus was named Amenophis (the Greek form of the name Amenhotep).[1] A whole chain of arguments thus seems to combine in favour of the early-date theory.

Amenhotep II. reigned some twenty-six years, dying about 1420,[2] and being interred like his ancestors in the Valley of the Kings. The Pharaoh of the Exodus is not distinctly stated in the Bible to have been drowned in the Red Sea, as is popularly imagined. Neither the historical record (Ex. xiv. 26 ff.), nor the unquestionably ancient Song of Triumph (Ex. xv.), gives any support to such a view. These passages only speak of his host and his chariots. The tomb of Amenhotep was discovered in 1898, and his body rests there to this day. He was buried in a rose-granite sarcophagus, which lies in a great rock-hewn chamber, with blue-gold starred roof, supported by square-sided columns. In 1901 an attempt to rifle the mummy was made by the tomb-robbers of Thebes, who cut through the wrappings in their search for royal treasure, but only to find that their Theban ancestors in the same craft 3000 years before had taken all that was of any value.

Objection has been taken by some to the date advocated on the ground that the Moses-narrative assumes the Pharaoh's residence to have been not far from the north-east frontier of Egypt and near the land of Goshen, whereas during the XVIIIth Dynasty Thebes was the principal seat of government and of royal residence, and so continued until the reign of Ramesses II. In a general sense this is true, for the Hyksos rulers had their capital at Avaris (believed to have been at or near Pelusium in the north-eastern Delta), but after their expulsion by the southern armies Thebes naturally became the chief centre of administration. There is a probability, however, almost

[1] See p. 116.

[2] The theory of Professor Tofteen (*Ancient Chronology*, i. p. 196) that Amenhotep II. died in 1447 B.C., after three years of co-regency with his father, has been shown by Dr. Hall to be an impossible one (*Proceedings of the Society of Biblical Archæology*, xxxiv. (1912), p. 107).

amounting to certainty, that the old capital was not abandoned by the Pharaohs of the XVIIIth Dynasty. Owing to the growing dominance of Egypt in foreign affairs, it was necessary that there should be a seat of power in the north-east of the Delta. It was for this very reason that the Hyksos centred their government in Avaris; and Thutmose and his son must have found it necessary also to have a residence and a seat of power there, within easy reach of their Asiatic dominions. There is evidence, moreover, that the kings had another capital in the Delta or on the borders of it, probably at or near Memphis. We know from a scarab, a picture of which is given by Petrie,[1] that Amenhotep II. was born at Memphis, not far from Goshen. "The reference to his birth," says Petrie, "is of interest as showing that the court probably resided at Memphis some time in his father's reign." In view of this fact, it is clear there must have been a royal residence and a seat of government in this city during the reigns of Thutmose III. and Amenhotep II. That there was a royal residence in this region during the XIXth Dynasty also seems corroborated by the Papyrus Anastasi V. (19. 6 to 20. 2),[2] where "the courts of the Royal Palace" are mentioned in such a connection that they must have been a journey of only about a day or a day and a half west or south-west of Theku [*i.e.* Tell el-Maskûta]. The translation says, "I was despatched from the courts of the Royal Palace on the ninth day of the third month of summer at eventide, in quest of those two servants. I reached the enclosure wall of Theku on the tenth day of the third month of summer; they told me that they had said in the south that they [the slaves] had passed on the tenth day of the third month of summer. And when I reached the fortress [*viz.* of Theku], they told me that the groom (?) had come from the desert [to say] that they had passed the north wall of the Migdol of Seti-Meneptah-is-beloved-like-Seth" (Seti I.). As Migdol was at Tell el-Hêr, between Pelusium and Tell el-Maskûta, it is clear that this Royal Palace

[1] *History of Egypt*, ii. p. 162.

[2] An excellent translation is given by Gardiner in the *Journ. of Egypt. Arch.*, vi. p. 109; cf. also H. M. Wiener, *Ancient Egypt*, 1923, p. 76.

could not have been at Pi-Ramasse (believed to be the Avaris of the Hyksos), for the *détour* from the latter place to Tell el-Hêr only some 6 or 7 miles away, *via* Maskûta, which was some 43 miles away, would obviously be absurd. The palace must have been at a point from which a traveller proceeding to the Egyptian frontier would pass through or near Maskûta; and Memphis, or at least the region immediately to the east of it, lies at the spot that would best suit this document. All this finds corroboration in the inscription of the famous stele of Tutankhamūn that Legrain discovered at Karnak in 1905.[1] The text informs us that the Pharaoh went to live for a time in the Great House which was in Per-Āakheperkarā. This palace has been placed near Thebes by some Egyptologists, but according to Wallis Budge and others it was situated "in a suburb of Memphis or in some district at no great distance from that city."[2] The king, owing to the Aten revolution which was fast collapsing, was not sure what kind of reception he might meet with in Thebes, and so he wisely went northward to Memphis or to that district. Viewed in this light, the frequent visits of Moses to Pharaoh at some palace near Goshen (whether at Avaris, Memphis, or some adjoining place) are quite understandable and in accord with Egyptian history.

There is another remarkable coincidence of this epoch with the narrative in Exodus. One can hardly help comparing the famous Queen Hatshepsut with the "Pharaoh's daughter" who rescued Moses from the basket of papyrus reeds (Ex. ii. 5 ff.). In the tomb prepared for her but never utilized,[3] she is described several times on the sarcophagus as "king's daughter." "O king's daughter, king's sister, wife of the god, great wife of the king, Hatshepsut!" If the story of Moses' birth and adoption be authentic, and not a Babylonian fairy-tale as some scholars

[1] See *Annales du Service*, v. (1905), p. 192; *Recueil de Travaux*, xxix. (1907), pp. 162 ff.

[2] Budge, *Tutankhamen*, p. 6.

[3] Discovered by Mr. Howard Carter, 1916 (*Journ. of Egypt. Arch.*, iv. (1917), pp. 107 ff.).

suggest,[1] the comparison is interesting and almost perfect. This wise, energetic, and peace-loving woman was the daughter of Thutmose I. (*c.* 1545–1514 B.C.). She is believed to have been born about 1532 B.C., and to have died about 1479 B.C.[2] She was one of the most interesting figures in history, and exercised rule for about 35 years altogether, *viz.* 13 before her brother (or nephew) Thutmose III. began to reign, and 22 years in association with him. She was a princess of strong character, and a very important factor in the politics of the time. For many years the fortunes of the country were in her hands until Thutmose III. obtained his independence at her death. So long as she lived, he was but a 'shadow-king,' and his desire for military glory and conquest had to be suppressed. She seems almost to have regretted that she was a woman, for she frequently had herself sculptured clothed as a king; yet her rule was womanly, and her energies were directed towards the welfare of her subjects at home, and to securing friendly relations with

[1] The stories relating the infantile hairbreadth escapes of Moses, Semiramis (*Diod.*, ii. 4), Perseus (*Apollod.*, ii. 4. 1), Cyrus (*Herod.*, i. 110 ff.), Romulus (*Livy*, i. 4), and other founders of nations (including even Japan) are believed by some to have their origin in the legend of Sargon I. (Sharru-kin), founder of the dynasty of Akkad, about 2752 B.C. According to the legend, he was the son of a poor woman who exposed him on the river in a basket of reeds smeared with pitch, from which he was rescued (cf. Maspéro, *Dawn of Civilization*, pp. 597 f.; Sayce, *The Early History of the Hebrews*, p. 161). But even though we accept this as a prototype of the Exodus story, there may still be some substratum of fact in the tradition connecting 'Pharaoh's daughter' with the deliverance and upbringing of Moses when a child. There must have been some connection, however vague, to give rise to the tradition.

[2] The date of her birth may be reached by one or two methods. According to Hall, Amenhotep began to reign in 1558 B.C. Egyptologists put the birth of Hatshepsut's father, Thutmose I., about two years before this, *i.e.* about 1560 B.C. (Petrie, *History of Egypt*, ii. p. 54). Assuming that Thutmose I. married at the age of twenty-one (*i.e.* about 1539 B.C.), and considering that he had several children (Breasted says four in his *History of Egypt*, p. 266), and that Hatshepsut is known not to have been the eldest of these, we must put Hatshepsut's birth, roughly speaking, at about 1532 B.C. The same result may be reached in another way. Hatshepsut is known to have been co-regent for thirteen years before Thutmose III. ascended the throne (Petrie, *History of Egypt*, p. 32), which according to Hall's date was in 1501 B.C. That is, she began to reign about 1514 B.C. If we assume her to have been eighteen years of age at the time, this places her birth about 1532 B.C.

foreign nations. The event of which we know most is her expedition to Punt, on the Somali coast, while Thutmose III. was still a youth. From here her ships returned laden with balsam, ebony, ivory, gold, panther skins, baboons, and other objects. She also ordered two magnificent granite obelisks with shining metal tops to be made, which should stand before the gate of her father and record her work for ever. Thutmose III. naturally chafed under her control and seems to have hated her profoundly. His first action, when she died, was to obliterate her name wherever he found it. Her cartouches and her figure were hacked from the walls of her own temple wherever possible, and a wall of masonry was built around the bases of her obelisks to hide her inscriptions. It seems a mean vengeance for a great monarch to take upon the memory and works of a great woman, but unfortunately it missed its aim, for she stands out in Egyptian annals as the most remarkable princess the Valley of the Nile has produced.

It is at least a very singular coincidence that, on the theory we are advocating, Moses must have been born about the very time that this " bold and clever " princess, as Brugsch calls her, was young and rising into power, and one cannot fail to connect her with the " Pharaoh's daughter " who is said to have adopted him. Josephus, it is true, gives the name Thermutis to the heroine of this incident, but if any weight must be attached to this, Thermutis may be identified with ' Thutmose,' the family name of the dynasty. If it were Thutmose III. who gave orders to throw all the new-born male children of Israel into the Nile, such a harsh edict could hardly have had the approval of this large-hearted princess, and one can understand her rescuing the Hebrew child.[1] Under her care, the boy when grown up would be sent to the Egyptian schools, where he would become skilled in writing and mathematics, as well as in legend, myth,

[1] The derivation of Moses' name (Hebrew, *Môshé*) given in Ex. ii. 10 (' drawn out ') is not accepted by Egyptologists, who are agreed that there is no passive participle corresponding to it. They favour the view that the name is the Egyptian *Mōsi* (' born ') which is found as an element in such names as Thutmose, Ahmose, etc.

and history, and her action had thus an undoubted influence on the course of the Jewish nation and on the welfare of the world in future millenniums.

We are told in the E-narrative that when Moses was grown up and had learned that he was an Israelite, he went to see how his people fared and slew an Egyptian who was ill-treating an Israelite, and when he found next day that his deed was known he fled to Midian in order to escape the wrath of Pharaoh (Ex. ii. 11–15, sometimes ascribed to J). The question as to how long he was in Midian has been much discussed. We read (Ex. ii. 23), " It came to pass in the course of those many days [*i.e.* the days of Moses' sojourn in Midian] that the king of Egypt died." Dillmann, Bäntsch, Driver, and others are probably right in regarding " many " as a redactional addition, on the ground that, according to the J-narrative, Moses seems to have married Zipporah not long after his arrival in Midian (Ex. ii. 21), and their son Gershom is represented as quite young at the time of Moses' return to Egypt (Ex. iv. 25 (J)). The J-narrative, indeed, implies that Moses did not stay in Midian more than a few years, certainly not more than twelve or thirteen. If we assume, as seems to be the case, that he returned on the death of Thutmose III. in 1447 B.C. (" Go return into Egypt, for all the men are dead which sought thy life," Ex. iv. 19), it follows that he must have fled to Midian about 1460 B.C. What was his age when he fled? If Hatshepsut rescued him from the Nile, she must have been about 30 years of age or a little over it at the time, for her actions imply that she was not a mere girl, but a woman of responsibility and power in the land. In this case Moses must have been born about 1500 B.C., and would thus be about 40 years of age when he fled to Midian. This agrees with the Rabbinical tradition referred to by Stephen (Acts vii. 23), " When a period of 40 years was completed for him." If the narrative of J, to which we have just referred be accepted, he would be about 13 years older (53) when he returned to Egypt as the deliverer of Israel. He was therefore a man in the vigour and prime of life, with a great knowledge acquired by long residence in Egypt and a rich spiritual experience gained by many years of association with Jethro. He was just at the age when gifts of leadership and statecraft are approaching their best, and we need not be surprised that within two or three years he had succeeded in leading his oppressed kinsmen out of bondage.

CHAPTER XV

CONCLUSION

OUR examination of the evidence for the date of the Exodus has revealed the weakness of the late-date theory, as well as of the Akhenaten one, and confirmed the earlier date. Beginning with Israel's consciousness of the Exodus as an historical fact, we have examined the question of Pithom and Raamses, together with the supposed Egyptian reconquest under the XIXth Dynasty, which are the two main supports of the late-date argument, but have not found in them sufficient satisfactory evidence to warrant the conclusions adopted. The same is true of the Akhenaten theory, so attractively put forward by Mr. Arthur Weigall and others: it has no historical foundation, being based largely upon sentiment, and being in contradiction to trustworthy Egyptian and Biblical history. None of these theories, moreover, offers any reasonable solution of the Ḫabiru-SA-GAZ question, or explains Merenptah's Israel stele, or solves the chronological difficulties. On the other hand, we have placed before the reader a combination of arguments—historical, Biblical, and chronological—which point clearly and unmistakably to the earlier date. The theory we advocate is not at all inconsistent with the building of Pithom and Raamses by the Israelites, nor does it conflict with the Egyptian campaigns of the XIXth Dynasty, while it certainly accords with the invasion of the Ḫabiru, accounts for the mention of Israel on the stele referred to, and agrees with a reasonable system of Biblical chronology.

The whole argument is manifold, consisting of a chain of corroborations, correspondences, and coincidences not found in the other theories, and in judging it this manifoldness must be taken into consideration as giving it a unique force and reasonableness. There are, of course, perplexities still, as there must be in dealing with any subject where the evidence is mainly indirect; and there is probably no point we have advanced on which some critics may not differ from us. Nevertheless, we believe that the view put forward in these pages, which has been advocated by many Biblical scholars and Egyptologists, is the one which best satisfies all the conditions and does least violence to history. There are signs that the old idea of an Exodus in the reign of Merenptah is losing its hold, and that the earlier date is being more generally accepted by scholars.

We willingly leave the result where we have put it, being confident that further archæological and documentary discoveries will only confirm the argument. We do not belong to the number of those who look askance at the results of modern Biblical criticism, or those who advocate theories drawn from mere Biblical chronology. Much harm is done by such writers. Nor are we inclined to dogmatize as to the exact year of the Exodus, but rather deprecate any such idea. Our conclusions lead us to a date about 1445 B.C., but this does not mean that the Exodus may not have taken place shortly before or after. At all events, the evidence points with peculiar persistency to this particular period as the correct one. There is good reason to believe that the Israelites made their attack on Canaan shortly after 1400 B.C., and entered on victorious possession between that time and 1370 B.C., during the lapse of Palestine from Egyptian government.

APPENDICES

I

TABLE OF DATES

THE following table gives a few of the more important dates connected with the early history of Israel, so far as these can be determined (approximately at least) from the facts discussed in this volume:

	DATE, B.C.
Migration of Abraham and Hebrew clans from Haran to Canaan	2090
Accession of Hammurabi (Langdon's date)	2067
Israelites entered Egypt	1875
Accession of Ahmose I. (the "new king who knew not Joseph"), who expelled the Hyksos	1580
Birth of Hatshepsut ("Pharaoh's daughter")	1532
Accession of Thutmose III., the Oppressor	1501
Birth of Moses	1500
Flight of Moses to Midian	1460
Death of Thutmose III. and return of Moses to Egypt	1447
Accession of Amenhotep II., the Pharaoh of the Exodus	1447
Exodus of the Israelites from Egypt	1445
Entry of Israelites into Canaan, shortly after	1400
Merenptah's forces in conflict with Israel	1228
Accession of Solomon	969
Foundation of Solomon's Temple	965

II

THE TWO ATEN HYMNS[1]

A. Hymn by the King

A Hymn of Praise to the Living Horus of the Two Horizons, who rejoiceth in the horizon in his name of "Shu, who is in the Aten," the giver of life for ever and ever, by the King who liveth in truth, the Lord of the Two Lands, Nefer-kheperu-Re Ua-en-Re, Son of Re, who liveth in Truth, Lord of the Crowns, Akhenaten, great in the duration of his life, giver of life for ever and ever. [He saith]:

Thou risest gloriously, O thou Living Aten, Lord of Eternity! Thou art sparkling (or coruscating), beautiful, [and] mighty. Thy love is mighty and great . . . thy light, of diverse colours, leadeth captive (or bewitcheth) all faces. Thy skin shineth brightly to make all hearts to live. Thou fillest the Two Lands with thy love, O thou god, who did[st] build [thy]self. Maker of every land, Creator of whatsoever there is upon it, [*viz.*] men and women, cattle, beasts of every kind, and trees of every kind that grow on the land. They live when thou shinest upon them. Thou art the mother [and] father of what thou hast made; their eyes, when thou risest, turn their gaze upon thee. Thy rays at dawn light up the whole earth. Every heart beateth high at the sight of thee, [for] thou risest as their Lord.

Thou settest in the western horizon of heaven, they lie down in the same way as those who are dead. Their heads are wrapped up in cloth, their nostrils are blocked, until thy rising taketh place at dawn in the eastern horizon of heaven. Their hands then are lifted up in adoration of thy Ka (or person); thou

[1] The translation of these hymns has been taken from Sir E. A. Wallis Budge, *Tutankhamen*, pp. 116 ff., with kind permission of the author.

vivifiest hearts with thy beauties (or beneficent acts), which are life. Thou sendest forth thy beams, [and] every land is in festival. Singing men, singing women, [and] chorus men make joyful noises in the Hall of the House of the Benben Obelisk, [and] in every temple in [the city of] Akhut-Aten, the Seat of Truth, wherewith thy heart is satisfied. Within it are dedicated offerings of rich food.

Thy son is sanctified (or ceremonially pure) to perform the things which thou willest, O thou Aten, when he showeth himself in the appointed processions.

Every creature that thou hast made skippeth towards thee, thy honoured son [rejoiceth], his heart is glad, O thou Living Aten, who [appearest] in heaven every day. He hath brought forth his honoured son, Ua-en-Re, like his own form, never ceasing so to do. The son of Re supporteth his beauties (or beneficent acts).

Nefer-kheperu-Re Ua-en-Re [saith]:

I am thy son, satisfying thee, exalting thy name. Thy strength [and] thy power are established in my heart. Thou art the Living Disk, eternity is thine emanation (or attribute). Thou hast made the heavens to be remote so that thou mightest shine therein and gaze upon everything that thou hast made. Thou thyself art Alone, but there are millions of [powers of] life in thee to make them (*i.e.* thy creatures) live. Breath of life is it to [their] nostrils to see thy beams. Buds burst into flower (?), [and] the plants which grow on the waste lands send up shoots at thy rising; they drink themselves drunk before thy face. All the beasts frisk about on their feet; all the feathered fowl rise up from their nests and flap their wings with joy, and circle round in praise of the Living Aten. . . .

B. Hymn by Ai, Master of the Horse of Akhenaten [1]

A Hymn of Praise of Herakhti, the Living One, exalted in the Eastern Horizon in his name of "Shu, who is in the Aten," who liveth for ever and ever, the living and great Aten, he who is in the Set-Festival, the Lord of the Circle, the Lord of the Disk, the Lord of heaven, the Lord of earth, the Lord of the House of the Aten in Akhutaten,

[1] This is the hymn which has been compared to the 104th Psalm.

> [of] the King of the South and the North, who liveth in Truth, Lord of the Two Lands (*i.e.* Egypt), Nefer-kheperu-Re Ua-en-Re, the son of Re, who liveth in Truth, Lord of Crowns, Akhenaten, great in the period of his life, [and of] the great royal woman (or wife) whom he loveth, Lady of the Two Lands, Nefer-Neferu-Aten Nefertiti, who liveth in health and youth for ever and ever. He (*i.e.* Ai) saith :

Thy rising [is] beautiful in the horizon of heaven, O Aten, ordainer of life. Thou dost shoot up in the horizon of the East, thou fillest every land with thy beneficence. Thou art beautiful and great and sparkling, and exalted above every land. Thy arrows (*i.e.* rays) envelop (*i.e.* penetrate) everywhere all the lands which thou hast made.

Thou art as Re. Thou bringest [them] according to their number, thou subduest them for thy beloved son. Thou thyself art afar off, but thy beams are upon the earth ; thou art in their faces, they [admire] thy goings.

Thou settest in the horizon of the west, the earth is in darkness, in the form of death. Men lie down in a booth wrapped up in cloths, one eye cannot see its fellow. If all their possessions, which are under their heads, be carried away, they perceive it not.

Every lion emergeth from his lair, all the creeping things bite, darkness [is] a warm retreat (?). The land is in silence. He who made them hath set in his horizon.

The earth becometh light, thou shootest up in the horizon, shining in the Aten in the day, thou scatterest the darkness. Thou sendest out thine arrows (*i.e.* rays), the Two Lands make festival, [men] wake up, stand upon their feet, it is thou who raisest them up. [They] wash their members, they take [their apparel], and array themselves therein, their hands are [stretched out] in praise at thy rising, throughout the land they do their works.

Beasts and cattle of all kinds settle down upon the pastures, shrubs and vegetables flourish, the feathered fowl fly about over their marshes, their feathers praising thy Ka (person). All the cattle rise up on their legs, creatures that fly and insects of all kinds spring into life, when thou risest up on them.

The boats drop down and sail up the river, likewise every road openeth (or showeth itself) at thy rising, the fish in the river swim towards thy face, thy beams are in the depth of the Great Green (*i.e.* the Mediterranean and Red Seas).

Thou makest offspring to take form in women, creating seed in men. Thou makest the son to live in the womb of his mother, making him to be quiet that he crieth not; thou art a nurse in the womb, giving breath to vivify that which he hath made. [When] he droppeth from the womb . . . on the day of his birth, [he] openeth his mouth in the ordinary manner, thou providest his sustenance.

The young bird in the egg speaketh in the shell, thou givest breath to him inside it to make him to live. Thou makest for him his mature form so that he can crack the shell, [being] inside the egg. He cometh forth from the egg, he chirpeth with all his might; when he hath come forth from it (the egg), he walketh on his two feet.

O how many are the things which thou hast made! They are hidden from the face, O thou One God, like whom there is no other. Thou didst create the earth by thy heart (or will), thou alone existing, men and women, cattle, beasts of every kind that are upon the earth, and that move upon feet (or legs), all the creatures that are in the sky and that fly with their wings, [and] the deserts of Syria and Kesh (Nubia), and the land of Egypt.

Thou settest every person in his place. Thou providest their daily food, every man having the portion allotted to him, [thou] dost compute the duration of his life. Their tongues are different in speech, their characteristics (or forms), and likewise their skins [in colour], giving distinguishing marks to the dwellers in foreign lands.

Thou makest Hāpi (the Nile) in the Tuat (Underworld), thou bringest it when thou wishest to make mortals to live, inasmuch as thou hast made them for thyself, their Lord who dost support them to the uttermost, O thou Lord of every land, thou shinest upon them, O Aten of the day, thou great one of majesty. Thou makest the life of all remote lands. Thou settest a Nile in heaven, which cometh down to them.

It maketh a flood on the mountains like the Great Green Sea, it maketh to be watered their fields in their villages. How beneficent are thy plans, O Lord of Eternity! A Nile in heaven art thou for the dwellers in the foreign lands (or deserts), and for all the beasts of the desert that go upon feet (or legs). Hāpi cometh from the Tuat for the land of Egypt. Thy beams nourish every field ; thou risest up [and] they live, they germinate for thee.

Thou makest the Seasons to develop everything that thou hast made : the season of Pert (*i.e.* Nov. 16–March 16) so that they may refresh themselves, and the season Heh (*i.e.* March 16–Nov. 16) in order to taste thee. Thou hast made the heaven which is remote that thou mayst shine therein and look upon everything that thou hast made. Thy being is one, thou shinest (or shootest up) among thy creatures as the Living Aten, rising, shining, departing afar off, returning. Thou hast made millions of creations (or evolutions) from thy one self, [*viz.*] towns and cities, villages, fields, roads and river. Every eye beholdeth thee confronting it. Thou art the Aten of the day at its zenith.

At thy departure thine eye . . . thou didst create their faces so that thou mightest not see. ONE thou didst make. . . . Thou art in my heart. There is no other who knoweth thee except thy son Nefer-kheperu-Re Ua-en-Re. Thou hast made him wise to understand thy plans [and] thy power. The earth came into being by thy hand, even as thou hast created them (*i.e.* men). Thou risest, they live ; thou settest, they die. As for thee, there is duration of life in thy members, life is in thee.

[All] eyes [gaze upon] thy beauties until thou settest, [when] all labours are relinquished. Thou settest in the West, thou risest, making to flourish . . . for the King. Every man who [standeth on his] foot, since thou didst lay the foundation of the earth, thou hast raised up for thy son who came forth from thy body, the King of the South and the North, Living in Truth, Lord of Crowns, Akhenaten, great in the duration of his life [and for] the Royal Wife, great of majesty, Lady of the Two Lands, Nefer-neferu-Aten Nefertiti, living [and] young for ever and ever.

III

ABDI-ḪIBA'S LETTERS

1. From Abdi-Ḫiba of Jerusalem to the King (Knudtzon, No. 287)

To the king, my lord, hath spoken Abdi-Ḫiba, thy servant: at the feet of my lord seven times and seven times do I fall. I have heard all the words which the king, my lord, has sent. . . . [Behold] the deed, which . . . has done . . . what shall I . . . news . . . brought to the city Kilti (Keilah). Let the king know that all lands have leagued in hostility against me; let the king therefore care for his land. Behold, the territory of Gazri (Gezer), the territory of Ashkaluna (Ashkelon), and the city of La[kisi] (Lachish), have given them oil, food, and all their necessaries. Let the king therefore care for the troops. Let him send troops against the people who have committed a crime against the king, my lord. If in this year there are troops here, then will the land and the local ruler[s] remain to the king, my lord; but if there are no troops here, then there will remain no lands and no local rulers to the king.

Behold this land of Jerusalem—neither my father nor my mother gave it to me; the mighty hand of the king gave it to me. Behold, this deed is the deed of Milki-ili, and the deed of the sons of Labaya, who have given the land of the king to the Ḫabiru. Behold, O king, my lord, I am innocent as regards the Kashi. Let the king ask the inspectors (*rabisûti*) if the house is very mighty (?). Indeed, they have aspired to perpetrate a very wicked crime; they have taken their implements and . . . sent to the land . . . servant; let the king take heed to them that they may support the land with their hand. Let the king demand for them much food, much oil, and many garments, until Pauru, the king's inspector (*rabis*) goes up to Jerusalem.

Adaja is in revolt together with the garrison, the officer (*ú-e-ú*) . . . the king. Let the king know that Adaja said to me:

"Behold, let me depart, but do not thou leave it (the city)." In this year send me a garrison, send the inspector (*rabisa*) of the king. I sent to the king, my lord, 5000 *asiru* . . . 318 (?) bearers for the caravans of the king; they were taken in the fields of Aijalon. Let the king, my lord, know that I am unable to send caravans to the king, my lord—this for thy information. Behold, the king has set his name in the land of Jerusalem for ever, therefore he cannot leave the land of Jerusalem in the lurch.

To the scribe of the king, my lord, hath spoken Abdi-Ḫiba, thy servant: At thy feet I fall. I am thy servant. Bring clearly before the king, my lord, these words. An officer (*ú-e-ú*) of the king am I. I am . . . And an evil deed has been done against me by the people of Kash. I was all but slain by the people of Kash in my house. Let the king ask . . . seven times and seven times . . . the king, my lord, to me.

2. From Abdi-Ḫiba of Jerusalem to the King (Knudtzon, No. 286)

To the king, my lord, hath spoken Abdi-Ḫiba, thy servant: At the feet of my lord, the king, seven times and seven times do I fall. What have I done to the king, my lord? They have slandered me before the king, my lord, [saying]: "Abdi-Ḫiba has revolted from the king, his lord." Behold, as for me, neither my father nor my mother appointed me in this place. The mighty hand of the king introduced me into my father's house. Why should I commit an offence against the king, my lord? So long as the king, my lord, lives will I say to the inspector (*rabis*) of the king, my lord: "Why do you love the Ḫabiru, and hate the local rulers (*ḫazianuti*)?" For this reason they slander me before the king, my lord. Because I say: "The territory of the king, my lord, will be ruined," therefore I am slandered before the king, my lord. Let the king, my lord, know that the king, my lord, had established a garrison, but . . . Yanḫamu has taken it . . . Egypt . . . king, my lord . . . there is no garrison there. May the king take care for his land! May the king take care for his land! The lands of the king, my lord, have all fallen away. Ilimilki is destroying the entire lands of the king. May the lord care for his land! I say: "I will go before the king, my lord, and see the eyes of the king, my lord." But the enemies are powerful against me, and I am unable to go before the king, my lord. So may it seem right to the king to send garrison-troops, and I will go and see the eyes of the king, my lord. So long as the king, my lord, lives, when an inspector (*rabis*) goes forth, I shall say: "The lands of the king, my lord, are going to ruin." But you do not listen to me. All the local rulers (*ḫazianu*) are lost; there remains not one local ruler to the king, my lord.

Let the king turn his face to the troops, and let the king, my lord, send troops! No territory remains to the king, my lord. The Ḫabiru are devastating all the lands of the king. If there be troops in this year, then the lands will remain the king's, my lord's; but if no troops arrive, the lands of the king, my lord, are lost.

To the scribe of the king, my lord: Abdi-Ḫiba, thy servant. Bring clearly before the king, my lord, [these] words: All the lands of the king, my lord, are going to ruin.

3. From Abdi-Ḫiba of Jerusalem to the King (Knudtzon, No. 288)

To the king, my lord, my sun, hath spoken thus Abdi-Ḫiba, thy servant. At the feet of the king, my lord, seven times and seven times I fall. Behold, the king, my lord, hath set his name upon the East and upon the West. It is a wickedness which they have wrought against me. Behold, I am not a local ruler (*ḫazianu*), I am an officer (*ú-e-ú*) of the king, my lord. Behold, I am a shepherd of the king, and one who brings tribute to the king. Neither my father nor my mother, [but] the mighty hand of the king, hath established me in my father's house . . . came to me. . . . I gave him ten slaves into his hand. When Shûta, the inspector (*rabis*) of the king, came to me, I gave him twenty-one maidservants and eighty (?) *asiru* . . . gave I into the hand of Shûta, as a present for the king, my lord. Let the king take care for his land! The whole king's land, which has begun hostilities against me, will be lost. Behold the land of Seir, as far as Gath-Carmel, its princes are wholly lost; and hostility prevails against me. If one could see (?)! But I do not see the eyes of the king, my lord, because hostility is established against me. As sure as there is a ship in the midst of the sea, the strong arm of the king will seize Naḫrima and Kapasi, but now the Ḫabiru are seizing the cities of the king. There is no local ruler left to the king, my lord; all are lost. Behold, Turbazu has been slain in the gate of Zilu, yet the king does nothing. As for Zimrida of Lachish, his [own] servants, become Ḫabiru, have slaughtered him. Jephthah-Hadad has been slain in the gate of Zilu, yet the king does nothing. . . . Let the king take care for his land, and let the king give his attention in regard to troops for the land of tribute (?). For if no troops come in this year, all the lands of the king, my lord, will be destroyed and in ruins. They must not say before the king, my lord, that the land of the king, my lord, is destroyed, and all the local rulers are destroyed. If no troops arrive in this year, then let the king send an inspector (*rabisa*) to take me to thee with my brothers, and we will die with the king, my lord.

To the scribe of the king, my lord, thus Abdi-Ḫiba, thy servant: At thy feet I fall down. Bring these words clearly before the king, my lord. . . . Thy son and thy servant am I.

4. From Abdi-Ḫiba of Jerusalem to the King (Knudtzon, No. 289)

To the king, my lord, [hath spoken] thus Abdi-Ḫiba, thy servant. At the feet of the king, my lord, seven times and seven times I fall. . . . Behold, hath not Milkilim revolted to Labaya's sons and to Arzaya's, so as to claim the land of the king for them? A ruler (*ḫazianu*) who has done this deed—why does not the king call him to account? Behold Milkilim and Tagi, the deed which they have done is this: after taking the city Rubuda, they are now seeking to take Jerusalem. If this land belongs to the king, why [delay] till the Ḫazati are at the king's disposal? Behold, the land of Gath-Carmel belongs to Tagi, and the people of Gath form a garrison in Beth-sâni (Debir); and the same will befall us now that Labaya and the land of Shechem have given everything to the Ḫabiru. Milkilim has written to Tagi and his sons: "As two are . . . , give to the people of Keilah all their desire." Shall we then let Jerusalem go? The garrison-troops which thou hast sent by the hand of Ḫaya, the son of Miarê, hath Addaia taken and placed in his house in Ḫazati (Gaza), and twenty men hath he sent to Egypt.

Let the king take heed that there is no garrison of the king with me. Such is the case as the king liveth. Puuru his . . .

he has departed from me and is in Ḫazati. Let the king keep this before him, and let the king send fifty garrison-men to protect his land. The whole land of the king is in revolt. Send Yanḫamu, and let him take heed for the land of the king.

To the scribe of the king, my lord, thus speaketh Abdi-Ḫiba, thy servant. Bring these words clearly before the king. I am in highest degree . . . to thee, thy servant am I.

5. From Abdi-Ḫiba of Jerusalem to the King (Knudtzon, No. 290)

To the king, my lord, hath spoken thus, Abdi-Ḫiba, thy servant: At the feet of the king seven times and seven times I fall. Behold the deed which Milki-ili and Shuwardata have done against the land of the king, my lord. They have . . . the soldiers (or people) of Gezer, the soldiers of Gath, and the soldiers of Keilah, and have taken the territory of Rubute. The land of the king is lost to the Ḫabiru. And now indeed a city of the territory of Jerusalem, called Beth-Ninib, has been lost to the people of Keilah. Let the king listen to Abdi-Ḫiba, thy servant, and send troops, that I may restore the king's land to the king. But if there are no troops, the land of the king will be lost to the Ḫabiru. This is the deed of Milki-ili . . . Shuwardata . . . and let the king take care for his land.

6. From Abdi-Ḫiba of Jerusalem to the King (Knudtzon, No. 285)

To the king [my lord, thus hath spoken] Abdi-Ḫiba, thy servant. [At] the feet [of the king, my lord] seven times and seven times I fall. Behold, I am not a [local ruler]; an officer (*ú-e-ú*) to the [king] am I. Why has the king . . . not sent a messenger . . . ? Under such circumstances Yanḫamu has sent . . . Let the king [hearken] to Abdi-Ḫiba, his servant. [Behold], there are no troops. Let the king, my lord, send an inspector (*rabisa*), and let him take the local rulers with him. The lands of the king . . . and people . . . who are . . . and Addaia, the inspector (*rabis*) of the king, [has] their house. . . .

Let the king take heed for them, and let him send a messenger quickly. When . . . I die . . .

IV

MUT-BAAL'S LETTER
(Knudtzon, No. 256)

Unto Yanḫamu, my lord, has thus spoken Mut-Baʿlu thy servant: At the two feet of my lord have I fallen down. How has Mut-Baʿlu spoken before thee, saying: Ayâb has fled as the king of Biḫishi has fled from before the inspectors (*rabizi*) of his lord, the king. May my lord, the king, live, may my lord, the king, live, if Ayâb is in Biḫishi (*i.e.* as the king liveth, Ayâb is *not* in Biḫishi). Behold! two months . . . Of a truth (?) ask Benenima, of a truth (?) ask Yadua, of a truth (?) ask Yashuya whether, since Silim-Marduk has stolen Ashtarti, he hath fled away, when all the cities of Gari, (*viz.*) Udumu, Aduri, Araru, Meshtu, Magdalim, Ḫinyanabi, and Zarki are hostile, and when Ḫawini and Yabishiba are captured. Further: behold, after thou hast written a tablet unto me, have I written unto him. Even before thine arrival from thy journey, then behold, he will have arrived in Biḫishi and will hear thy words.

V

SHUWARDATA'S LETTER

(*Louvre Museum*, AO 7096)

To THE KING, my lord, my sun, say this: Thus speaks Shuwardata thy servant, the servant of the king and the dust of his two feet, the ground that thou treadest on. At the feet of the king, my lord, the sun in the heavens, seven and seven times have I cast myself, both on the belly and the back. Let the king, my lord, know that the SA-GAZ are carrying [war] into the territory which the god of the king, my lord, has given me, and that I have defeated them. Moreover, let the king, my lord, know that all my brothers have forsaken me, and that I and Abdi-Ḫiba are making war on the SA-GAZ. Zurata, the ruler (*amêlu*) of the city of Akka, and En-dar(?)-uta, the ruler (*amêlu*) of the city of Akshapa, these are the helpers [come] to me with fifty chariots. Behold, they are with me in the war. Let it please the king, my lord, to send Yanḫamu, so that we may finish the war, and that thou mayst give back the territory of the king, my lord, to its . . .

VI

PARALLELS OF SA-GAZ AND ḪABIRU IN THE BOGHAZ KEUI TREATIES

A LARGE number of gods and goddesses are mentioned in the Treaties. We give here a few of the names immediately preceding and following the mention of the gods of the SA-GAZ or Ḫabiru (in the exact order in which they occur), so that a proper comparison may be made. The dates of the Treaties cannot be fixed with any accuracy, and those here given must be regarded as somewhat vague and only provisional.[1] Tushratta, king of Mitanni, the father of Mattiuâza, seems to have died about 1367 B.C., and Shuppiluliu about 1364 B.C. Tuppi-Teshup I., king of Amurru, was the second successor after Aziru (the first being Idin-Teshup) and appears to have reigned c. 1355–1330 B.C.

The square brackets contain words inserted where the reading on the tablets is illegible or injured.

[1] Dr. Ernst F. Weidner, to whom the author has submitted the Treaty-dates here given, has expressed his agreement with them. "Sie sind daher mit dem grössmöglichen Masse von Wahrscheinlichkeit berechnet, und ich stimme ihnen völlig zu."

INDEX

NOTE.—Such prefixes as Mt., Jebel (' Mountain '), Tell (' Mound '), Wady (' Torrent '), Nahr (' River '), as well as the Arabic article (el-), are omitted in the alphabetical arrangement.